Illuminate
Publishing

WJEC/Eduqas
Media
Studies

for A Level Year 1 & AS

Revision Guide

Christine Bell • Lucas Johnson

Published in 2020 by Illuminate Publishing Limited, an imprint of Hodder Education, an Hachette UK Company, Carmelite House, 50 Victoria Embankment, London EC4Y 0DZ

Orders: Please visit www.illuminatepublishing.com
or email sales@illuminatepublishing.com

British Library Cataloguing-in-Publication Data
A catalogue record for this book is available from the British Library

ISBN 978-1-911208-87-7

Printed by: Oriental Press, Dubai

08.22

The publisher's policy is to use papers that are natural, renewable and recyclable products made from wood grown in sustainable forests. The logging and manufacturing processes are expected to conform to the environmental regulations of the country of origin.

Eduqas examination questions are reproduced by permission from WJEC.

Editor: Dawn Booth
Design and layout: Kamae Design
Cover design: Nigel Harriss
Cover image: iStock / dem10

Author acknowledgements
Thanks as always to Eve, Dawn, Steph, Rick and everyone at Illuminate Publishing for all their hard work, patience and encouragement.

Dedication
For my sister, Anna – LJ

Contents

Introduction

How to Use this Revision Guide

This revision guide is designed for those learners following the Eduqas Media Studies specification in England and Northern Ireland. It accompanies the WJEC/Eduqas Media Studies A Level Year 1 & AS student book. The purpose of this guide is to support your revision across all three components and to prepare you for the assessments.

The revision guide revisits the key elements of the theoretical framework and applies them to the set forms in the A Level Year 1/AS Media Studies specification. It includes a range of examples from the set products to support your revision and also features additional examples from the set forms to help prepare you for the analysis of the unseen product in the Component 1 exam. The guide explores how each component is assessed, explaining the structure of the examination papers, the assessment objectives and their application across the components.

This guide incorporates a range of activities and revision tasks, enabling you to practise analysis and demonstrate knowledge and understanding of the theoretical framework.

The aim of this guide is to help you to structure an effective revision programme.

Key Features of this Guide

The guide is divided into chapters focusing on the key elements of the specification and the individual components. Each chapter incorporates the following features to aid your revision:

Reminder

Lists of important details about the content of the specification, the requirements and the assessment.

Checklist

Reminders of the aspects of the specification and the theoretical framework you have studied during your course. They will also remind you of the main requirements for each component, containing essential information to guide your revision.

Top Revision Tip

Essential pieces of advice that will help you to structure your revision and prepare effectively for assessment in the different components.

Top Revision Tip

Revising relevant terminology related to the media forms you have studied will help to enhance your examination responses.

Top Revision Tip

While the focus of this revision guide is the Year 1/ AS assessment, many of you will be following the linear A Level course. This guide will also revise elements of the theoretical framework relevant to the A Level course. Highlighted sections provide you with links to the additional set products and theories required for the Year 2/A Level assessment.

Top Revision Tip

Completing the Quickfire Revision questions and the Apply it! activities as you work through sections of the guide will reinforce your knowledge and understanding of the theoretical framework.

Top Revision Tip

For the Apply it! tasks, where you are required to match terminology to definitions you may need to refer to the relevant sections of the Year 1/AS student book or engage in some independent research to find the correct answer.

Quickfire Revision

Questions and tasks designed to test your existing knowledge and understanding of the theoretical framework, set forms and products, and additional examples studied. They will reinforce your learning and guide you to make connections between elements of the theoretical framework and the products you have studied. The answers to these can be found at the end of this book and are also on a dedicated WJEC/Eduqas Media Studies webpage: www.illuminatepublishing.com/Media_AS_RG_Answers.

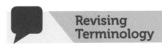

Apply it!

A range of tasks and activities designed to encourage you to apply the knowledge and understanding you have acquired in this guide and throughout your course. The aim is to enhance your ability to discuss media products, their contexts and relevant theoretical perspectives to enable you to produce successful examination responses.

Take it Further

Activities designed to broaden your knowledge and understanding of the theoretical framework and the set media forms and products. They may introduce you to new resources, including recent newspaper articles, or give suggestions and encourage you to revisit products by applying a different focus to your analysis. The questions in this section will challenge you and encourage you to engage in independent extended research related to the theoretical framework.

Revising Terminology

Some of the sections include vocabulary lists related to the set forms and theoretical perspectives.

Mind map

Mind maps are included in the guide at the end of each section in Chapters 1, 2 and 3. They are a very useful revision tool as they sum up the key points covered in the section, remind you of the main requirements and cover the relevant theories and contexts to be studied. These are also available to download from a dedicated WJEC/Eduqas Media Studies webpage: www.illuminatepublishing.com/Media_AS_RG_Answers.

Link

Throughout the guide there will be links to more detailed sections in the Year 1/AS student book, to the Year 2/A Level products, theories and theoretical perspectives and to other useful areas of the revision guide. These will help to consolidate your learning and revision.

The Structure of this Guide

This revision guide is comprised of ten chapters, each with a specific focus.

Chapters 1 and 2

Chapters 1 and 2 offer an overview of the main information related to this Year 1/AS specification. They are a reminder of the theoretical framework including:

- Media Language
- Representation
- Media Industries
- Audiences.

Having an overview and understanding the requirements of the specification will help to focus your revision.

Chapter 1 provides a concise overview of the individual components that comprise this specification, the set products, theories and contexts, and how you will be assessed.

Chapter 2 focuses on revision of the theoretical framework, which underpins the specification, across all three components. Key terminology, theoretical perspectives and relevant contexts are reinforced through the exploration of the set products. Additional examples are also introduced in preparation for the unseen element of Component 1.

Chapters 3 and 4

Chapters 3 and 4 form a review of Component 1: Investigating the Media. They revisit the requirements of this component and the assessment.

Chapter 3 prepares you for the examination through the consideration of the set products in Section A and B. Revision checklists are given, referring to the 'spec' (specification), to help focus your revision. It also gives you opportunities to practise examination-style questions in relation to the set products and new examples of unseen products across the forms required for Section A. Each section is accompanied by a revision mind map.

Chapter 4 consolidates the products, theories and contexts required for each of the set forms, offering a straightforward reference guide.

Chapters 5 and 6

Chapters 5 and 6 focus on Component 2: Investigating Media Forms and Products.

Chapter 5 gives an overview of the set products you will study and how you will be assessed. As in Chapter 3, revision checklists are given, referring to the 'spec' (specification), to help focus your revision. Tasks and revision tips will help to reinforce and consolidate your learning. Examples from the set products and their forms are revisited in relation to relevant aspects of the theoretical framework.

Top Revision Tip

Over your course of study you will have analysed a range of unseen products in preparation for Section A of Component 1. As part of your revision you should revisit your notes for these products.

Link

Additional examples of products to prepare you for the unseen element of Component 1 can be found in Chapter 3 of the Year 1/AS student book.

Chapter 6 provides an overview of the Component 2 examination paper, explaining how you will be assessed and the specific requirements of the different sections of the examination paper.

Chapters 7 and 8

The main focus of this revision guide is the examination components. However, Chapter 7 gives a brief overview of the non-examination assessment (NEA). This includes a concise overview of the requirements, a deconstruction of a brief from the Sample Assessment Material, ideas for research and planning tasks and production tips appropriate to all briefs.

Chapter 8 explains how to complete the different elements of the cover sheet successfully, including tips for writing the Statement of Aims and Intentions.

Chapter 9

Chapter 9 revises the key skills you require for the two examinations. This includes a quick guide to the Assessment Objectives, tips for writing examination questions and revision checklists. In addition, a selection of questions is deconstructed and there are examples of candidate responses and related activities to help you see how marks are awarded. Further activities include planning your own tasks to help you tackle the extended response questions.

Chapter 10

The final chapter of this guide offers a refresher of the main theories and theoretical perspectives.

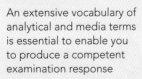

Top Revision Tip

An extensive vocabulary of analytical and media terms is essential to enable you to produce a competent examination response

This revision guide helps you to approach your revision in an organised manner, enabling you to consolidate your learning through tasks, tips and activities.

What is Expected from You

The purpose of this guide is to support your revision programme and help in preparing you for your final assessments. However, you should also take responsibility for your own learning and use this guide alongside the Year 1/AS student book and the work you have done in class.

- During your course of study you will have explored each of the set forms, set products and additional examples where appropriate. The review of the theoretical framework and the activities in this guide can be used to analyse the new products introduced here, as well as refreshing your understanding of the products you have already studied in class.

- Be organised! Spend time sorting out the notes, worksheets, resources and other useful materials you have gathered over the year. Use the revision checklists in Chapter 9 of this guide to help you plan a revision programme.

- It is important that you engage with the activities in this guide and be an active learner, as they will enable you to reinforce your knowledge and understanding in a useful and memorable way. Consider how you can record what you have learned in an easily accessible way, for example flash cards can be revisited throughout the revision period.

- The overview of theories, theoretical perspectives and contexts included in this guide is a meaningful way of reminding yourself of this more challenging element of the specification. Consider ways that work for you in remembering and applying the theories appropriately. For example, the 'What might … have said?' in Chapter 3 may help to reinforce the key elements of a particular theory.

- Use this guide and the student book to familiarise yourself with the requirements of the different sections of the examination papers. Knowing what to expect and where will help focus your revision and build your confidence. Engaging with the planning activities included in this guide will help to consolidate your learning. The 'Design your own questions' grid in Chapter 9 is a useful way of demonstrating your understanding of the different question requirements and the assessment objectives.

- You can support your independent revision by visiting the Eduqas section of the WJEC website, where you will find additional support materials. Past papers, mark schemes and the examiners' reports for the main components will also provide valuable information to guide your revision.

Top Revision Tip

Practise writing timed examination responses. Check the usual mark tariff for the question by consulting past papers and work to a mark a minute. Where you are required to respond to an unseen product you will need to add extra time to prepare for this.

The WJEC Media Studies Specification

This revision guide focuses on the Eduqas specification. Centres in Wales will follow the WJEC specification, which differs in content and structure from the Eduqas qualification.

However, this revision guide does contain some content, tips and revision activities that will be relevant to WJEC candidates:

- The theoretical framework, incorporating the exploration of Media Language, Representation, Media Industries and Audiences, underpins any study of the media and as such is relevant to both specifications. The review of the theoretical framework in Chapter 2 reinforces relevant analytical skills and subject-specific terminology.

- Chapters 3 and 5 of this revision guide explore forms and some products relevant to both specifications. While there are differences in the products studied, the revision of key codes and conventions and relevant terminology for print and audio-visual forms is transferable to the products studied for the WJEC specification.

- The activities related to approaching examination responses, deconstructing questions and designing your own examination questions found in Chapter 9 can be easily applied to examples of past questions from WJEC papers.

- Similarly, the ideas for planning and research tasks and the generic production tips for the non-examination assessment covered in Chapter 7 of this guide provide information applicable to the WJEC production unit.

The Media Studies Specification

The aim of this chapter is to remind you of the key elements of the Media Studies A Level Year 1 & AS specification and how you will be assessed.

Reminder

The theoretical framework is made up from four interrelated areas:

- **Media Language**: how the media through their forms, codes, conventions and techniques communicate meaning.
- **Representation**: how the media portray events, issues, individuals and social groups.
- **Media Industries**: how the media industries' processes of production, distribution and circulation affect media forms and platforms.
- **Audiences**: how media forms target, reach and address audiences, how audiences interpret and respond to them and how members of audiences become producers themselves.

Checklist of key points

In studying this specification, you will have done the following:

- ⊘ Developed your understanding of the media by analysing a range of set media products as well as additional products chosen by your centre.
- ⊘ Used the theoretical framework to help you explore and analyse media products, the representations contained in them, the industry that produced them and the audiences that consume them.
- ⊘ Made connections between the forms and the products and their contexts.
- ⊘ Studied the relevant social, cultural, political, economic and historical contexts in relation to the media products.
- ⊘ Used your knowledge and understanding of the theoretical framework to make connections between theory and practical work through the creation of your own media product.

Link

The specification overview is covered in more detail on pages 46–57 of the Year 1/AS student book and will be referred to in the separate sections of this revision guide.

Top Revision Tip

Make sure that you revise all the elements of the theoretical framework and are familiar with how and where they are assessed.

Quickfire Revision

1.1 Why is it important to explore additional products as well as the set products?

In class and independently you will have studied all aspects of the theoretical framework.

Products and Forms

Across Components 1 and 2 you will have studied products from the following media forms:

- Advertising and marketing
- Newspapers
- Music video
- Radio
- Film
- Video games
- Television
- Magazines
- Online media

These products will:

- have social, cultural and historical significance
- reflect different historical periods and global settings
- illustrate different industry contexts
- be constructed for different audiences
- reflect contemporary and emerging developments in the media.

Top Revision Tip

The forms and products have been chosen to offer you a broad and more detailed understanding of the media. As part of your revision you should ensure that you are aware of the significance of the different products you have studied in relation to the theoretical framework.

Take it Further

1.1 You can develop your knowledge and understanding of the theories and theoretical perspectives required by conducting your own independent research.

Theories and Contexts

In addition to analysing the set products, you will also have applied set theories and theoretical perspectives to advance and inform your understanding. These will include the theories and theoretical perspectives set for study by WJEC/Eduqas and may also include supplementary relevant theories explored in class or as part of your independent study.

Media products do not stand in isolation, they invariably reflect the contexts of the time in which they were produced. During your course you will have developed your knowledge and understanding of a range of media products in relation to the following contexts:

- social and cultural
- economic
- political
- historical.

Independent research to develop your understanding is an important aspect of your revision.

Ensure that you are aware of the demands of the different areas of the examination papers.

⇲ The Components

The Media Studies specification is made up of three components covering all elements of the theoretical framework.

Component 1: Investigating the Media

Reminder

- This component is 35% of the qualification and is worth 60 marks.
- It covers a range of media products and forms in breadth.
- It is divided into Section A and Section B.
- Section A has a focus of Media Language and Representation.
- Section B focuses on Media Industries and Audiences.

Section A: Investigating Media Language and Representation

Checklist of key points

☑ For this section of Component 1 you will have studied the set forms and products and additional examples.

☑ You will be required to analyse the products, considering how media language is used to create meanings and how representations are constructed.

☑ You will be required to apply theories and theoretical perspectives in order to analyse the products in more sophisticated detail.

☑ You will use appropriate subject-specific terminology when analysing media products.

☑ You will be aware of the demands of the examination and know when it is important to construct an extended response that develops a sustained line of reasoning.

Section A Set Products

For Section A of Component 1 you are required to study the products in the following table and additional products from the same forms to prepare you for the unseen resources in the examination. These products may be reviewed and changed at times, but the forms will stay the same.

Advertising and marketing	Music video	Newspapers
Tide print advertisement (1950s)	*Formation*, Beyoncé (2016)	*Daily Mirror* (10 November 2016)
WaterAid audio-visual advertisement (2016)	OR	Front page and article on the US election
The Kiss of the Vampire film poster (1963)	*Dream*, Dizzee Rascal (2004)	

Apply it!

1.1 Think of an example of a product you have studied in relation to each of the contexts. For example, *Tide* in Component 1 for historical context.

Quickfire Revision

1.2 What do you understand by the social and cultural contexts of a media product?

For assessment from 2021 onwards, the newspaper set product will change. It will still be the *Daily Mirror* but the set edition will be 13 March 2019.

Theories and Contexts Revision

Remember that not all theories and contexts need to be applied to all the products. The following table illustrates the theories and theoretical perspectives required for the specific products in Section A and the suggested contexts.

Product	Media Language theories	Representation theories	Suggested contexts
Tide	Semiotics (including Roland Barthes)	Representation (including Stuart Hall) Identity (including David Gauntlett)	Historical Social and cultural
WaterAid	Semiotics	Representation Identity	Social and cultural Economic Political
The Kiss of the Vampire	Semiotics	Representation Identity	Historical Social and cultural
Formation	Semiotics	Representation Identity	Social and cultural
Dream	Semiotics	Representation Identity	Social and cultural
Daily Mirror (set front page and article)	Semiotics	Representation	Social and cultural Economic Political

Consider the effect of historical contexts on the representations constructed in the set products.

Section B: Investigating Media Industries and Audiences

Checklist of key points

- ☑ For this section of Component 1 you will have studied the forms and products set by WJEC/Eduqas.
- ☑ You will be required to analyse the products considering key aspects of media industries and audiences.
- ☑ The focus of Section B is not textual analysis; the set products need to be studied as examples of the relevant media industries and audience issues that they illustrate.
- ☑ You will be required to apply theories and theoretical perspectives in order to explore relevant aspects of industry and audience.
- ☑ You will use appropriate subject-specific terminology.
- ☑ You will be aware of the requirements of this section: Film as a set form should only be studied in relation to Media Industries; Advertising is only studied in relation to Audiences.

Audience is a key focus of Component 1 Section B.

Section B Set Products

Reminder

Some of these set products and forms are the same as the ones you have studied for Section A; some are different. Where the products are the same, you will be focusing on different aspects.

Advertising	Film	Newspapers	Radio	Video games
Tide print advertisement (1950s) AND *WaterAid* audio-visual advertisement (2016)	*Straight Outta Compton* (2015)	*Daily Mirror* • one complete print edition (different from the one studied in Section A) • selected pages from the paper's website	*Late Night Woman's Hour*, Home (28 October 2016)	*Assassin's Creed III: Liberation* (2012)

For assessment from 2021 onwards there will be some changes to the set products. The Film set product will change to *Black Panther*. For *Late Night Woman's Hour* there will be no set episode; instead you will be required to consider extracts from at least one podcast. This can be the 'Home' episode or a different one.

No wonder you women buy more TIDE than any other washday product!

TIDE'S GOT WHAT WOMEN WANT!

NO SOAP-NO OTHER SUDS-NO OTHER WASHING PRODUCT KNOWN-WILL GET YOUR WASH AS CLEAN AS TIDE!

ONLY TIDE DOES ALL THREE!

TIDE GETS CLOTHES CLEANER THAN ANY OTHER WASHDAY PRODUCT YOU CAN BUY!

Quickfire Revision

1.3 Give an example of an aspect of Media Industries that you have studied in relation to the set products.

Theories and Contexts Revision

The following theories, theoretical perspectives and contexts should be explored in relation to the Section B set products.

Product	Media Industries theories	Audiences theories	Suggested contexts
Tide		Cultivation theory (including George Gerbner) Reception theory (including Stuart Hall)	Historical Social and cultural
WaterAid		Cultivation theory Reception theory	Social and cultural Economic Political
Straight Outta Compton	Power and media industries (including James Curran and Jean Seaton)		Economic Political
Daily Mirror	Power and media industries	Cultivation theory Reception theory	Social and cultural Economic Political
Late Night Woman's Hour	Power and media industries	Reception theory	Social and cultural Economic
Assassin's Creed III: Liberation	Power and media industries	Media effects Reception theory	Social and cultural Economic

Radio is explored in relation to Media Industries and Audiences in Section B.

Apply it!

1.2 In order to inform your study of media forms and products you will have developed your understanding of media contexts. Match the following contexts with the relevant statement.

Context	Statement
A. Economic	**1.** This context may be reflected through specific bias or orientation as well as through themes, values and messages.
B. Political	**2.** How and why particular groups, in a national and global context, may be under-represented or misrepresented.
C. Historical	**3.** The significance of patterns of ownership and control and factors such as funding.
D. Social and cultural	**4.** The relationship of recent technological change and media production, distribution and circulation.

Link

Refer to pages 44–45 of the Year 1/AS student book or page 10 of the AS specification to help you with this task.

Component 1 Assessment

Reminder

This component assesses:

- Media Language
- Representation
- Media Industries
- Audiences
- Media contexts

Section A is worth 35 marks and will assess Media Language and Representation in relation to two of the forms you have studied. There are two questions:

- **One question** will assess Media Language, requiring analysis of an unseen audio-visual or print product taken from any of the forms you have studied in this section.
- **One question** will assess Representation and will require you to compare a set product with an audio-visual or print unseen product from any of the forms you have studied for Section A. This unseen product may be in the same or a different form from the set product. You may be required to compare products from the same media form or from different forms. This is an **extended response question**.

Across Section A, there will always be one unseen audio-visual resource and one unseen print-based resource: Question 1 will relate to an audio-visual resource and Question 2 will relate to a print-based resource.

Top Revision Tip

You will be required to discuss the contexts of the set products in Components 1 and 2 of the examination, so it is important that you understand this aspect of the theoretical framework.

Top Revision Tip

The Representation question requires you to compare, discussing similarities and differences between the set product and an unseen product. Make sure you understand how to structure a comparative response. This is covered in Chapter 9 of this Revision Guide.

Quickfire Revision

1.4 What is meant by an extended response question?

Quickfire Revision

1.5 What is a stepped question?

Top Revision Tip

Stepped questions require you to manage your time carefully. You should avoid spending too long on the lower tariff questions to allow you more time for the questions that require extra detail and structure. Use the general guide of a mark a minute to help you.

Link

More detailed information about Component 2 can be found on pages 52–55 of the A Level Year 1/AS student book and in Chapter 5 of this revision guide. Revision tips regarding the additional media products that are only studied at A Level can be found in the Year 2/A Level revision guide.

Quickfire Revision

1.6 What is meant by studying the media forms in depth?

It is important to plan your time carefully in the examination.

Section B is worth 25 marks and will assess your knowledge and understanding of media industries, audiences and media contexts in relation to any of the forms studied for this section. There are two questions in this section:

- **Question 3** will be a **stepped question** that will assess your knowledge and understanding of Media Industries in relation to one of the forms studied.
- **Question 4** will be a stepped question that will assess your knowledge and understanding of Audiences. This will focus on a different form from Question 3.

Component 2: Investigating Media Forms and Products

Reminder

- This component is 35% of the qualification and is worth 60 marks at AS Level.
- You will have studied three media forms **in depth**, covering all areas of the theoretical framework.
- These forms are television, magazines and online media (blogs and vlogs).
- There are options of media products in each form; your teacher will have selected which products you will study.
- You will be required to apply your knowledge and understanding of theories and theoretical perspectives to the set products.

Section A: Television

Checklist of key points

In studying your television set product, you will have explored:
- ☑ The importance of genre in the production, distribution and consumption of media products.
- ☑ How the product appeals to the audience and how audiences may respond.
- ☑ How media language positions audiences.
- ☑ The significance of economic and industry contexts.
- ☑ The marketing strategies employed to promote the set product.
- ☑ Representations and how they convey attitudes and beliefs.

Set Options for Television: A Reminder

Option 1	Option 2	Option 3
Life on Mars (UK, 2006) Series 1, Episode 1	*Humans* (UK/US, 2015) Series 1, Episode 1	*The Jinx: The Life and Deaths of Robert Durst* (US, 2015) Episode 1: 'A Body in the Bay'

Applying Theories: Television

These are the theories that you will have studied in relation to your set television product at AS Level or in the first year of your A Level:

Media Language theories	Representation theories	Media Industries theories	Audiences theories
• Narratology (including Tzvetan Todorov) • Genre (including Steve Neale)	• Theories of representation (including Stuart Hall)	• Not required for this section at AS Level	• Reception theory (including Stuart Hall)

Section B: Magazines

 Checklist of key points

In studying your magazine set product, you will have explored:

☑ The significance of the economic and industry contexts in which magazine products are produced.

☑ How magazine publishers target, attract, reach and address particular audiences.

☑ The effect of social, cultural and historical contexts on the representations constructed by the magazine.

☑ How media language and representations convey values, attitudes and beliefs.

Set Options for Magazines: A Reminder

Option 1	Option 2	Option 3
Woman 23–29 August 1964 IPC	*Woman's Realm* 7–13 February 1965 IPC	*Vogue* July 1965 Condé Nast

 Apply it!

1.3 Consider how you applied Neale's theory when analysing your chosen television product.

 Top Revision Tip

Familiarise yourself with the relevant theories related to the products and forms you have studied. Remember that a question in the examination may refer directly to a theory or theorist.

The magazine options can give us an insight into the role of women in the 1960s and the values, attitudes and beliefs of the time.

Quickfire Revision

1.7 Give an example of a specification requirement covered through the study of the specific magazine options shown in the table at the bottom of page 19.

Apply it!

1.4 Look back at the magazine product you have studied and consider its historical context.

Applying Theories: Magazines

The following theories and theoretical perspectives are ones relevant to the study of the magazine options.

Media Language theories	Representation theories	Media Industries theories	Audiences theories
• Semiotics (including Roland Barthes)	• Theories of identity (including David Gauntlett)	• Power and media industries (including James Curran and Jean Seaton)	• Cultivation theory (including George Gerbner) • Reception theory (including Stuart Hall)

Section C: Online Media

Checklist of key points

In studying the set online product, you will have explored:

- ⊘ How the world has become increasingly dominated by digital technology.
- ⊘ How online, social and participatory media, including blogs and vlogs, have become an integral part of the media landscape.
- ⊘ The impact of digital technologies on media language.
- ⊘ The impact that digital technologies have on audience consumption, participation and interaction.
- ⊘ The potential offered by these digital platforms for self-representation.

Digital technology has enabled bloggers to become influencers.

Set Options for Online Media: A Reminder

Option 1	Option 2
Alfie Deyes/*PointlessBlog* www.youtube.com/user/PointlessBlog	*Zoella* www.zoella.co.uk

Applying Theories: Online Media

These are the theories that you will have studied in relation to your set online product at AS Level or in the first year of your A Level:

Media Language theories	Representation theories	Media Industries theories	Audiences theories
• Semiotics (including Roland Barthes)	• Theories of representation (including Stuart Hall) • Theories of identity (including David Gauntlett)	• Not required for this section at AS Level	• Cultivation theory (including George Gerbner)

Component 2 Assessment

Reminder

- This component assesses your knowledge and understanding of:
  - Media Language
  - Representation
  - Media Industries
  - Audiences
  - Media contexts
- You will also be assessed on your ability to apply relevant theories and theoretical perspectives and your use of subject-specific terminology.
- The AS Level paper consists of three sections, each worth 20 marks.
- In each section there will be one two-part question or one extended response question on the set product you have studied.
- The extended response questions, as with Component 1, require you to construct and develop a sustained line of reasoning and be able to substantiate your points with specific reference to the set products or theories.

Your ability to understand and apply theory and theoretical perspectives is an important part of the Component 2 assessment.

Component 3: Media Production

As this is a revision guide focusing on the examination components and Component 3 is the non-exam assessment, what follows is only a brief overview to remind you how this component fits into the overall qualification.

Reminder

- This is the non-exam component.
- It is 30% of the qualification and worth 60 marks.
- You will complete this component later in your course, alongside the other components.
- You need to choose one of the briefs released by Eduqas.

Checklist of key points

In Component 3 you will have:

☑ Applied your knowledge and understanding of the theoretical framework through the creation of an individual media production for a specific audience detailed in the brief.

☑ Produced research and planning relevant to your production.

☑ Followed the brief closely, completing all the required elements.

☑ Submitted a Statement of Aims and Intentions showing how you have applied the theoretical framework and targeted the specified audience.

☑ Completed a cover sheet.

☑ Completed a production in the chosen set form.

Component 3 Assessment

The total number of marks for this component is 60:

- 10 marks for the Statement of Aims and Intentions.
- 20 marks for creating a media product that meets the requirements of the set brief, including suitability of the chosen form, genre, industry context and target audience.
- 30 marks for creating a media product that uses media language to communicate meaning and construct representations.

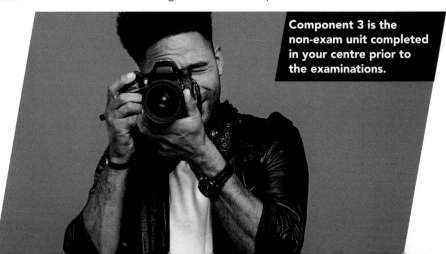

Component 3 is the non-exam unit completed in your centre prior to the examinations.

Revising the Media Studies Theoretical Framework

2

Reminder

The Media Studies A Level Year 1/AS specification is based on a theoretical framework that underpins all three components and comprises four interrelated areas:

- Media Language
- Representation
- Media Industries
- Audiences.

You need to clearly understand all areas of the theoretical framework and how they help to analyse media products.

Revising the Theoretical Framework: Media Language

Reminder

- This is one of the key elements of the Media Studies framework and will form the focus of one of the Component 1 Section A examination questions, as well as being assessed in Component 2. Media Language is part of your Analysis Toolkit, as it helps you to explore a range of media products in detail.

Link

Media Language is covered in more detail on pages 14–27 of the Year 1/AS student book.

Checklist of key points

- ☑ Media language is the means by which the media, through their forms, codes, conventions and techniques, communicate meanings.
- ☑ All media products are constructed. Media producers communicate messages through the use of media language, incorporating technical, visual and language codes.
- ☑ The creators of media products use media language to encode messages, meanings and ideas within the products.
- ☑ Audiences will decode the messages contained within the product differently and may respond to them in different ways.

Top Revision Tip

It is important that you understand the different elements of media language and their purpose, and that you are able to use this understanding to analyse the unseen examples and set products you have studied in class.

Revising Terminology

- Codes
- Connotation
- Decoding
- Denotation
- Encoding
- Polysemic
- Signification
- Signs

Quickfire Revision

2.1 What affects the way in which an audience may respond to signs and codes?

Link

Refer to pages 14–19 of the Year 1/AS student book for help with this task.

Consider how the Union flag is a polysemic sign.

Apply it!

2.2 Explain in your own words, using examples, how signs can be polysemic.

2.3 Choose a film poster you have studied in preparation for the unseen element of Component 1 Section A. Explore how the product communicates meaning through semiotics.

Revising Key Theories: Semiotics

Reminder

- One of the main theories you need to apply when analysing elements of media language is semiotics. This is the way in which texts use signs and codes to communicate meanings.

Checklist of key points

- ☑ The named theorist related to your study of semiotics is Roland Barthes.
- ☑ He put forward the idea that all texts communicate their meanings through a series of signs, the meanings of which are decoded by the audience.
- ☑ He argued that signs function at the level of denotation and connotation.
- ☑ Signs can communicate the ideology of a society and as such become accepted because they appear natural through repetition over time.
- ☑ Audiences will not decode signs in the same way; their response will be affected by a range of other factors.

Apply it!

2.1 Match the following terms with the correct definition.

Term	Definition
A. Semiotics	**1.** The meaning associated with the ~~sign~~.
B. Denotation	**2.** The process through which an audience interprets the messages contained within the product.
C. Polysemic	**3.** These are signs contained within a media product that give clues to its meaning.
D. Connotation	**4.** The process through which the product's creator communicates meaning through signs and codes.
E. Decoding	**5.** Something that stands in for or represents something else. It is not the same as the actual object.
F. Encoding	**6.** A sign that has more than one meaning and thus can be interpreted differently by different audiences.
G. Sign	**7.** The language of codes and signs used to communicate messages to an audience.
H. Codes	**8.** The literal or common sense meaning of the sign.

Revising Media Language: Visual Codes

All media products are constructed and have a purpose. Visual codes are used by the creators of media products to convey messages and meanings to an audience.

The main visual codes are:

- clothing
- colour
- expression
- gesture
- graphics
- iconography
- images
- **technique**.

Apply it!

2.4 How do visual codes communicate meanings in the following stills from *Humans* (top) and *Formation* (bottom)?

Consider how this image has been constructed using visual codes.

Quickfire Revision

2.2 What is meant by the code of technique?

Top Revision Tip

Revisit the unseen examples of media products you have studied in class and the set products, then consider how you could develop your analysis by using the terminology related to semiotics.

Revising Media Language: Technical Codes

Link

Technical codes are covered in more detail on pages 15–17 of the Year 1/AS student book.

Top Revision Tip

When exploring technical codes, it is essential that you avoid just naming or describing the technique employed. You should discuss the purpose and effect of it.

Quickfire Revision

2.3 Give an example of how a technical code may reflect the product's genre.

Reminder

- Technical codes are one of the ways in which meanings are constructed in media products. In audio-visual products this refers to the way in which camera shots, angles and movement are edited together to communicate messages.
- In print products, technical codes include design and layout, graphics and key features.
- You should be able to discuss the technical codes of a range of products, including the set products and those you study in class in preparation for the unseen resources.
- You will need to use your Analysis Toolkit – the set of key points you should refer to when analysing technical codes.
- Technical codes often reflect the genre of the product.

Apply it!

2.5 Consider the following questions when exploring the **technical codes** used in the following stills:

1. What type of shot is used and how does it communicate meaning to an audience?
2. What is the purpose of the technical code used?
3. How does the technical code used relate to the genre?
4. How does the technical code suggest the narrative?
5. Can you suggest what type of audio code may accompany the image where appropriate?

Revising Technical and Audio Codes

Apply it!

2.6 Complete the following table, considering the examples of technical and audio codes you have explored in the set products and the additional examples from the set forms you have analysed. Some examples have been completed for you as a reminder.

Technical code/ audio code	Purpose and effect When might this technical code be used and how does it communicate meanings?	Give an example from one of the set or unseen products you have studied in class to show how this technical code is used to communicate messages
Close-up		In the *WaterAid* advertisement, the close-up of the smiling face of Claudia challenges preconceived ideas about charity adverts.
Establishing shot	A rapid way of advancing the plot by showing the audience where the narrative is about to take place.	
Tracking shot		
Zoom		
Tilt		
Low angle		In the trailer for *The Jinx*, Robert Durst is shot from a low angle to make him seem more intimidating, reinforcing the idea that he is dangerous.
Lighting	In both audio-visual and print products the choice of lighting communicates messages about the form, genre and narrative.	
Colour		
Post-production techniques		
Diegetic sound		
Non-diegetic sound	This is sound that has been added post-production and is used to suggest the mood of the scene and create an atmosphere.	

(continued)

Technical code/ audio code	Purpose and effect When might this technical code be used and how does it communicate meanings?	Give an example from one of the set or unseen products you have studied in class to show how this technical code is used to communicate messages
Sound effects		
Dialogue		
Voice-over		
Music		The choice of the song in *WaterAid* reinforces the positive message of the advertisement and makes the audience feel engaged.

Top Revision Tip

Be prepared to discuss how technical and audio codes communicate messages in the products you have studied.

Top Revision Tip

With regard to the unseen product you will view in the examination, ensure that you make notes about how the product uses aspects of media language, for example technical and audio codes, to convey meaning.

Quickfire Revision

2.4 How does editing contribute to the construction of meaning in a media product?

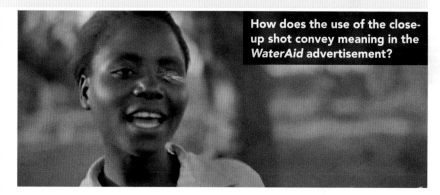

How does the use of the close-up shot convey meaning in the *WaterAid* advertisement?

Apply it!

2.7 Select a product you have studied in class. Write at least two paragraphs analysing how technical and audio codes have been used to construct meaning.

Apply it!

2.8 Study the still below from the television crime drama *Killing Eve* and consider how visual, technical and audio codes may work together to communicate messages to an audience.

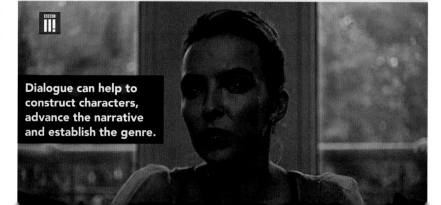

Dialogue can help to construct characters, advance the narrative and establish the genre.

Revising Language and Mode of Address

Checklist of key points

☑ Language in this sense refers specifically to the written language of print products and the spoken language of audio-visual products, and as such is different from the media language discussed earlier in this chapter.

☑ The language used by a media product can communicate meanings about the target audience, genre and purpose of the product.

☑ Mode of address is the way in which the print or audio-visual product 'speaks to' the audience and it can be direct or indirect.

☑ Language and mode of address are used in media products to convey meanings to an audience.

☑ Language features can be linked to specific media products and become recognisable and hence expected by audiences, for example the use of alliteration in advertising slogans.

☑ The lexis and mode of address used within a product may involve or exclude some audiences.

Link

Language and mode of address are covered in more detail on pages 21–22 of the Year 1/AS student book.

Revising Terminology

Language in Media Products

- Alliteration
- Colloquialism
- Hyperbole
- Lexis
- Puns
- The imperative

Apply it!

2.9 Consider the language features and mode of address used in the set and additional products you have studied for Components 1 and 2, and analyse their purpose and effect on an audience.

Complete the following table as part of your revision of the set products for Component 2.

Language feature/mode of address	Give an example of how it is used and the effect on an audience in a product you have studied
Hyperbole	
Subject-specific lexis	
Puns	
The imperative	
Slang/colloquialisms	
Informal mode of address	
Formal mode of address	
Direct mode of address	
Indirect mode of address	

Quickfire Revision

2.5 How can the lexis used within a product involve an audience?

Take it Further

2.1 Revisit the newspaper set products and a selection of one day's papers. Consider how they engage the reader through language features and mode of address.

Newspaper front pages are often very creative in the way that they use language in order to attract their audience.

Revising Genre

Link

Genre is covered in more detail on pages 22–24 of the Year 1/AS student book and is referred to when discussing specific forms and products in this revision guide and in the student book.

Quickfire Revision

2.6 What is a hybrid genre?

Checklist of key points

- ☑ In the application of your knowledge and understanding of media language you may need to discuss genre.
- ☑ This element may be specifically assessed in the Component 2 examination, where you will be expected to be aware of the dynamic and historically relative nature of genre.
- ☑ In Component 1 Section A you may be expected to demonstrate knowledge and understanding of the generic codes and conventions of the set media forms.
- ☑ Each genre has a repertoire of elements that are recognisable to audiences due to repetition over time.
- ☑ However, some contemporary media products may be less easy to categorise, they may belong to sub-genres or **hybrid genres**.
- ☑ The typical codes and conventions may also be subverted by the creator of the product in order to challenge audience expectations while still including familiar elements.
- ☑ The set theorist for this element of media language is Steve Neale. His theory will be explored in more detail later in this revision guide.

Apply it!

2.10 **Steve Neale – What can you remember?**

Fill in the missing words below.

Steve Neale stated that genres are instances of .... and ....

Genres are marked by ...., variation and ....

Genres change, ... and .... as they .... from one another.

Genres with set codes and .... are an advantage to media .... as they have a predetermined audience and therefore are easy to .... This helps to ensure the .... success of the product.

Apply it!

2.11 Study the film poster below for *Warm Bodies* and consider:

1. How are the typical codes and conventions of the film genre used in the poster?
2. What elements of hybridity are evident in the poster?
3. How is the **repertoire of elements** subverted in order to appeal to a specific audience demographic?
4. How does the poster illustrate elements of Steve Neale's theory?

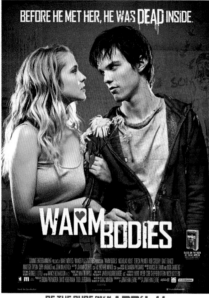

Quickfire Revision

2.7 What is included in the repertoire of elements of any genre?

Top Revision Tip

In preparation for the Components 1 and 2 assessments, consider how the set products and the other examples you have studied use genre conventions.

Revising Narrative

Checklist of key points

☑ All media products, both audio-visual and print, have a structure or a narrative. Narratives are important in constructing meanings. The narrative is a way of organising a text so that it makes sense to an audience.

☑ Narratology is the study of narrative and is an aspect of media language you will need to apply to the study of media products.

☑ The set theorist related to the study of narratology is Tzvetan Todorov.

☑ Narratology is specifically assessed in relation to the Component 2 set products, but is also relevant when analysing elements of media language in relation to the Component 1 Section A products.

Link

Narrative is covered in more detail on pages 24–27 of the Year 1/AS student book and is referred to when discussing specific forms and products in both this revision guide and the student book.

Revising Terminology

- Disruption
- Enigma codes
- Equilibrium
- Flexi-narratives
- Linear
- Manipulation of time and space
- Non-linear
- Privileged spectator position
- Three-strand narratives

Take it Further

2.2 Revisit the products you have studied and consider how the narrative conveys meaning to an audience.

Apply it!

2.12 Consider how narrative conventions are used in audio-visual and print products you have studied.

Narrative convention	Explain the purpose and effect of the narrative techniques used in a product you have studied
Flashback	
Apparently impossible position	
Privileged spectator position	
Enigma code	
Point-of-view shot	
Headlines	
Images and captions	
Use of language	

Apply it!

2.13 Write a caption for the following image that constructs a narrative.

Images in newspapers rapidly construct a narrative and are often accompanied by a caption to anchor the meaning of the image.

Narrative

» Narrative structures, forms and techniques used in audio-visual and print products, e.g. enigma codes

» The narrative codes and conventions of different media forms and products

Technical and Audio Codes

» Camera angles
» Camera shots
» Dialogue
» Diegetic sound
» Editing
» Layout and design
» Music
» Non-diegetic sound
» Post-production
» Sound effects
» Techniques
» Voice-overs

Where is it Assessed?

» Component 1 – unseen product
» Component 2 – all forms and products
» Component 3 – through knowledge and understanding of the TF

Points to Remember

» Narrative and genre are only assessed in Component 2

» In Component 1, media language is assessed in relation to the unseen product

» This question may be Q1 or Q2, according to the form of the unseen

» Discuss purpose and effect when exploring the product

Media Language

How the media communicates through their forms, codes and conventions and techniques

KEY THEORIES/THEORETICAL PERSPECTIVES

» Semiotics: Roland Barthes
» Narratology: Tzvetan Todorov
» Genre: Steve Neale

Genre

» Codes and conventions of specific types of media product

» The dynamic nature of genre and how genres change and adapt over time

» The influence of genre on the production, distribution and reception of media products

Visual Codes

» Clothing
» Colour
» Expression
» Gesture
» Graphics
» Iconography
» Images
» Technique

Language Codes

» Mode of address
» Language features, e.g. puns, alliteration
» Subject-specific lexis
» Language related to a specific form, e.g. the use of the imperative in magazines

Revising the Theoretical Framework: Representation

Link

Representation is covered in more detail on pages 28–34 of the Year 1/AS student book and is referred to when discussing specific forms and products in this revision guide and in the student book.

Revising Terminology

- Construction
- Context and purpose
- Decoding
- Encoding
- Mediation
- Selection
- Stereotypes

Quickfire Revision

2.8 What key point does Stuart Hall make about stereotyping in relation to power?

Reminder

- This is one of the key elements of the media studies framework and one that will form the focus of one of the Component 1 Section A examination questions, as well as being assessed in relation to the Component 2 set products.

Checklist of key points

- ☑ Representation is the way in which aspects of society and social identity, issues and events are re-presented or portrayed to an audience.
- ☑ All media products are constructions, they do not simply reflect the real world and the representations within them are also constructions as they are not real but are often accepted as such by an audience because they give an illusion of reality.
- ☑ The creators of media products make choices about how representations are constructed through selection and combination.
- ☑ The representation is controlled by the product's creators and as such encodes values, attitudes and beliefs.
- ☑ The repetition by the media of a particular representation may result in that representation being accepted as normal.
- ☑ Representations are affected by the context and purpose.
- ☑ Media products may construct stereotypes which can be both positive and negative.
- ☑ Representations position audiences differently and audience responses may vary.
- ☑ The key theorists to study in relation to representation are Stuart Hall (theories of representation) and David Gauntlett (theories of identity).

Newspapers construct representations of people, issues and events that clearly reflect their values, attitudes and beliefs. These are regularly reinforced across different issues of the newspaper.

Revising Representation

Apply it!

2.14 Match the following representation terms with the correct statement.

Representation term	Statement
A. Stereotype	**1.** The way in which the representation has been put together by the product's creators in order to give an illusion of reality.
B. Construction	**2.** The choices available to individuals, through, for example, technological developments, about how to construct representations of themselves.
C. Mediation	**3.** Representations and the way in which audiences may respond will change according to where the representations appear and the desired effect upon the audience.
D. Self-representation	**4.** A construction whereby the traits of a social group are exaggerated in order to be easily recognised by an audience, thus communicating messages and meanings more rapidly.
E. Context and purpose	**5.** The process a product may go through before it is shown to an audience, including the encoding of meanings through selection and construction.

The reinforcement and repetition of negative representations in charity advertisements constructs a particular view of developing countries that becomes accepted as the truth by audiences.

Quickfire Revision

2.9 What key point did David Gauntlett make about the way in which the representation of gender identity has changed in the media?

2.10 How is mediation evident in newspaper front pages and articles?

2.11 In which of your set products are you most likely to see examples of self-representation?

Link

Refer to pages 28–30 of the Year 1/AS student book for help with this task.

Take it Further

2.3 Revisit the newspapers you have studied alongside the set products and consider where mediation has occurred and the effect upon the reader.

Self-representation gives the individual control over the way in which they re-present themselves. But is it the truth?

Reinforcement of negative representations makes them appear the norm.

Top Revision Tip

In Component 1 Section A the representation question will require you to compare an unseen example with a set product. This could be in the same or a different form.

Top Revision Tip

It is important, when writing about the products in the examination in relation to representation, that you avoid simple assertions about positive and negative. Instead, explore how the representations are constructed through the use of media language, how they relate to contexts and how meanings are conveyed.

Apply it!

2.15 Choose one of your set products and write a short analysis exploring how representations of gender are constructed. Try to incorporate key terminology and support your points with specific examples.

Representations of Gender

Reminder

- This is one of the aspects of representation that you will need to study both in relation to the set products for Component 1 Section A and Component 2, and in preparation for the unseen product in Component 1 Section A.

Representations of Women in the Media

Checklist of key points

- ☑ The representation of women has developed to reflect changes in society in relation to women's roles, creating more realistic representations and positive role models.

- ☑ However, stereotypical representations of women still exist in some media forms and products. The more unrealistic representations of women that appear tend to define women by how they look and their relationships. This creates unattainable aspirations for the audience.

- ☑ Where women are constructed in a more positive way, challenging outdated stereotypes, they are seen as more active and have a key role in shaping the narrative. They are defined by what they do, rather than what they have done to them.

- ☑ Some theorists argue that, while women's roles and representations in the media have changed, they are equally limiting, as women are expected to be 'strong' and indeed to demonstrate masculine attributes.

- ☑ Representations of women change in order to reflect cultural shifts in relation to gender and to satisfy audience expectations.

How much have representations of women in beauty advertisements changed over time?

Representations of Men in the Media

Checklist of key points

- Similar to the representations of women in the media, the representation of **masculinity** has changed and adapted in order to reflect social and cultural change.

- There is now a range of representations of men in the media and the role of men within society has been called into question and examined in the light of the #MeToo campaign.

- As is the case with representations of women, while there have been some fundamental changes in representations, essentially masculinity tends to be defined by physical strength, sexual attractiveness, success in relationships and power. This is reflected in some media forms more than others, for example advertising.

- Other forms, for example the music video, while reinforcing some typical male characteristics, have also been a platform that allows men to present themselves as more rounded, realistic individuals.

Quickfire Revision

2.12 What is the definition of masculinity?

Apply it!

2.16 Consider how the representations of masculinity constructed by the products you have studied reflect social contexts.

The media today offer a more diverse range of representations of masculinity to reflect what is happening in society and audience expectations.

New terms have been introduced in order to define different aspects of masculine representation. One of these is toxic masculinity:

Toxic masculinity refers to harmful behaviour and attitudes commonly associated with some men, such as the need to repress emotions during stressful situations, and to act in an aggressively dominant way. (Sabrina Barr (2019, 17 January) 'What is Toxic Masculinity and How Can it Be Addressed?', the *Independent*, www.independent.co.uk/life-style/toxic-masculinity-definition-what-is-boys-men-gillette-ad-behaviour-attitude-girls-women-a8729336.html)

Take it Further

2.4 It is important to keep up to date with what is happening in the media. Read the article 'What is Toxic Masculinity and How Can it Be Addressed?', in the *Independent* and watch the Gillette advertisement to further your understanding of the issues surrounding modern masculinity.

In the wake of the criticism around modern masculinity, media forms that traditionally represented men in stereotypically unattainable ways, have re-evaluated their ideas. In 2019 Gillette produced a self-reflective advertisement, 'The Best a Man Can Be', referencing its original advertisement, 'The Best a Man Can Get'. The advertisement examines the different ways in which masculinity can be defined in modern society.

> *It is completely necessary to show men – and especially boys – that there are many ways of 'being a man'; ways in which strength can be reimagined as calling out a friend who tells a sexist joke or resilience can be seen as an acceptance of one's vulnerability.* (Ben Hurst, project coordinator, cited in Sabrina Barr (2019, 17 January) 'What is Toxic Masculinity and How Can it Be Addressed?', the *Independent*, https://www.independent.co.uk/life-style/toxic-masculinity-definition-what-is-boys-men-gillette-ad-behaviour-attitude-girls-women-a8729336.html)

Take it Further

2.5 The Gillette advertisement had a mixed response. Why do you think some people were unhappy with how the advertisement represented men?

THE BEST A MAN CAN GET

Gillette, in its advertisement, attempted to challenge as well as define what it means to be a man in 2019.

Representations of Ethnicity in the Media

 Checklist of key points

- Just as with gender, the representation in the media of people from different cultures has changed in order to reflect changes in society. Many areas of the media offer positive representations of minority groups and there are fewer instances whereby these social groups are defined as being 'other'.

- However, the construction of stereotypes and the misrepresentation and under-representation of these social groups in certain areas of the media continues to be problematic, as the way ethnicity and race are presented in the media is often the only experience of these cultures that an audience may encounter and so will accept it as the truth.

- Certain stereotypical representations are reinforced across different forms. For example, black and Asian people are often represented as exotic in magazines, advertisements and music videos. Some newspapers demonise young black males, defining them in terms of gang culture and violence. This perpetuates a negative representation of certain social groups.

- Other media forms offer more positive representations of minority ethnic groups, including music videos and some television crime dramas.

Name check
How a remix can help get a foot in the office door

Damien Gayle

In youth centres across Britain, music is being remixed in studios. But at the Moving on Up project of Hackney Council for Voluntary Service (HCVS), young men searching for a job are remixing their names.

Oluwatosin Adegoke, 23, who graduated from Bristol University this year, was an early adopter of this strategy. He's been called Peter, the last of his middle names, since he was a child. "My African parents wanted it to be easier for me in school," he said. "But in the past two to three years I've had to start thinking about it a bit more. One, it's instinct; and two, whenever I go by Oluwatosin I have to spell it, and sometimes I get referred to as Oliver – even after I spell it out."

Adegoke is in precarious work. But many young black men who visit the project are unemployed. They have that in common with more than a quarter of black 16-24-year-olds – the highest of any ethnic group, and more than double the 11% rate for white youths. Black males are understood to be the worst affected but data – while apparently collected – were not readily available.

At Moving on Up, they aim to do something about that. "The difference is getting a foot in the door," said Deji Adeoshun, an HCVS youth worker, who advises Adegoke and other graduates. "I've had some guys who have had to change their surname because that was an issue," he says, describing one in particular who was applying for an IT job.

"Same job: applied with his actual surname and didn't get a call back, applied with a 'Christian' name and got an interview."

The strategy Adeoshun advocates may seem radical but in the context of a workplace culture that often excludes black men, radical action may be necessary. Prof Binna Kandola, a business psychologist, argues that offices are prone to a deep-seated racist culture. "There's a racial hierarchy," Kandola says. "It was developed during the course of the slave trade and it's a hierarchy of human beings. And wherever I looked, whether it was Brazil or North America or Europe – [or] even South Africa, where black people are the majority – the hierarchy is always the same. It's white at the top, black at the bottom."

This bias has clear consequences economically. The poverty rate for ethnic minorities is double that of white groups, according to research last year by the Joseph Rowntree Foundation, which also noted that black and brown workers were concentrated in low-paid sectors. And that's despite generally higher standards of academic attainment than among most white groups.

And it is young black men who suffer the brunt of the exclusion – in particular thanks to stereotypes around aggression and fecklessness.

"Aggression and violence is the strongest stereotype that research has shown is associated with black men," Kandola says.

Connor Robinson, a mixed-race 18-year-old from south Croydon, has been working with Talent Match Croydon, a local project to help disadvantaged young people into work. "Being brown or being black has been a big affect on my life," says Robinson. "I think white people are very stereotyping towards me because I'm brown, because they think I'm a rudeboy or a gangster. White people are very quick to judge black and brown people."

Such barriers mean that by the time young black men find their way into work, they have been forced to severely moderate their ambitions. As a result, they – and particularly black African workers – are more likely to be overqualified for their roles. Adeoshun is a prime example. A law graduate, he passed his bar exams only to find he was unable to secure a pupillage at a chambers.

And for those who stay stuck on the scrapheap, the lure of the illicit economy is strong. One young man in Croydon spoke of how, in an effort to raise a couple of hundred pounds, he became involved in a scam and was convicted of fraud. Now he is barred from any job in a bank, further limiting his prospects.

What are the solutions? Many companies, including the Guardian, have introduced training for senior managers in how to recognise unconscious bias that may put them off hiring ethnic minorities.

But young black men are not sitting back and waiting for change. Lamide Olusegun, 23, who has a diploma in animation, is among them. After finding no openings at established production companies, he started his own business, selling items based on his cartoon characters. "I've seen the light in self-employment; it's helped me build some resilience," he said. "I've learned so much of how to run a business, how to market yourself. These are things I had a little idea about but I'd never had a chance to practise. And I'm seeing results."

> 'Whenever I go by Oluwatosin I have to spell it ... I can get referred to as Oliver even after I spell it'
>
> **Oluwatosin Adegoke**
> *Recent graduate*

Some newspapers include articles that highlight the issues related to particular social groups.

Apply it!

2.17 Create a revision podcast discussing how the representation of gender or ethnicity has changed over time. Support your points with reference to specific products you have studied.

Create your own podcast.

Representations of Issues and Events in the Media

Apply it!

2.18 Revision questions

Consider the following questions when you are exploring the way in which issues and events are represented in the media.

1. How has the representation been constructed through the use of media language?

2. Does the way in which the representation of the issue/event has been constructed convey any values or attitudes or a specific viewpoint?

3. How do the decisions that have been made regarding what has been selected to construct the representation offer a particular view of the issue/event? How might this affect an audience response?

4. Is there evidence that mediation has occurred? Have messages and meanings been encoded into the product reflecting the dominant ideology?

5. What has been selected and what has been left out in order to construct the representation and convey meanings?

6. Does the way in which the product has been constructed encourage the audience to focus upon a particular aspect of the issue/event, therefore offering a selected viewpoint?

Quickfire Revision

2.13 Which of the media forms you have studied will be more likely to offer representations of issues and events?

2.14 Give an example from one of the media forms or products you have studied of how a media product may encourage the audience to focus on a particular aspect of the event/issue.

2.15 What is meant by opinion leaders?

Apply it!

2.19 Revisit the set and additional products you have studied that construct representations of issues or events, for example the music videos and newspaper pages you have prepared for Component 1 Section A. Use the revision questions on page 39 as a guide.

Apply it!

2.20 **Revising the representations of issues and events**

Decide which of the following statements are true and which are false. Support your decisions with specific examples from the products you have studied.

Statement	True or false? Support with examples
Some newspapers make their dominant ideology evident in their front pages or inside articles.	
Documentaries can be biased and selective in the information they give about an issue or event.	
Newspapers are a source that audiences go to when they want true facts about an issue or event.	
Some media forms are creative in the way in which they represent issues and events and give a very personal viewpoint.	
The way in which the media represents issues and events has no effect on how the audience views them.	
Certain media forms have a very powerful influence and can become **opinion leaders**.	
How we view an issue or event in the media is exactly the same as if we witnessed it in real life.	
The way in which some media forms represent an issue actually magnifies or creates the issue itself.	
Media personalities, for example bloggers, have very little influence with regard to how their followers may respond to an issue or event.	
In the representation of an issue or event by the media it is as much to do with what is left out as what is selected for inclusion.	

Are newspapers opinion leaders?

Men

» Masculinity has a very specific meaning
» The contemporary media offers a range of representations of masculinity
» Like women, representations of men have changed over time as their role in society has developed

Issues and Events

» The way in which issues/events are represented will reflect the viewpoint of the product and its creators
» The representation of the issue/event is a construction, not real life. Mediation will have taken place

Where is it Assessed?

» Component 1 Section A – comparison of one set product and an unseen print or audio-visual product from any of the forms studied. This is an extended response with a higher mark tariff
» Component 2 – all forms and products
» Component 3 – through knowledge and understanding of the TF

Points to Remember

» All representations are constructed through a process of selection, combination and the use of elements of media language. They do not simply reflect real life but are a version of reality
» Representations are affected by social and cultural contexts
» Representations convey and reinforce beliefs about the world
» Stereotypes can be used positively and negatively to communicate messages about particular social groups

Representation

The way in which aspects of society and social identity, including gender, age and ethnicity, are re-presented or portrayed by the media

KEY THEORIES/THEORETICAL PERSPECTIVES

» Theories of representation: Stuart Hall
» Theories of identity: David Gauntlett

Women

» The representation of women has changed in order to reflect changes in society
» However, while some products construct more positive, realistic representations, others still rely on outdated stereotypes

Key Terminology

» Construction
» Context and purpose
» Decoding
» Encoding
» Mediation
» Selection
» Stereotypes
» Tokenism

Ethnicity

» Representation of non-white cultures has changed dramatically but there is still a tendency for aspects of the media to focus on difference and otherness
» Some ethnic groups are mis- and under-represented
» Certain media forms construct and reinforce stereotypical representations

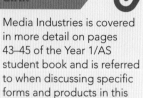

Link

Media Industries is covered in more detail on pages 43–45 of the Year 1/AS student book and is referred to when discussing specific forms and products in this revision guide and in the student book.

Quickfire Revision

2.16 What did Curran and Seaton say about more socially diverse patterns of ownership?

Revising Terminology

- Circulation
- Conglomerate
- Cross-platform marketing
- Distribution
- Horizontal integration
- Production
- Vertical integration

Top Revision Tip

The focus of the questions for this element of the theoretical framework will be related to the industry that produces the product, not the product itself. You will not be required to analyse the product textually, but to discuss it in relation to its industry. Be aware of that when you are planning your revision.

The key focus in Section B Question 3 is industry.

Revising the Theoretical Framework: Media Industries

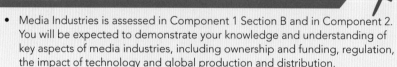

Reminder

- Media Industries is assessed in Component 1 Section B and in Component 2. You will be expected to demonstrate your knowledge and understanding of key aspects of media industries, including ownership and funding, regulation, the impact of technology and global production and distribution.
- The focus of Component 1 Section B is on the set products as examples of the output of the related media industries. You should not engage in textual analysis of the set products but study them in relation to the industry factors and issues they illustrate.
- Advertising is not assessed in relation to media industries in Component 1 Section B.
- The key theorists you have studied for this section of the theoretical framework are Curran and Seaton (power and media industries).

Checklist of key points

You will need to demonstrate your knowledge and understanding of the following in relation to the media industries you have studied:

- ☑ How media organisations, groups and individuals produce, distribute and circulate their products, and how this may differ according to the institution and the audience.
- ☑ How media organisations use marketing in order to maintain audiences.
- ☑ The ways in which developments in technology have had an impact on the production, distribution and circulation of media products.
- ☑ How the different media industries are regulated.
- ☑ The different patterns of ownership and control and the impact this has on the industry.

Apply it!

2.21 Match the following Media Industry terms with the correct definition and form/industry application.

Media Industry term	Definition	Apply it to a set form/industry
A. Distribution	**1.** A larger organisation that has interests spanning across a number of different businesses and industries.	**i.** A magazine publisher that owns a printing company has greater control over distribution of the product.
B. Production	**2.** When different companies that produce and sell similar products join together to facilitate production and create economic stability.	**ii.** Falling print sales have meant fewer newspapers being produced in the traditional form. This has forced the newspaper industry to adapt the way in which it produces and distributes the product.
C. Circulation	**3.** Where one company acquires another involved at a different level of the industry. This facilitates distribution.	**iii.** BBC Radio promotes its programmes on BBC television and the BBC website. Likewise, BBC Radio programmes review and market BBC television output.
D. Cross-platform marketing	**4.** The link between the producer and the audience. This element refers to everything employed in the promotion of the product.	**iv.** Facebook acquired Instagram in 2012. These are both social media platforms and their merger strengthened Facebook's market position and reduced competition.
E. Vertical integration	**5.** The factors that combine to make a media product, for example filming, sound, etc.	**v.** *Straight Outta Compton* was produced by Legendary Pictures. It was distributed by Universal Pictures owned by NBC Universal, part of an even larger company – Comcast.
F. Horizontal integration	**6.** When one media form is advertised on another media platform to maximise audience reach.	**vi.** In a music video this would entail filming across different locations and managing both sound and audio-visual elements.
G. Conglomerate	**7.** How many copies of a particular publication are produced and distributed.	**vii.** With regard to the film industry, this refers to the film itself and its marketing, including the trailers, posters, online marketing and global promotion of the product.

Apply it!

2.22 Hot seating

Work in groups. Each member of the group becomes an 'expert' on an area of Media Industry. Each person in turn takes the 'hot seat' and is questioned.

'Hot seating' is a useful revision strategy that helps both the 'expert' and the questioners.

Top Revision Tip

In your revision, be sure you understand the different key terms related to Media Industries – they may be the focus of an examination question.

Take it Further

2.6 Engage in independent reading and research in order to keep up to date with the latest developments in the industries you are studying.

Top Revision Tip

In Component 1 Section B the questions will be stepped, some will be lower tariff and test your knowledge or your knowledge with some understanding. Some questions will demand a more detailed response, supported by references to set forms and products. In your revision you should anticipate the different types of questions that may appear.

Revising Media Industries

Apply it!

2.23 Challenge grid

Working with a partner, answer the questions in the grid below, trying to accumulate as many points as you can.

1 mark	2 marks	3 marks	5 marks
Name the media organisation that owns the *Daily Mirror*.	Identify two ways in which newspapers are distributed.	Explain what is meant by cross-platform marketing.	Explain vertical integration in relation to one of the set forms you have studied.
What is horizontal integration?	Give two examples of media production processes.	Explain how the film industry is regulated.	Explain, using a specific example, how horizontal integration is beneficial to media industries.
Name the set theorists who suggested the links between media industries and power.	Give two examples of how television programmes are marketed.	Explain how the video games industry is regulated.	Explain how one of the media organisations you have studied reaches a global market.
What is a conglomerate?	Give two ways in which magazines are funded.	Explain the regulation of the television industry.	Explain the significance of economic factors to an industry you have studied.
What is meant by distribution?	Give a statement related to media industry theory that you are expected to know.	Explain how television programmes are marketed.	Explain the impact of recent technological change in relation to online media. Support your points with examples.

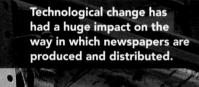

Technological change has had a huge impact on the way in which newspapers are produced and distributed.

Regulation

» The names of the regulatory bodies
» The ways in which different industries are regulated, including recent changes
» The impact of new digital technologies on media regulation
» The issues surrounding the regulation of particular media industries and individual producers

Key Terminology

» Circulation
» Conglomerate
» Cross-platform marketing
» Distribution
» Horizontal integration
» Ownership
» Production
» Vertical integration

Where is it Assessed?

» Component 1 Section B
» Component 2 all forms and products
» Component 3 through knowledge and understanding of the TF

Points to Remember

» The focus of Component 1 Section B is on the set products as examples of the related media industries. You should not engage in textual analysis of the set products
» You will be expected to demonstrate your knowledge and understanding of key aspects of Media Industries in Components 1, 2 and 3. This will be specifically assessed in lower tariff questions in Component 1 Section B
» Advertising is not assessed in relation to Media Industries in Component 1 Section B

Media Industries

How the media industries' processes of production, distribution and circulation affect media forms and platforms

KEY THEORIES/THEORETICAL PERSPECTIVES

» Power and media industries: James Curran and Jean Seaton

Technological Change

» The relationship between technological change and media production, distribution and circulation
» How digital platforms have facilitated the distribution and circulation of products
» How technology has changed the way in which audiences access and use products

Ownership

» The significance of patterns of ownership and control
» Conglomerate ownership
» Vertical and horizontal integration

Industry Processes

» Global production, distribution and circulation by organisations, groups and individuals
» How media organisations maintain national and global audiences

Revising the Theoretical Framework: Audiences

Link

Audiences is covered in more detail on pages 35–42 of the Year 1/AS student book and is referred to when discussing specific forms and products in this revision guide and in the student book.

Revising Terminology

- Active
- Appeal
- Attract
- Demographic
- Participatory culture
- Passive
- Positioning
- Prosumer
- Psychographic
- Reach
- Target

Reminder

- Audiences is one of the key elements of the media studies framework and one that will form the focus of one of the Component 1 Section B examination questions, as well as being assessed in relation to the Component 2 set products.
- Audiences will not be assessed in relation to film for Component 1 Section B.

Checklist of key points

- ☑ The relationship between the audience and the media product changes in order to reflect social and technological developments.
- ☑ Developments in technology mean that audiences have higher expectations but are also easier to reach across different platforms.
- ☑ The way in which audiences access media products has changed dramatically and media industries have had to adapt the way in which they target and reach audiences.
- ☑ Audiences are not a mass, they are made up of individuals. Audiences will not respond in the same way to media products, the response will be affected by social and cultural factors.
- ☑ There is a range of theories and theoretical perspectives that will help you to understand the relationship between the product and the audience.
- ☑ The set theorists you need to study are Albert Bandura (media effects), George Gerbner (cultivation theory) and Stuart Hall (reception theory).
- ☑ You are not required to study all these theorists in relation to all of the set products in Components 1 and 2.

The ways in which audiences consume media products have changed as technology has progressed.

Developments in technology have enhanced the viewing experience for audiences.

BINGE-WATCHING

Apply it!

2.24 Match the following Audience terms with the correct definition.

Audience term	Definition
A. Audience positioning	**1.** A way of categorising audiences according to factors, including age, income and occupation. This helps industries to determine how to target the audience.
B. Target audience	**2.** An audience who are more likely to accept the preferred meaning of the product. This audience are less likely to challenge encoded meanings.
C. Demographic	**3.** The elements of the product that resonate with a particular audience and persuade them to engage with the product.
D. Active audience	**4.** When media products manipulate audiences to respond in a particular way.
E. Participatory culture	**5.** The specific group at whom the media product is aimed.
F. Audience reach	**6.** A relatively small audience with specialised interests, tastes and backgrounds.
G. Prosumer	**7.** Whereby individuals not only consume the media product but also contribute to existing products and produce their own.
H. Passive audience	**8.** A way of categorising audiences based on factors including values, attitudes and lifestyle choices.
I. Niche audience	**9.** An audience who engage with the media product and respond to the messages encoded in it.
J. Appeal	**10.** The number and range of different people who can access and are exposed to a media product.
K. Psychographics	**11.** Related to marketing, this term describes individuals who comment on, create and adapt existing content and then distribute it digitally.

Top Revision Tip

When preparing for the examination you need to consider all the elements of audiences in relation to the set products. Remember that the focus of the question could be how the product works on the audience, or how the audience engages with the product.

Quickfire Revision

2.17 Why is demographic profiling seen to be a less reliable way of grouping audiences by some media industries?

2.18 Which media industries still rely on demographic profiling of audiences and why?

2.19 Who first used psychographic profiling as a means of categorising audiences?

2.20 Give examples of the main groups created as part of psychographic profiling.

Take it Further

2.7 Explore the more recent research that has been conducted into how audiences are categorised, for example Rachel Pashley's work on new female tribes.

Rachel Pashley conducted new research into categorising contemporary women.

What do I need to know about audiences?

Audiences are categorised by the media industry in order to make them easier to research and target. Different ways of grouping audiences include:

- **Demographic profiling**: this categorises audience groups from A to E according to class, occupation and income. Categories A and B contain the most wealthy groups in society with the highest disposable income. Age and gender are also factors used in constructing demographic groups. This method of audience profiling is seen to be outdated but is still used by some media industries.

- **Psychographic profiling**: this method defines an audience by their values, attitudes and lifestyles, considering how cross-cultural consumer characteristics can be used to group people depending on their motivational needs. This method considers that audiences are more complex than demographic profiling would suggest.

- **Tribes**: this is a more recent method of categorising audiences and often incorporates self-identification as a means of grouping them. This method is used in targeting audiences by grouping together people with the same mindset, attitudes and goals.

How media products target, attract, reach, address and construct audiences.

All media products have a specific target audience, some products target a broad audience and some a niche one. Depending on the audience, the product will use a range of techniques to engage this audience with the product, including:

- **Technical and audio codes**: the choice of shots and editing style.

- **Language and mode of address**: use of lexis and tone may be target-audience specific.

- **How the product is constructed**: the choice of images and the way in which the product is put together may appeal to a particular audience.

- **The marketing and distribution of the product** determines the audience reach and will differ according to the target audience.

- **The way in which the audience is positioned by the product** will encourage the audience to engage with the product and accept the encoded meanings.

Advertisements construct an idea of who the audience is and the lives they may lead.

- **The way in which the product is created and its marketing**: construct the idea of the audience they are targeting. Over time, advertisements have constructed an image of an audience which may not reflect the actual consumer. The audience sees an aspirational image of themselves that can be persuasive.

- **Some products produce profiles** of their audience to target them more effectively and to provide potential advertisers with information.

The different ways in which media products position audiences.

Audience positioning refers to the relationship between the product and the audience and how the way in which they are positioned affects their response.

Apply it!

2.25 Consider how audiences are positioned in the products you have studied.

How audiences are positioned	Specific example from a set product and the effect on the audience
Technical codes	
Audio codes	
Language and mode of address	
The construction of the product	

The different ways in which audiences respond to media products.

An audience is made up from individuals who may respond to the same media product in different ways. Their response will be affected by:

- gender
- age
- ethnicity
- culture and cultural experience
- cultural competence
- situated culture.

How audiences interact with the media and become producers themselves.

- Modern technology allows audiences greater opportunities to interact with media products across a range of platforms. This has facilitated the creation of a participatory culture whereby audiences are not only the consumers of media products but also contribute to existing products and produce their own.
- Audiences are also given a range of opportunities to engage actively with media products and 'have their say' through the use of social media platforms, for example Twitter. This allows them to potentially influence media content.

Quickfire Revision

2.21 Give an example of how a product constructs the idea of an audience.

Top Revision Tip

Make sure that you understand the difference between the keywords target, attract, reach, address and construct in relation to the products you study and the industry that produces them.

The way in which a product is constructed can position an audience emotionally.

Individuals now have the means to create and distribute their own content.

Citizen journalists contribute content to media products.

Quickfire Revision

2.22 What did Stuart Hall suggest were the three main ways that an active audience may respond to a media product?

Apply it!

2.27 Choose one of the set products you have studied and apply the three ways audiences may respond to media products as suggested by Stuart Hall.

- Media products, for example newspapers, will use content produced by citizen journalists on their mobile phones, as they have had more immediate access to an event.
- There is a clear, interactive relationship between media producers and their audience.
- The internet and social media have facilitated the coming together of online communities with shared interests, for example fan sites. Bloggers and vloggers also have easy access to an audience and can be a lucrative means of advertising where more traditional platforms are less so. Consumers have become prosumers.

Revising Audiences

Apply it!

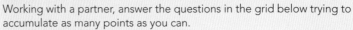

2.26 Challenge grid

Working with a partner, answer the questions in the grid below trying to accumulate as many points as you can.

1 mark	2 marks	3 marks	5 marks
What is a target audience?	Identify two ways in which media organisations categorise audiences.	Explain what is meant by a demographic audience profile.	Explain cultural experience in relation to one of the set forms you have studied.
Name the ad agency that first used psychographic profiling.	Give two examples of the psychographic groups identified by the ad agency.	Explain what is meant by a psychographic audience profile.	Explain why categorising audiences is useful to media organisations.
Name the set theorist whose focus is reception theory.	Give two examples of factors that could affect audience response.	Explain the effect of positioning on an audience.	Explain cultural competence in relation to one of the set forms you have studied.
Name the set theorist whose focus is media effects.	Briefly explain what is meant by a prosumer.	Explain what is meant by media effects.	Explain some of the ways in which an audience can interact with media products.
Name the set theorist whose focus is cultivation theory.	Give one of the statements related to cultivation theory that you are expected to know.	Explain what is meant by cultivation theory.	Explain cultivation theory, referring to one of the set newspapers you have studied.
What is a niche audience?	Give two ways in which an audience can be positioned.	Explain what is meant by an interactive audience.	Explain how one of the set products positions audiences.

Audience Responses

» How audiences interpret and respond to the media
» How audiences may respond to and interpret the same media product in different ways
» What affects the way in which an audience interprets and responds to a media product, e.g. gender, age

Key Terminology

» Active
» Appeal
» Attract
» Demographic
» Participatory culture
» Passive
» Positioning
» Prosumer
» Psychographic
» Reach
» Target

Where is it Assessed?

» Component 1 Section B
» Component 2 all forms and products
» Component 3 through knowledge and undertanding of the TF

Points to Remember

» The relationship between the audience and the media product changes in order to reflect social and technological developments
» The way in which audiences access media products has changed dramatically
» Audience will not be assessed in relation to film for Component 1 Section B

Audiences

How media forms target, reach and address audiences, how audiences interpret and respond to them and how audience members become producers

KEY THEORIES/THEORETICAL PERSPECTIVES

» Media effects: Albert Bandura
» Cultivation theory: George Gerbner

Audience Categorisation

» Demographic: age, gender, class, income
» Psychographic: lifestyle (Young and Rubicam)
» Tribes
» How grouping helps the industry to effectively target the audience

Audience Appeal Strategies

» What is meant by the target audience?
» The techniques used by media industries to target audiences, e.g. content, appeal, marketing, distribution and circulation of products
» How media producers reach, attract and address audiences
» How audiences are positioned by media products
» The ways in which media producers construct audiences

Audience Interaction

» Passive and active audiences
» The impact of technology in facilitating audience consumption of and response to the media
» The role of the audience as prosumers and their importance to the success of a product
» How participatory culture has enabled audiences to contribute to existing products and create their own

Link

Contexts are covered on pages 44–45 of the Year 1/ AS student book and are referred to when discussing specific forms and products in this revision guide and in the student book.

Quickfire Revision

2.23 What is meant by contexts?

2.24 Give an example of the effect of funding in the film industry.

Apply it!

2.28 Select a media product you have studied. Write at least two paragraphs on how it reflects a particular context.

Apply it!

2.29 Consider how the film and newspaper products you have studied reflect a political context.

Top Revision Tip

Political contexts are most relevant when discussing newspapers and film.

Revising the Theoretical Framework: Contexts

Reminder

In order to inform your study of the media forms and products you will have developed your knowledge and understanding of the products in relation to the following **contexts**:

- economic
- historical
- political
- social and cultural.

Certain contexts are more relevant to specific media forms and products.

Checklist of key points

Historical contexts

Ø The ways in which genre reflects the time and so is historically relative.

Ø The effect of historical context on representations.

Ø The impact of technological change on media production distribution and circulation.

Social and cultural contexts

Ø How the values and attitudes of society at the time affect media products.

Ø How these values and attitudes may affect the way in which audiences respond to media products.

Ø How, within a social and cultural context, social groups may be under-represented or misrepresented.

Ø How media products are shaped by cultural influences and will change and adapt in order to reflect the ideas of the time.

Economic contexts

Ø How production, distribution and circulation both nationally and globally relate to economic contexts.

Ø The importance and relevance of ownership and control.

Ø The impact of funding, sales and consumers.

Political contexts:

Ø How the representations, values and messages encoded in certain media products reflect the political contexts in which they were made.

Ø How a range of industry aspects, including ownership, political viewpoint, production, distribution, marketing and audience consumption, can reflect the political context of the product.

Revising the Theoretical Framework: A Summary

The framework consists of four inter-related areas:

Media Language: how the media, through their forms, codes, conventions and techniques, communicate meanings. Studied in: Component 1 Section A, Component 2 and Component 3.

Representation: how the media portray events, issues, individuals and social groups. Studied in: Component 1 Section A, Component 2 and Component 3.

Media Industries: how production, distribution and circulation processes in different media industries affect media forms, platforms and products. Studied in: Component 1 Section B, Component 2 and Component 3

Audiences: how media forms target, reach and address audiences, how audiences interpret and respond to forms and products, and how audience members may become producers of media content. Studied in: Component 1 Section B, Component 2 and Component 3.

These areas are applied to a range of forms and products in Components 1, 2 and 3, and to your own production work in Component 3.

Top Revision Tip

It is very important to be aware of which elements of the theoretical framework are relevant to which components. This will help to guide your revision and prepare you for the different sections of the examination papers.

Top Revision Tip

Familiarise yourself with the key theorists, the theoretical perspectives and the statements from the specification. You should also be able to apply these to the relevant forms and products.

Take it Further

2.8 Exploring the theorists and theoretical perspectives in greater detail will develop your knowledge and understanding and your ability to apply their ideas.

Who Said That?

Revising Theory and Theoretical Perspectives

Apply it!

2.30 Match the following theorists/key figures with the correct theory/theoretical perspective and explanatory statement.

Theorist/key figure	Theory/theoretical perspective	Explanatory statement
A. Stuart Hall	**1.** Semiotics	**i.** The idea that stereotyping, as a form of representation, reduces people to a few simple characteristics or traits.
B. Steve Neale	**2.** Media effects	**ii.** The idea that all narratives share a basic structure that involves a movement from one state of equilibrium to another.
C. Roland Barthes	**3.** Theories of identity	**iii.** The idea that genres change, develop and vary as they borrow from and overlap one another.
D. Albert Bandura	**4.** Narratology	**iv.** The idea that while, in the past, the media tended to convey singular, straightforward messages about ideal types of male and female identities, the media today offer a more diverse range of stars, icons and characters from whom you may pick and mix different ideas.
E. Stuart Hall	**5.** Cultivation theory	**v.** The idea that the media can implant ideas into the minds of the audience directly.
F. Tzvetan Todorov	**6.** Power and media industries	**vi.** The idea that texts communicate their meanings through a process of signification.
G. George Gerbner	**7.** Reception theory	**vii.** The idea that more socially diverse patterns of ownership help to create the conditions for more varied and adventurous media productions.
H. David Gauntlett	**8.** Genre theory	**viii.** The idea that there are three hypothetical positions from which messages and meanings can be decoded.
I. Curran and Seaton	**9.** Representation	**ix.** The idea that exposure to repeated patterns of representation over long periods of time can shape and influence the way in which people perceive the world around them.

Component 1: Investigating the Media

Reminder

This component has:

- introduced you to the key aspects of the theoretical framework: Media Language, Representation, Media Industries and Audiences
- developed your ability to apply relevant theories and theoretical perspectives
- developed your understanding of media forms through the study of additional products from the set forms
- developed your understanding of how media products relate to key contexts: social and cultural, historical, political and economic
- developed your **subject-specific terminology**.

Checklist of key points

- ☑ In Component 1 you will have studied a broad range of forms and products set by WJEC/Eduqas.
- ☑ These forms are advertising and marketing, music video, newspapers, film, radio and video games.
- ☑ Component 1 is divided into Section A and Section B. Section A has a focus of media language and representation and Section B focuses on media industries and audiences.
- ☑ In Section A you will be required to analyse unseen products in the examination. You will have prepared for this by studying other examples in each form to familiarise yourself with aspects of the theoretical framework.

≫ Section A: Investigating Media Language and Representation

Media language and representation are the focus for the exploration of the forms and products you will study for Section A.

In investigating these elements of the theoretical framework across both the set products and the additional examples, you will be aware that you need to cover the statements set out in the specification in relation to the theoretical framework. These statements will be referred to in the different sections of this revision guide.

Link

There is a reminder of the set products you are required to study in Chapter 1 of this revision guide. Remember that some of the set products will change for assessment in 2021.

Link

There is an overview of what you are required to know about media language in Chapter 2 of this revision guide.

Quickfire Revision

3.1 Which of the Component 1 Section A products have you studied in relation to political contexts?

3.2 What is meant by subject-specific terminology?

Top Revision Tip

You will probably have analysed a range of additional media products from the forms you have studied over the year. When you are revising make sure you use these examples to help you to prepare for the unseen resources in the examination.

Revising Media Language Statements

Link

The additional statements required for Media Language in Year 2/A Level are covered in the Year 2/A Level revision guide.

Top Revision Tip

The statements in the Apply it! below, related to the different areas of the theoretical framework, will form the basis for the examination questions.

Apply it!

3.1 In the following table, tick to show that you understand the statement. An example for each one has been given for you. Demonstrate your understanding by giving a different example of how you have applied the statement to an additional form or product you studied in Section A.

Statement	✓	Example	Different example
How the various modes and language associated with different media forms communicate multiple meanings.		How visual codes, for example in print advertising, communicate polysemic meanings.	
How the combination of elements of **media language** influence meaning.		How the combination of images and text on a newspaper front page anchor meaning.	
How developing technologies affect media language.		How computer-generated imagery (CGI) may affect the ways in which music videos are produced.	
The codes and conventions of media forms and products, including the **processes** through which media language develops as genre.		Genre codes and conventions are common to media forms and are recognisable to audiences, for example the elements of the front page of a newspaper.	
The processes through which meanings are established through intertextuality.		The way in which media producers make intertextual references to other media products to communicate meanings. For example, the references to the New Orleans floods in *Formation*.	
How audiences respond to and interpret the above aspects of media language.		The way in which the elements above may affect audience understanding of and responses to a product. For example, the combination of elements of media language on the front page of a newspaper may cause a negative audience response depending on their viewpoint.	

Quickfire Revision

3.3 What is meant by media language?

3.4 What is meant by media processes?

Apply it!

3.2 Choose one of the additional products you have studied in class from any of the Section A forms.

Construct a question from one of the statements.

Answer it, spending approximately 15 minutes on your response.

Top Revision Tip

Practise writing responses to questions under timed conditions to prepare effectively for the examination.

The *Formation* music video uses intertextuality to communicate meanings.

Link

The additional statements required for Representation in Year 2/A Level are covered in the Year 2/A Level revision guide.

Revising Representation Statements

Apply it!

3.3 In the following table, tick to show that you understand the statement. An example for each one has been given for you. Demonstrate your understanding by giving a different example of how you have applied the statement to a form or product you studied in Section A.

Statement	✓	Example	Different example
The way events, issues, individuals (including self-representation) and social groups (including social identity) are represented through a process of selection and combination.		Media producers will select and combine elements of media language in order to construct a particular representation, for example the selection of positive images and audio track in the *WaterAid* advert.	
The way the media, through re-presentation, construct versions of reality.		What we see in the media is not real life, even when it purports to be. News events are re-presented differently in different newspapers.	
The processes that lead media producers to make choices about how to represent events, issues, individuals and social groups.		The media organisation can influence how an event or social group is represented, for example the political leanings of a newspaper will affect representations.	

(continued)

Statement	✓	Example	Different example
The effect of social and cultural context on representations.		Media products reflect the time in which they were made. The *Tide* advertisement reflects the culture of the 1950s in relation to gender.	
How and why stereotypes can be used positively or negatively.		Stereotypes are used to communicate messages rapidly as they are easily recognised by audiences. *WaterAid* challenges the more usual stereotypes of charity campaigns to construct a more positive message.	
How and why particular **social groups**, in a national and global context, may be under-represented or misrepresented.		Images of the developing world tend to be negative, particularly in charity campaigns as their aim is to target a more privileged audience with power.	
How media representations convey values, attitudes and beliefs about the world and how these may be systematically reinforced across a wide range of media representations.		For example, social and cultural attitudes regarding gender within society at a specific time. You may have studied other examples of 1960s film posters that reinforce a particular representation of women at that time.	
How audiences respond to and interpret media representations.		Audiences are individuals, not a mass. Several factors will affect the way in which they may respond to representations in the media.	
The effect of historical context on representations.		The ideas and values of the time in which it was made will affect the representations in a product. The *Tide* advert represents gender in a particular time period.	

Quickfire Revision

3.5 Give an example of a social group.

Newspapers re-present events to construct different versions of reality.

Quickfire Revision

3.6 What aspects might affect how an audience interprets or responds to representations?

Revising the Set Forms and Products: Advertising and Marketing

Link

The additional Year 2/A Level theories will be explored in detail in the Year 2/A Level revision guide.

Revising Terminology

- Brand identity
- Demonstrative action
- Hard sell
- Hyperbole
- Iconic representation
- Intertextuality
- Mode of address
- Product endorsement
- Soft sell
- Typography and graphics
- Unique selling point

Reminder

- Advertising and marketing is studied in Component 1 Section A in relation to media language and representation.
- The products you will have studied are:
  - *Tide* print advertisement (1950s)
  - *WaterAid* audio-visual advertisement (2016)
  - *The Kiss of the Vampire* film poster (1963).
- Advertisements use media language and construct representations in order to communicate meanings about their products and services.
- Advertising has subject-specific terminology that you need to use in your analysis of advertising products.
- The set theory/theorist for Media Language in Year 1/AS and Year 2/A Level is semiotics/Roland Barthes.
- The set theories/theorists for Representation in Year 1/AS are: theories of representation/Stuart Hall; theories of identity/David Gauntlett.
- The products remain the same in Year 2/A Level. In Year 2/A Level you will study additional theories, including structuralism/Claude Lévi-Strauss for Media Language. For Representation you will explore feminist theories, including van Zoonen and bell hooks, and theories around ethnicity and postcolonial theory, including Paul Gilroy.

Checklist of key points

Print and audio-visual adverts have a limited amount of time to catch the attention of the audience. The aim of an advertising campaign is to establish a brand identity which will be included in all elements of the campaign.

The producers of campaigns use a range of persuasive strategies to appeal to the audience, including:

- ⊘ Visual codes to communicate messages rapidly. Advertisements use non-verbal communicators that are recognisable to audiences.
- ⊘ Persuasive language including hyperbole and alliteration to engage the attention of the audience. Slogans that are memorable and reinforce elements of the product.
- ⊘ A narrative. Many adverts are similar in style to short films, their aim is to involve the audience in the story.
- ⊘ Soft and hard sell techniques, depending on the genre of the advert.
- ⊘ Establishing the codes and conventions of the advertising genre.
- ⊘ Creating a brand identity through, for example, the name, the logo, a slogan and often a celebrity endorsement.

The *WaterAid* advertisement constructs a narrative that challenges more conventional representations in charity advertisements, so involves the audience in a positive, personal story.

Revision Checklist: Media Language in Advertising and Marketing

It is important to familiarise yourself with the key statements related to the different elements of the Year 1/AS specification.

What it says in the spec	What you need to know
How the different modes and language associated with different media forms communicate multiple meanings.	• The different ways in which visual codes, sound, speech and mode of address convey meaning in advertising products. For example, the way that colour conveys meaning.
How the combination of elements of media language influence meaning.	• How elements of media language, such as technical and audio codes, work together in advertising products to construct meaning.
The codes and conventions of media forms and products, including the processes through which media language develops as a genre.	• The **repertoire of elements** used across marketing products from different genres, for example to establish a brand identity for a film. • The predictable elements that belong to a specific genre, for example the use of a dark colour palette for a film poster in the horror genre.
The processes through which meanings are established through intertextuality.	• The way in which adverts may create meanings by referencing another media product. For example, replicating memorable scenes from an iconic film or television programme, related to the cultural database of the audience, within the advert.
How audiences respond to and interpret the above aspects of media language.	• The different ways in which audiences may respond to the way in which media language is constructed to persuade them within advertising. For example, with a charity campaign, an **active audience** may donate their time or money.
How developing technologies affect media language.	• How, for example, special effects, CGI and graphics can combine to create meaning in an advertisement.

Link

Advertising and marketing is covered in more detail on pages 60–71 of the Year 1/AS student book.

Quickfire Revision

3.7 What is meant by a repertoire of elements?

Predictable dark colours and a repertoire of elements typical of the genre are used for this horror film poster.

Quickfire Revision

3.8 How would you define an active audience?

Apply it!

3.4 What strategies are used in the images from the advertising campaigns below?

Apply it!

3.5 Match the following advertising terms with the correct definition.

Advertising term	Definition
A. Hard sell	**1.** The use of 'ordinary' people or celebrities in the advertisement. The audience may be convinced by this person to listen to the message or buy the product.
B. Brand identity	**2.** The element that makes the product different from its competitors, for example a new ingredient, flavour or a claim for what the product can do.
C. Soft sell	**3.** This is 'in your face' advertising. These advertisements are usually short, may be loud and employ a direct mode of address as part of their selling strategy.
D. Demonstrative action	**4.** This is what distinguishes one product or service from another and creates an image for the campaign. It establishes a recognisable association with the consumer and may include the logo, font style or colour palette.
E. Mode of address	**5.** This is where the product is seen to be used in the advertisement. The aim is to convince the audience how effective the product is.
F. Product endorsement	**6.** This refers to how the advertisement communicates with the audience, for example some of the people may look directly at the audience to personalise the message.
G. Unique selling point	**7.** This is where the audience are sold a lifestyle, not just a product. The actual product is often not the focus, may not appear or only be alluded to briefly.

Revising Media Language: Charity Campaigns

Reminder

- Charity campaigns are a genre of advertising.
- Charity campaigns use the codes and conventions of the advertising form, but also share recognisable conventions that are particular to charity advertisements.
- Charity campaigns have a different aim from those for consumable products. This is to raise awareness and elicit an immediate response from the audience.
- Charity campaigns can be more explicit in their images and more hard-hitting than those from other genres.

Apply it!

3.6 Use the following table to revise the elements of Media Language with reference to the set product, *WaterAid*, and another charity campaign you have studied. Consider the purpose and effect of the technique used.

Element of Media Language	Example from *WaterAid* Purpose and effect	Additional example Purpose and effect
Technical codes		
Audio codes		
Visual codes		
Language and mode of address		
Narrative		
Codes and conventions of the advertising sub-genre		

Take it Further

3.1 To expand your understanding of the charity advertising genre, research an example of an advertisement that you have not studied in class.

Apply it!

3.7 Using your additional example, answer the following question:

How does media language communicate meaning in the advertisement?
[10 marks]

Spend approximately 10–15 minutes on your response.

Top Revision Tip

The Media Language question will always relate to an unseen audio-visual or print resource. However, your detailed study of the set forms and products will help to prepare you for this. The unseen will always be taken from one of the forms you have studied for Section A.

Apply it!

3.8 Watch the 2018 Save the Children charity advertisement on YouTube: *Censored*, www.youtube.com/watch?v=oBl5l6d993M. Analyse how media language is used to communicate meaning in it.

1. How do the **technical codes** construct meaning in the advertisement?

Consider:

- camera shots: how they involve the audience
- editing: how this conveys the panic to an audience who will have no experience of the situation.

3. How does the combination of **visual codes** influence the meaning in the advertisement?

Consider:

- expression
- clothing
- colour palette
- technique
- gesture.

5. How do the **audio codes** in the advertisement establish meaning?

Consider:

- diegetic and non-diegetic sound
- the voice-over
- the ambient sounds
- sound effects.

7. What **paradigmatic choices** have been made by the producers of this advertisement?

2. How do **language** and **mode of address** establish meanings in the advertisement?

Consider:

- the on-screen graphics and their effect
- how the camera positions the audience
- how the advert speaks to the audience
- the use of language devices.

4. How do **setting** and **iconography** convey meaning in the advertisement?

Consider:

- recognisable settings seen in other forms, for example news
- images related to war and conflict
- binary opposites – children within the war zone.

6. What recognisable **codes** and **conventions** of the charity campaign sub-genre are evident in this advertisement?

Consider:

- the aim to raise audience awareness
- the use of apparently 'real people'
- the setting and iconography related to an issue
- the name of the advert/campaign
- the use of a personalised narrative.

Apply it!

3.8 Using the Save the Children advertisement *Censored*, answer the following Section A Media Language question:

How do codes and conventions communicate meaning in this charity advertisement? [10 marks]

Spend approximately 10–15 minutes on your response.

Revising Media Language: Print Advertising Products

Reminder

- The set print product at the time of writing is the *Tide* advert from the 1950s.
- In studying this and other print advertisements you will have prepared for the unseen element of Section A, where you may be required to analyse a print advertisement.
- Your study of the set product and additional examples will have familiarised you with the codes and conventions of the advertising form and of products within the different advertising genres.

Checklist of key points

Print advertisements share common conventions with audio-visual examples, which makes them part of the same media form. However, they also employ elements specific to the print advertising form including:

☑ Print adverts have less space and time to persuade the audience to engage with the product than audio-visual adverts. They must therefore use strategies to arrest the attention of the audience.

☑ Layout and design – the construction of the advert and the **paradigmatic** choices that have been made to communicate meaning.

☑ The use and construction of still images, some of which may have been manipulated to create a version of reality.

☑ Typography and graphics – font styles are chosen to communicate messages about the product or service.

☑ Visual codes, including colour, gesture, expressions and technique.

☑ Technical codes, including camera shots, the use of lighting and post-production editing.

☑ Language and mode of address.

Link

There is an analysis of a Maybelline advertisement on page 65 of the Year 1/AS student book.

Apply it!

3.10 Consider how media language constructs meaning in the following advertisement for *Alien* perfume.

Take it Further

3.2 Apply your knowledge and understanding of semiotics to the Save the Children and Alien advertisements included in this chapter.

Quickfire Revision

3.9 What is a paradigm?

Apply it!

3.11 Role of the expert

Working in groups, each member independently researches an example of a historical and contemporary advertisement. They then discuss their research with the group.

The group should be active listeners considering:

- use of subject-specific terminology
- understanding of media language
- reference to specific examples from the chosen products
- application of theory, for example semiotics
- understanding of the codes and conventions of the advertising form.

Give constructive feedback to the presenter, referring to the positive aspects and what could have been improved. To avoid giving unhelpful negative feedback, use the traffic light system:

Green: better then I could have done it.

Amber: the same as I would have done it.

Red: I could have done it better. Here you should give specific suggestions as to what you would have said.

Quickfire Revision

3.10 What is a syntagm?

Apply it!

3.12 Use your study of the *Tide* advertisement to analyse the historical advertisement below. Remember to use your understanding of semiotics.

1. What are the connotations of the **visual codes** used in the advertisement?

Consider:

- clothing
- expression
- gesture
- colour palette.

2. What can you say about the **language** and **mode of address** used in the advertisement to persuade the 1950s audience to buy the product?

Consider:

- language devices, for example the use of hyperbole and superlatives
- other examples of persuasive language.

3. How is **brand identity** established in the advertisement?

4. What other techniques are used by the producer of the advertisement to persuade the 1950s housewife to purchase the product?

5. What can you say about the way in which this advertisement has been constructed?

Consider:

- layout and design
- technical codes
- paradigmatic choices
- the **syntagm** of the advert and how this produces meaning.

6. Although this is a 1950s advertisement, what advertising strategies used in it are still evident in contemporary advertisements?

Revising Film Posters: Media Language

Reminder

- The promotion of films through film posters is another element of advertising and marketing.
- Film posters from all genres use a recognisable set of codes and conventions that establish the form.
- The set film poster for Section A in Year 1/AS and Year 2/A Level is *The Kiss of the Vampire* (1963).
- The choice of this poster allows you to discuss the main elements of the vampire/horror genre. Your study of similar and more contemporary posters will prepare you for the unseen element of this section and allow you to explore how the genre has developed over time.

Apply it!

3.13 Revisit a film poster you have explored in class in preparation for the Component 1 Section A examination. Annotate the poster, illustrating how the product uses media language to convey meaning to an audience. Use subject-specific terminology in your analysis.

Revising Film Posters: Codes and Conventions

Apply it!

3.14 Match the following film poster terms with the correct definition and illustrative image example from the film poster for *Crucible of the Vampire* (2019).

Film poster term	Definition	Example
A. Tag line	**1.** This connotes the film's genre by the inclusion of recognisable visual codes, for example clothing and expression.	i.
B. Star billing	**2.** This will have been carefully chosen and positioned in order to suggest the narrative of the film and introduce the central characters.	ii. ★★★★☆ "JOYOUS NOSTALGIA EXPERTLY DELIVERED" DIABOLIQUE MAGAZINE
C. Central image	**3.** The memorable phrase or slogan that becomes associated with the film and is used as part of the branding.	iii. NEIL MORRISSEY FLORENCE CADY BRIAN CROUCHER
D. Expert criticism	**4.** The use of the director's name or reference on the poster to previous films is included to convince the audience of the film's quality.	iv.
E. Iconography and setting	**5.** Positioning of the names or images of the actors in the film, this is usually according to their star quality.	v. AN ANCIENT BLOOD CURSE FINDS A NEW BEGINNING
F. Mark of quality	**6.** Quotes from newspapers, film magazines and reviews suggesting the quality of the film and persuading potential audiences.	vi. CRUCIBLE OF THE VAMPIRE
G. Typography and graphics	**7.** The font style chosen for the poster, which may connote the genre of the film.	vii.

Link

Structuralism, the additional Section A Media Language theory, will be explored in relation to the set and additional products in the Year 2/A Level revision guide.

Top Revision Tip

It is important when analysing media products to apply theories and theoretical perspectives. Avoid describing or explaining the theories in isolation, they are there to help you make sense of the forms and products.

Apply it!

3.15 Consider how you could use semiotics to develop your analysis of the set and additional advertising products you have studied.

Applying Theory and Theoretical Perspectives: Semiotics

Reminder

- Semiotics, including Roland Barthes, is the set theory for Media Language in Year 1/AS Component 1.
- You may also have studied other relevant theories and theorists related to semiotics that could enhance your response.

Checklist of key points

Semiotics, Roland Barthes

✓ **Statement**: The idea that texts communicate their meanings through a process of signification.

Application: As advertisements must communicate messages rapidly, they use signs and codes that signify messages to audiences. For example, the code of clothing – dressing someone in a particular way – will quickly resonate with an audience, who will have expectations of how that person relates to a product. A woman in evening wear in a perfume advert signifies a sophisticated fragrance.

✓ **Statement**: The idea that signs can function at the level of denotation, which involves the 'literal' or common-sense meaning of the sign, and at the level of connotation, which involves the meanings associated with or suggested by the sign.

Application: In advertisements and film posters colours are used to communicate messages. The denotation of red is a primary colour, but in an advert or film poster it may connote passion, power or danger depending on the product, genre and context.

✓ **Statement**: The idea that constructed meanings can come to seem self-evident, achieving the status of myth through a process of naturalisation.

Application: For example, the cultural myth encoded in film posters and advertisements that wearing red has connotations of being sexually attractive, or that red cars have more speed and power.

The red dress worn in advertisements has a recognisable constructed meaning synonymous with sexual attraction. Here the dress and snowflake iconography also connote typical codes of Christmas.

Analysing Media Language in Film Posters

The set product is *The Kiss of the Vampire*, a historical vampire/horror film poster. In your preparation for this part of the examination you will have explored other examples of film posters, both historical and modern. Analyse how visual codes have been used to communicate messages in this film poster for *Burying the Ex* (2015).

Apply it!

3.16

1. How is **iconography** used to communicate the film genre?

   Consider:
   - recognisable images related to the genre
   - the significance of the chosen iconography
   - iconography related to parody.

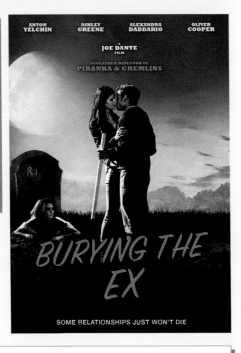

2. What are the **connotations** of the colours used?

   Consider how colours convey messages:
   - the connotations of the colours used
   - the purpose and effect of the muted colour palette.

3. How do the codes of **gesture** and **expression** both reinforce the genre and establish **intertextuality**?

   Consider:
   - mode of address
   - clues to narrative
   - links to other films in the genre and other genres
   - the use of parody.

Top Revision Tip

When you are analysing the unseen example for the Media Language question in the examination, you will need to transfer your knowledge and understanding gained through studying both the set product and unseen examples you have explored in class and independently.

Top Revision Tip

Remember that the mark allocation is a guide to how much you will need to write in the examination. You also need to plan time to study the unseen product and make a few example notes in preparation.

Quickfire Revision

3.11 What is meant by intertextuality?

Link

Look back at Chapter 2 of this revision guide for an overview of Representation.

Link

Representation in advertising and marketing is covered in more detail on pages 68–71 of the Media Studies Year 1/AS student book.

Take it Further

3.3 Read Chapters 3–5 in Gauntlett's book, *Media, Gender and Identity*, where he discusses representations in the past and present along with modern notions of identity.

Top Revision Tip

David Gauntlett is one of the set theorists related to representation. Reading some of his ideas will further your understanding of his theoretical perspective.

Revising Representation: Advertising and Marketing

Reminder

- Representation is one of the key elements of the theoretical framework.
- It needs to be studied in relation to all the forms and products in Section A of Component 1.
- You will have explored how events, issues, social groups and individuals are represented in media products.
- You will have considered how representations relate to social and cultural, historical, political and economic media contexts.
- There will always be a representation question in the examination for Section A of Component 1. You will be required to compare one of the set products with an unseen product from one of the forms studied in this section.

Checklist of key points

- Advertisements, including film posters, have a limited amount of time and space to communicate messages, so frequently use shortcuts, including stereotypes and easily identifiable visual codes and iconography.
- Stereotypes work as they are recognisable to audiences, but they also tend to reinforce rather than challenge, common representations.
- Stereotypes can be positive or negative.
- New stereotypes appear to reflect changes in society. In the past, it was women who were pressurised by the 'beauty ideal'; this pressure is now extended to men.

   Today men are also expected to spend time in the gym, working to develop 'tight, toned bodies'. Women who have these well-toned bodies are likely to expect – equitably enough – that men will put in a similar effort. (David Gauntlett (2008) *Media, Gender and Identity*)

   This is apparent in the changing representations of masculinity in adverts.
- Representations are constructions and, depending on the product, may convey values, attitudes and beliefs about the world.
- The representations in media products do not give a true version of reality; they re-present the world and mediate messages and meanings.

This advertisement has been constructed to encode messages about modern masculinity.

Revision Checklist: Representation in Advertising and Marketing

It is important to familiarise yourself with the key statements related to the different elements of the Year 1/AS specification.

What it says in the spec	What you need to know
The way events, issues, individuals (including self-representation) and social groups (including social identity) are represented through processes of selection and combination.	• All adverts and marketing materials are constructions, the aim is to sell a product or service. The paradigmatic choices made construct a version of reality in order to persuade an audience.
The way the media through re-presentation construct versions of reality.	• Beauty and fragrance advertisements, both historical and contemporary, construct aspirational representations of gender that are not a reflection of reality but can be persuasive.
The processes which lead media producers to make choices about how to represent events, issues, individuals and social groups.	• These choices may be related to the purpose of the advertisement. For example, charity campaigns often include emotive images of children in their representation of an issue to persuade the audience to donate.
The effect of social and cultural context on representations.	• The attitudes and beliefs of the society of the time will influence the construction of representations in media products. *Tide* and *The Kiss of the Vampire* both convey messages about gender roles and as such reflect historical contexts.
How and why stereotypes can be used positively or negatively.	• Advertisements and film posters have a limited time to convey their message so may use recognisable, although not necessarily negative, stereotypes. For example, the female superhero is a positive representation that uses some stereotypical elements. *WaterAid* subverts stereotypes to construct a positive representation of developing countries.

(continued)

Apply it!

3.17 Consider how the representations in the *Tide* advertisement are affected by social and cultural contexts.

What it says in the spec	What you need to know
How and why particular social groups, in a national and global context, may be under-represented or misrepresented.	• The dominant, powerful groups in society largely control what is produced. As a result, minority groups are marginalised. Consider the under-representation and misrepresentations of minority ethnic groups in both the film industry and certain advertising genres.
How media representations convey values, attitudes and beliefs about the world and how these may be systematically reinforced across a wide range of media representations.	• Some advertisements, particularly those for beauty products, continue to reinforce ideas about how women should look and behave. This representation is also evident in some film genres and is related to the perceived place of women in society.
How audiences respond to and interpret media representations.	• Audiences are not passive and will respond to media products in different ways. The *WaterAid* advert was produced as a result of research which suggested that audiences were becoming desensitised, so responded negatively to the more stereotypical representations of developing countries in charity campaigns.
The effect of historical context on representations.	• Historical context may affect the representations in terms of a specific period or event, for example the post-war era in the *Tide* advert or the changing role of women in the 1960s, as evident in *The Kiss of the Vampire*.

Revising Representation: Gender in Advertising and Marketing

1. How is media language used to construct representations of gender in the set products and additional examples you have studied? Consider the process of selection and combination evident in the products.

2. How do the gender representations in the historical set products *Tide* and *The Kiss of the Vampire* convey the values, attitudes and beliefs about the world at the time they were produced?

3. How do the contemporary examples of adverts and film posters you have explored illustrate the way the representation of gender has developed to reflect social and cultural changes?

4. Is there evidence in your research of the continued existence of stereotypical representations of gender in modern adverts and film posters?

5. How do the products you have studied reflect social and cultural contexts in relation to gender?

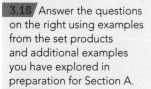

Apply it!

3.18 Answer the questions on the right using examples from the set products and additional examples you have explored in preparation for Section A.

3.19 Consider how the representations of social groups are constructed in the additional examples of charity campaigns you have studied. How can this be said to reflect the attitudes and values in society?

Consider how the above advertisements for Nike and Dior:

- use stereotypes – do the images in the advertisements reflect reality and real women? How do they use media language to construct versions of reality?
- reflect a social and cultural context – how do these examples reinforce values, attitudes and beliefs about gender?
- convey values, attitudes and beliefs about the same contemporary world
- may elicit different audience interpretations and responses.

 Apply it!

3.20 Using *The Kiss of the Vampire* film poster and either the Nike or Dior advertisement above, **plan** a response to the following representation question:

> Compare the choices that have been made in the representation of gender in the film poster and the advertisement. [25 marks]

Spend 25–30 minutes on your response.

In your answer you must consider:

- how gender is represented through processes of selection and combination
- the similarities and differences in the representations of gender
- how far the representations relate to relevant media contexts.

 Top Revision Tip

The Representation question may require you to compare products in the same or different forms. You will also be required to demonstrate your understanding of media contexts.

 Top Revision Tip

You need to plan your time carefully:

- Study the unseen resource:
  - If it is audio-visual you will watch it three times and should make notes during the second and third viewing.
  - If it is print you need to spend time studying and making notes in relation to the question.
- You need to respond to all the bullet points in the question. They are there to help you to plan your response and will form the mark scheme for the examiner.

 Quickfire Revision

3.12 What do you need to remember about the mark tariff for the Representation question in Section A?

Quickfire Revision

3.13 What are some of the more typical codes and conventions employed by charity campaigns?

Take it Further

3.4 In 2019, Comic Relief came under criticism for employing the white saviour stereotype, whereby white celebrities are pictured with black, usually African, 'victims' in order to raise money:

David Lammy MP hit out at the 30-year-old charity for portraying Africa as a continent of poverty-stricken victims and stereotypes who don't speak for themselves. The organisations had 'tattooed images of poverty in Africa' on to people's minds, he said. (Karen McVeigh (2018, 23 March) 'Comic Relief to Ditch White Saviour Stereotype Appeals', the *Guardian*, www.theguardian.com/global-development/2018/mar/23/comic-relief-to-ditch-white-saviour-stereotype-appeals)

Read the full article and explore how *WaterAid* subverts stereotypes.

MP David Lammy criticised Comic Relief for perpetuating the white saviour myth.

Revising Representation: Ethnicity and Issues in Advertising and Marketing

The relevant set product to explore representations of ethnicity and issues is *WaterAid*.

Checklist of key points

Ø You will have explored how representations are constructed in this advertisement and for what purpose.

Ø This advertisement challenges more typical representations of developing countries and their issues through the central character Claudia.

Ø The construction also combines upbeat audio codes, a bright colour palette and codes of expression and clothing that create a positive representation.

The *WaterAid* advertisement constructs positive images of developing countries.

Ø The advertisement avoids using the emotive and negative terms usually evident in similar campaigns, for example 'famine', 'drought' and 'disaster'. This was in response to research suggesting that such shock tactics were becoming less effective.

Ø The technical codes also contribute to the representation, including camera shots and editing that establish the independence of Claudia and involve the audience in her journey. In this way the creators of the product avoid constructing her as a victim, unlike other similar campaigns.

Claudia challenges stereotypical representations by not being a victim.

Ø Other charity campaigns are more likely to create a representation of non-Western cultures as distanced from us and 'other'. The choice of Claudia, a young woman who is part of a wider community of women, is a more modern and culturally relevant representation.

650 million people still don't have access to clean drinking water

The audience can see the result of donations and are given facts, not emotive language.

Ø The purpose of this positive representation is to show an audience the effect their donation may have on communities.

Apply it!

3.21 Use the following table to compare representations of ethnicity in the *WaterAid* advertisement and the film poster for *The Hate U Give*.

TWO WORLDS
ONE VOICE
NO GOING BACK

THE
HATE
U
GIVE

IN CINEMAS
OCTOBER 22

Key point	WaterAid	The Hate U Give
How the representations of ethnicity are constructed through the selection and combination of elements of media language.		
The similarities in the representations of ethnicity.		
The differences in the representations of ethnicity.		
How far the representations relate to relevant contexts.		

Apply it!

3.22 Using the completed table above and your knowledge of the set forms and product, write an answer to the following question under timed conditions:

Compare the representations of ethnicity in the *WaterAid* advertisement and the film poster for *The Hate U Give*.   [25 marks]

- Consider the similarities and differences in the representations.
- Make judgements and draw conclusions about how far the representations relate to relevant media contexts.

Top Revision Tip

As part of your revision it is important to practise writing responses to questions under timed conditions. This will enable you to manage the examination paper effectively.

Link

The additional Year 2/A Level theories related to Representation are explored in the Year 2/A Level revision guide.

Apply it!

3.23 Produce a short podcast exploring how you can apply either of these theories of representation to two of the advertisements or film posters you have studied in class.
Share the podcasts with your peers.

Applying Theory: Representation and Identity

Checklist of key points

Theories of representation, Stuart Hall

⊘ **Statement**: The idea that representation is the production of meaning through language, with language defined in its broadest sense as a system of signs.

Application: *This is true of advertising and marketing where media language is used to communicate messages through rapidly recognisable signs and codes that are interpreted by the audience. For example, the use of colour and font style to establish the genre in a film poster.*

⊘ **Statement**: The idea that stereotyping, as a form of representation, reduces people to a few simple characteristics or traits.

Application: *Advertisements, in particular, have always used stereotypes as shortcuts to convey meaning. They isolate key characteristics that are recognisable to audiences, who will then predict behaviour and narrative. For example, the apron, glamorous clothing and delighted code of expression helped to construct the 'happy housewife' stereotype used in 1950s adverts.*

⊘ **Statement**: The idea that stereotyping tends to occur where there are inequalities of power, because subordinate or excluded groups are constructed as different or 'other'.

Application: *Consider how far this statement is true in relation to women in the 1950s and to a large extent in the 1960s (Tide and The Kiss of the Vampire), whose roles were very clearly defined by a patriarchal society. This statement can also be applied to many charity campaigns, in relation to ethnicity, which seek to reinforce differences in order to appeal to the seemingly more privileged Western audience.*

Theories of identity, David Gauntlett

⊘ **Statement**: The idea that the media provide us with 'tools' or resources that we use to construct our identities.

Application: *Audiences are greatly influenced by the media. Advertisements construct versions of reality that appear attainable and are used by some consumers to model their lives. Consider how identities are constructed in the additional examples you have studied.*

⊘ **Statement**: The idea that while in the past the media tended to convey singular, straightforward messages about ideal types of male and female identities, the media today offer us a more diverse range of stars, icons and characters from whom we may pick and mix different ideas.

Application: *In the past, both film posters and advertisements provided role models for men and women that were largely aspirational even when anchored in the domestic sphere. This is evident in the advertisement for Tide. However, The Kiss of the Vampire [TKOTV] from 1960 does herald a change in that women were represented as more diverse and in control. While contemporary advertisements do reflect cultural change, there is still evidence of gender stereotyping.*

Representation

- » **Social Groups:** e.g., gender, age, ethnicity. The representations may reflect social and cultural change, including in relation to gender
- » **Issues:** this is particularly relevant to charity campaigns, e.g., social and political issues of the time, including poverty, abuse, famine
- » **Events:** charity campaigns re-present events in order to target an audience, e.g. natural disasters

POINTS TO CONSIDER

- » How the representation is constructed through selection and combination of elements
- » How the re-presentation constructs a version of reality (aspirational beauty adverts)
- » How the representations are influenced by social, cultural and historical contexts
- » How the representation reflects the values, attitudes and beliefs of the time
- » How stereotypes are used (positive and negative)
- » How audiences may respond to and interpret the representations

CONTEXTS

- » Social and cultural
- » Economic/political: *WaterAid* and other similar campaigns
- » Historical: *Tide/The Kiss of the Vampire* and similar examples

Points to Remember

- » **Advertising** and **marketing** is studied in Component 1 Section A in relation to Media Language and Representation
- » You may be asked to respond to an extract from an unseen print or audio-visual advert or a film poster in a Media Language question. This question is worth 10 marks and you should use your knowledge and understanding of the form
- » Or, in a representation question, you may be required to compare the set product with another unseen in a different form, or with a print or audio-visual advert or film poster
- » When the unseen source is audio-visual, you will see it three times and be given time to make notes. Read the question carefully first
- » Use key terminology related to the form and semiotics

Advertising and Marketing

KEY THEORIES/THEORETICAL PERSPECTIVES

- » Media Language:
  Semiotics: including Roland Barthes
- » Representation: Stuart Hall
- » Theories of identity: David Gauntlett

Media Language

CODES and CONVENTIONS of the form

- » The repertoire of elements of the form, e.g.:
- » **Film posters:** tag line, film title, central image, expert criticism, promises of pleasure, typography and graphics, setting and iconography
- » **Print and audio-visual adverts:** use of language, slogan, images, use of colour, typography and graphics
- » Consider the connotations of these conventions

VISUAL CODES

- » Non-verbal communicators, e.g. colours and their connotations
- » Clothing – what rapid messages are conveyed?
- » Gesture and expression
- » Iconography related to the advertising genre, e.g. parched ground in a charity advert, recognisable objects from the vampire genre

TECHNICAL AND AUDIO CODES

- » Selection and combination of camera shots and editing that may relate to the advertising genre of the product
- » Use of close-ups to engage the audience
- » Layout and design
- » Choice and use of music, dialogue and voice-over (diegetic and non-diegetic)
- » Paradigmatic choices related to the form

LANGUAGE AND MODE OF ADDRESS

- » Persuasive language: including hyperbole and alliteration
- » Slogans and tag lines that are memorable and reinforce elements of the product
- » How the audience is positioned by the mode of address

Revising the Set Forms and Products: Music Videos

Link

The additional Year 2/A Level music video product, *Riptide* by Vance Joy, and theories will be explored in detail in the Year 2/A Level revision guide.

Quickfire Revision

3.14 How has media language in music videos been influenced by developments in technology?

3.15 What is meant by star persona?

Music genres have a recognisable set of codes and conventions.

Reminder

- Music video is studied in Component 1 Section A in relation to Media Language and Representation.
- The set products you will have studied are either *Formation*, Beyoncé (2016) **or** *Dream*, Dizzee Rascal (2004).
- You will also have studied additional examples of music videos in preparation for the unseen element of Section A.
- The set theory/theorist for Section A Media Language in Year 1/AS and Year 2/A Level is semiotics, including Roland Barthes.
- The set theories/theorists for Representation at Year 1/AS are: theories of representation, including Stuart Hall, and theories of identity, including David Gauntlett.
- In Year 2/A Level you will study an additional music video: *Riptide*, Vance Joy (2013).
- In addition, in Year 2/A Level you will also study additional theories, including structuralism/Claude Lévi-Strauss for Media Language. For Representation you will explore feminist theories, including van Zoonen and bell hooks, and theories around ethnicity and postcolonial theory, including Paul Gilroy.

Checklist of key points

- Music videos use media language and construct representations in order to communicate messages, establish the music genre and create a brand identity and **star persona** for the artist or band. They also interpret the lyrics and engage the audience.
- Music videos are an integral part of the marketing strategy for a band or artist. They establish the image of a new performer and can be used to signal a change in the image of an existing artist or band.
- There are different styles of music video, including: performance, narrative and thematic. Some are a combination of styles.
- Different music video genres share a repertoire of elements that are recognisable to audiences.
- Although music videos may belong to a specific genre, the form itself also has a recognisable set of codes and conventions which differentiates it from other media forms.
- The music video as a form has developed over time and has been influenced by many things, including social and cultural contexts and technological developments.

A performance element in a music video can establish the music genre and the persona of the band or artist.

Revision Checklist: Media Language in Music Videos

It is important to familiarise yourself with the key statements related to the different elements of the theoretical framework in the Year 1/AS specification.

What it says in the spec	What you need to know
How the different modes and language associated with different media forms communicate multiple meanings.	• The different ways in which visual codes, sound, speech and mode of address convey meaning in music videos. For example, the way in which colour conveys meaning about the music genre.
How the combination of elements of media language influence meaning.	• How elements of media language, such as technical and audio codes, work together in music videos to construct meaning.
How developing technologies affect media language.	• How more sophisticated filming and editing techniques, CGI and special effects can affect how meanings are communicated.
The codes and conventions of media forms and products, including the processes through which media language develops as a genre.	• The repertoire of elements used across music videos from different genres, for example the artist in performance. • The predictable elements that belong to a specific genre, for example the use of codes of clothing related to a music genre.
The processes through which meanings are established through intertextuality.	• The way in which music videos may create meanings by referencing another media product. For example, replicating memorable scenes from an iconic film or television programme, related to the cultural database of the audience, within the music video.
How audiences respond to and interpret the above aspects of media language.	• The different ways in which audiences may respond to the way in which media language is constructed in music videos. This will be influenced by demographics and engagement with the artist/band.

Link

There is an analysis of an additional music video – Taylor Swift's *Bad Blood* – on page 74 of the Year 1/AS student book.

Quickfire Revision

3.16 Give two reasons why an artist or band may incorporate performance into their music video.

George Ezra regularly incorporates performance into his music videos and engages in direct mode of address with the audience, as seen in these shots from the *Shotgun* (above top) and *Paradise* (above bottom) videos.

Revising Music Videos: Codes and Conventions

Apply it!

3.24 In the following table, find examples of the codes and conventions of different music styles in relation to the set product and an additional example you have studied. Some examples have been completed for you as a reminder. Consider the purpose and effect of the conventions.

Style: performance	Dream OR Formation	Additional example
Clips from live performance, including shots of the band/artist playing and cutaways to the audience to show their enjoyment of the spectacle.		The Lumineers' music video *Ophelia* starts and ends with the band in live performance and features a band member as the main protagonist in the narrative.
Clips of the band/artist in rehearsal, performing in a more informal situation.		
Close-ups of the performer(s) creating a spectacle and engaging directly with the audience.		In George Ezra's music videos *Shotgun* and *Paradise*, he performs directly to the audience, establishing a relationship with his fanbase.
Shots focusing on iconography or a recognisable motif related to the music genre or the artist.		
Performance in different settings to engage the audience and establish the genre.		For Beyoncé and Jay-z's music video, *Apes**t – The Carters*, they rented the Louvre, illustrating their power as artists.
Filming and editing that interpret the lyrics in some way. This may challenge audience expectations.	In *Dream*, the intertextual reference to the original song *Happy Talk* is subverted to make a social comment.	

(continued)

Style: performance	*Dream* OR *Formation*	Additional example
The artist may appear as a character in the narrative, play themselves in performance, or be absent from the video entirely, using actors instead.	In *Dream*, Dizzee Rascal is an integral part of the narrative, as his story is told directly to the audience.	In Ed Sheeran's music video, *The Shape of You*, he is an actor in the narrative, he does not appear as a performer. His character reflects the indie sub-genre.
The narrative may resemble a mini film. The production values may be high and the editing and technical codes will create a sophisticated storyline.		Pink's music video, *Walk Me Home*, demonstrates high production values and illustrates how media language is affected by developments in technology.
Just as in a film, enigmas may form part of the narrative to hold the audience's attention.		In Avicii's music video, *Wake Me Up*, the tattoo is an enigma within a complex and intertextual narrative.
Stereotypes may be used to transmit messages rapidly to the audience. These may relate to the music sub-genre.		
Intertextuality may be used to add to the complexity of the narrative.	In *Formation* a range of historical and contemporary intertextual references are incorporated into the narrative to reinforce the theme of racial discrimination.	
The narrative may make a social comment on a topic of concern to the artist.		Childish Gambino's video, *This Is America*, depicts scenes of senseless violence in order to make a social comment about gun laws in the USA. It had a big social impact.

Take it Further

3.5 Independently research some of the additional examples of music videos mentioned in this table. This will further your understanding of the codes and conventions of the form.

Avicii's music video, *Wake Me Up*, uses enigmas and cinematic intertextual references to construct meaning.

Apply it!

3.25 Consider how media language communicates meaning in the Zedd and Katy Perry music video, *365*, which can be found on YouTube: www.youtube.com/watch?v=YrbgUtCfnC0.

1. How do **technical codes** communicate meaning in the music video?

Consider:

- the purpose and effect of camera shots
- editing
- use of graphics.

2. How are meanings established through **intertextuality**?

Consider the visual and language references to:

- the science fiction genre
- the creation of a dystopian universe
- *Black Mirror*
- *Humans*
- *The Stepford Wives*.

3. How do **visual codes** communicate meanings in the music video?

Consider:

- the paradigmatic choices made by the producers of the video
- the codes of clothing and how they establish characters
- the codes of expression and gesture
- the colour palette – how it helps to establish the genre and character roles
- setting and iconography.

4. How is the **narrative** constructed in this music video?

Consider:

- the equilibrium
- disruption
- resolution
- how the characters are constructed and contribute to the storyline
- the dual role of Katy Perry the 'star' and the actor within the story.

Apply it!

3.26 Choose a 2-minute extract from the Katy Perry video and answer the following Media Language question:

How are meanings established through intertextuality in the music video for *365*?   [10 marks]

Spend approximately 10–15 minutes writing your response.

Applying Theory and Theoretical Perspectives: Semiotics

Reminder

- Semiotics, including Roland Barthes, is the set theory for Media Language in Year 1/AS and Year 2/A Level.
- You may also have studied other relevant theories and theorists related to semiotics that could enhance your response.

Checklist of key points

Semiotics, Roland Barthes

⊘ **Statement**: The idea that texts communicate their meanings through a process of signification.

Application: Music videos communicate messages using signs and codes that are recognisable and signify messages to audiences. For example, the code of clothing and iconography, including the use of motifs, will help to establish the music sub-genre. The hoodie and track suit bottoms worn by Dizzee Rascal in Dream *are indicative of rap/hip hop/grime.*

⊘ **Statement**: The idea that signs can function at the level of denotation, which involves the 'literal' or common-sense meaning of the sign, and at the level of connotation, which involves the meanings associated with or suggested by the sign.

Application: In Dream, *the code of clothing of the woman playing the piano has the denotation of a smart, older woman. The connotation is related to the cultural differences between her world and that of Dizzee Rascal: the matriarchal presenter and the black urban youth. In* Formation, *the code of clothing of the antebellum dresses signifies the postcolonial legacy and has connotations of the power of the white plantation owners in contrast to the black slaves.*

⊘ **Statement**: The idea that constructed meanings can come to seem self-evident, achieving the status of myth through a process of naturalisation.

Application: In Formation, *for example, the audience recognise the signs and codes related to black oppression, both historical and contemporary, as they have been repeated over time in other media products. In* Dream, *this idea relates to the use of iconography related to urban youths, for example the hoodie, which over time has come to signify rebellion and social deviance in the mainstream media.*

Apply it!

3.27 Choose one of the additional examples of music videos you have studied in class, or Zedd and Katy Perry's *365*, and consider how you could apply Barthes' statements about semiotics to it.

Apply it!

3.28 Consider the signification of clothing, gesture and expression in these stills from either *Dream* or *Formation*.

Top Revision Tip

You can use your understanding of media language to analyse how representations are constructed.

Representation in Music Videos

Reminder

- This aspect of the theoretical framework will be assessed through comparison of a set and an unseen product in the same or different forms. For example, you may be required to compare the set music video you have studied with another music video or a film poster.
- You may also be required to compare any of the other set products for Section A with an unseen music video.
- Your exploration of representation as a key concept and additional examples of the form will prepare you for the unseen resource.

Checklist of key points

- ☑ Similar to the advertisements you have studied, music videos have a relatively short time in which to attract an audience and deliver their message.
- ☑ Stereotypes may be used in order to transmit messages quickly.
- ☑ Different music genres will construct representations of social groups, issues and events in different ways.
- ☑ The representations contained within the music video may reflect social and cultural contexts in relation to the time in which they were produced.
- ☑ As well as representing social groups, issues and events, music videos often offer a representation of the artist or band which is constructed to establish their star persona, or to explore a theme which is personal to them. In her video *Delicate*, Taylor Swift explores her own concerns about the restrictions to her life and behaviour that fame has brought. Similar to Beyoncé, Taylor Swift has also used her music videos to introduce new representations of herself and new musical themes.
- ☑ Representations of gender in music videos can sometimes be ambiguous and contradictory. Women can be powerful and sexually objectified in the same product. It is important to consider who is in control of the representation and what is its purpose.

Taylor Swift is an artist who frequently uses the music video form to construct representations of herself and aspects of her life.

Revision Checklist: Representation in Music Videos

It is important to familiarise yourself with the key statements related to the different elements of the theoretical framework in the Year 1/AS specification.

Link

Representations in music videos is explored on pages 75–77 of the Year 1/AS student book.

What is says in the spec	What you need to know
The way events, issues, individuals (including self-representation) and social groups (including social identity) are represented through processes of selection and combination.	Some music videos, including *Dream* and *Formation*, construct versions of reality. They make paradigmatic choices through the selection and combination of technical codes and editing in order to communicate a viewpoint.
The way the media through re-presentation construct versions of reality.	Artists/bands may construct a representation of an event or social group which they present as the truth. The band/artist will construct a star persona that appears real to fans but is a re-presentation of who they are in real life.
The effect of social and cultural context on representations.	The attitudes, beliefs and concerns of the society of the time will influence the construction of representations in media products. In *Formation*, Beyoncé overtly refers to the floods in New Orleans to raise wider social points about racial inequality. Dizzee Rascal uses the form to send a positive social message to young black teenagers.
How and why stereotypes can be used positively or negatively.	Stereotypes can be used as a cultural shortcut, but reinforcement over time can make them appear normal. Music videos often challenge accepted stereotypes and construct more positive representations of social groups.
How and why particular social groups, in a national and global context, may be under-represented or misrepresented.	The dominant, powerful groups in society largely control what is produced. As a result, a dominant ideology is communicated and minority groups are often marginalised. Although music videos as a form reflect social changes in the way in which they represent gender and ethnicity more positively, some music sub-genres continue to under- and misrepresent certain social groups.
How media representations convey values, attitudes and beliefs about the world and how these may be systematically reinforced across a wide range of media representations.	Some artists/bands will use the music video form to reinforce representations evident in other media products, for example concerns about social ills and climate change. In 2019 Coldplay announced they would cancel all tours until concerts could be more sustainable.
How audiences respond to and interpret media representations.	Active audiences will engage with the representations constructed in music videos. This will be influenced by the audience demographic and their relationship with the band/artist. Often, fans cannot separate the constructed representation from the actual person.

Apply it!

3.29 Use the following table to explore how representations are constructed in the set product. Another example, Zedd and Katy Perry's *365*, has been used to illustrate key points.

Question	Example from *Dream* OR *Formation*	Additional music video key points: *365*
What are the main areas of representation featured in the music video?		Gender and issues (the developing place of technology in society). There are examples of both powerful and vulnerable women in the video.
How have the representations been constructed? What paradigmatic choices have been made?		Paradigmatic choices have been made in the representation of gender with regards to clothing and setting. The trans-human, Katy Perry's character, wears two main costumes, both of which objectify her. As the robot in the lab she is controlled by the scientists and wears a skin-tight jumpsuit, with emphasis on the breasts. As the AI woman she wears red, signifying passion and danger, but the back of the costume reveals her underwear.
Have stereotypes been used and to what effect?		The white clothing of the scientists is a stereotype, although there is a positive representation as the leader of the experiment is female and mixed race. There is stereotypical behaviour when the android malfunctions. The constructions of the vulnerable female and the ambivalent male are stereotypical. The audience are positioned through the mode of address to empathise with the robot.
How do the representations relate to the lyrics and music genre?		This music is from the pop sub-genre and the theme of many such songs is love. Katy Perry's style is recognisable, including high production values and the creation of a motif and Easter egg-laden narrative, of which she is the central focus.
How has the performer used the music video for self-representation?		Katy Perry invariably appears in her music videos, where she is central to the narrative. She establishes a motif which is then used for marketing. The face of the AI woman in direct mode of address is memorable.
How have the representations in the music video been affected by contexts?		Social and cultural context is relevant in the future advances in technology and the idea of power and relationships.
How have the representations in the music video been mediated to convey values, attitudes and beliefs?		Katy Perry is making a social comment regarding love and obsession and the future of technology. The music video constructs an ironic narrative whereby the android has stronger emotions than the human male. However, it also reinforces the stereotypical representation of the female as more vulnerable and emotional, even when a robot.

Applying Representation Theories: David Gauntlett and Stuart Hall

Reminder

- Theories of identity, including David Gauntlett, and theories of representation, Stuart Hall, are the set theories for representation in Year 1/AS.
- You may also have studied other relevant theories and theorists related to representations.

Consider how these theories can be applied to the set music video products you have studied:

- Fans engage with artists and bands and their work, as it resonates with them and their attitudes and beliefs. In this way, music videos may be said to provide a 'tool' through which identities can be constructed. How may this be both positive and negative?

- How far is it true that, compared to older examples, contemporary music videos offer a diverse range of representations of gender and ethnicity with which an audience can engage? What examples have you found in your study of the form?

- Are stereotypes reinforced across the examples of music videos you have explored? Have you analysed music videos where stereotypes have been challenged or subverted?

- Are certain social groups in music videos constructed as 'different' or 'other' or have you found evidence of greater diversity in modern music videos?

- How are representations in music videos constructed using recognisable polysemic signs and codes. How does this influence the way in which audiences may respond to the representations?

Top Revision Tip

You can use your understanding of Audiences from Section B to explore how audiences may respond to the representations in the products.

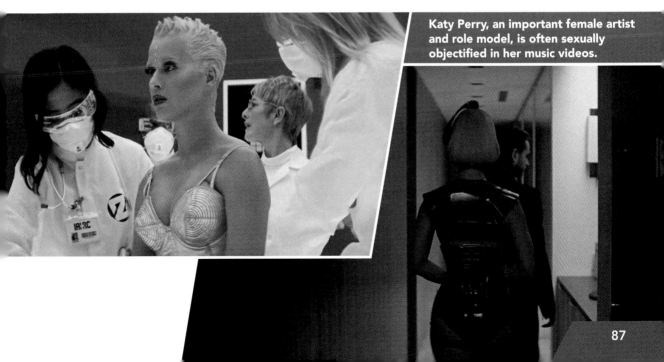

Katy Perry, an important female artist and role model, is often sexually objectified in her music videos.

Revising Contexts: Social and Cultural

Music videos, as you will have found in your study of other media products, reflect the time in which they were made and the issues and events prevalent at that time. They frequently offer social commentary through their themes and narratives. Consider how *Dream* or *Formation* relate to social and cultural contexts.

Dream	*Formation*
• Reflects Britain in the early 2000s in comparison to the world of the 1950s. • References 1950s children's television to construct a seemingly innocent time in contrast to the depiction of contemporary social issues. However, the video positions the audience to question this white, matriarchal post-war society when many people were moving to Britain to work from other areas of the world. • Highlights the conflict between urban youths and the police, illustrating contemporary social problems. • Reflects the multi-cultural society and offers a largely positive message. Dizzee Rascal subverts the stereotypes by celebrating his success and offers encouragement to the youth of society.	• The video is set against the backdrop of the New Orleans floods and social comment is being made about the lack of help for the largely black victims of Hurricane Katrina. • The video addresses the racial tensions in the aftermath of this event between the police and the black community. • References are also made to the civil rights movement and Martin Luther King and contemporary black activists. • Black culture is celebrated through the codes of language and gesture, including dance. • The video explores issues relating to the experience of living in modern-day America as part of a black community. • The video refers to and also subverts racial hierarchies, which are seen to be evident in past and present American culture.

No wonder you women buy more TIDE than any other washday product!

TIDE'S GOT WHAT WOMEN WANT!

NO SOAP–NO OTHER SUDS–NO OTHER WASHING PRODUCT KNOWN–WILL GET YOUR WASH AS CLEAN AS TIDE!

ONLY *TIDE* DOES ALL THREE!

TIDE GETS CLOTHES CLEANER THAN ANY OTHER WASHDAY PRODUCT YOU CAN BUY!

3.30 Using the *Tide* advertisement and the music video *365*, answer the following Section A Representation question:

Compare the choices that have been made in the representation of gender in the advertisement and the music video.   [25 marks]

In your answer you must consider:

• how gender is represented through processes of selection and combination
• reasons for the choices made in the representations of gender
• the similarities and differences in the representations of gender
• how far the representations relate to relevant media contexts.

Music Videos

Representation

» **Social groups:** e.g., gender, age, ethnicity

» **Events:** these may be of concern to the artist/band or may be historical (Beyoncé *Formation*/Dizzee Rascal *Dream*)

» **Issues:** e.g., social issues of the time and of concern to the artist/band, e.g. diversity, racism, social media

» **Self-representation:** the way in which the band/artist uses the music video form to construct a star persona

CONSIDER:

» How the representation is constructed through selection and combination of elements

» How the re-presentation constructs a version of reality

» How the representations are influenced by social, cultural and historical contexts

» How the representation reflects the values, attitudes and beliefs of the artist/band

» How stereotypes are used

» How audiences may respond to and interpret the representations

CONTEXTS

» Social and cultural

Points to Remember

» **Music videos** are studied in Component 1 Section A in relation to media language and representation

» You may be asked to respond to an extract from an unseen music video in a Media Language question. This question is worth 10 marks and you must use your knowledge and understanding of the music video form

» Or, in a Representation question, you may be required to compare the set product with another unseen music video extract, or with a product in a different form. This is an extended response question worth 25 marks and requires you to refer to media contexts

» When the unseen source is audio-visual, you will see the music video three times and be given time to make notes. Read the question carefully first

» Use key terminology related to the form and semiotics

KEY THEORIES/THEORETICAL PERSPECTIVES

» Media Language:
Semiotics: including Roland Barthes

» Representation: Stuart Hall

» Theories of identity: David Gauntlett

Media Language

CODES and CONVENTIONS of the form

» The repertoire of elements used to reflect the music video styles and music genres, e.g.:

» **Performance video:** shot of the band/artist live, close-ups, direct mode of address, focus on themes and motifs

» **Narrative:** interpretation of the lyrics through the creation of a story, role of the artist, use of intertextuality, creation of a star persona, enigmas

» Consider how music videos use media language to construct the brand identity of the artist/band (Beyoncé dancing, Dizzee Rascal rapping to camera)

VISUAL CODES

» Colour codes reflecting the music genre

» Codes of gesture, clothing and expression reinforcing the style of music and the identity of the artist/band

» The use of themes and motifs as part of the marketing

TECHNICAL CODES

» Selection and combination of camera shots and editing which may relate to the music genre

» Production values

» How technical codes are used to interpret the lyrics and to establish the band's identity (independent, more serious musicians will employ close-ups of band members playing instruments to reinforce credibility)

LANGUAGE AND MODE OF ADDRESS

» Direct mode of address used to establish connection with audience and star persona

» Language related to the music genre or to reflect cultural contexts (Beyoncé's use of dialect in *Formation*)

Link

Newspapers are covered in relation to Section A on pages 77–81 of the Year 1/ AS student book.

Link

The Times, the additional Year 2/A Level newspaper product, will be covered in the Year 2/A Level revision guide.

Quickfire Revision

3.17 What is meant by right and left wing?

3.18 What is the political leaning of the *Daily Mirror*?

Revising Terminology

- Central image
- Gatekeepers
- Headline
- Jump line
- Masthead
- Plug/puff
- Pull quote
- Splash
- Standalone
- Standfirst
- Strapline
- Subheadings

The newspaper front page is designed to attract the attention of the reader.

Revising the Set Forms and Products: Newspapers

Reminder

- Newspapers are studied in Component 1 Section A in relation to Media Language and Representation.
- The set product you will have studied in Year 1/AS is the *Daily Mirror* (10 November 2016), front cover and article on the USA election.
- You will also have studied additional examples of pages from different newspapers to broaden your understanding of the form and to prepare you for the unseen element of Section A.
- The set theory/theorist for Section A Media Language in Year 1/AS and Year 2/A Level is semiotics/Roland Barthes.
- The set theories/theorists for Representation at Year 1/AS and Year 2/A Level are theories of representation, including Stuart Hall.
- In Year 2/A Level you will study an additional newspaper: *The Times*, 10 November 2016, front and back pages.
- For assessment from 2021 there will be a different front page of *The Times*: 13 March 2019.
- In Year 2/A Level you will also study additional media language theories, including structuralism/Claude Lévi-Strauss.
- There are no additional representation theories to study in relation to newspapers in Year 2/A Level.

The AS/Year 1 set newspaper product for assessment from 2021 will be: the *Daily Mirror* (13 March 2019), front page and article on the 'Brexit' vote. The newspaper front page has been updated to make the set product more current, and reflective of issues more relevant than the previous set version.

Although this set product is different, the newspaper form remains the same and the information and revision tasks included in this revision guide will still be relevant.

Checklist of key points

- ⊘ Newspaper front pages are the shop window of the publication, they are constructed in order to catch the attention of the potential reader through a range of media language techniques.
- ⊘ The front page may use media language to encode information about the values, attitudes and beliefs of the newspaper. Newspapers are opinion leaders and are powerful in their ability to persuade readers to follow a particular viewpoint.
- ⊘ Despite their differences in terms of views and opinions, newspapers share a set of common codes and conventions that make them recognisable as the newspaper form: a large, commanding headline and central image.
- ⊘ Newspapers can, for example, be categorised in different ways according to their political allegiance (**right or left wing**), their reporting style (popular or quality) and size (tabloid or broadsheet).

⊘ Newspapers reflect what is happening nationally and globally, but they are not a window on the world. The stories chosen and how media language is employed in their presentation will reflect the attitudes and values of the newspaper, both political and social.

⊘ More ethnocentric newspapers tend to only report on global events when they may directly affect the UK.

⊘ Newspapers mediate the news using media language to encode the values, attitudes and beliefs of the publication. This will generally reinforce the beliefs already held by their readers.

Newspapers chronicle national and global events.

Revision Checklist: Media Language Statements in Newspapers

It is important to familiarise yourself with the key statements related to the different elements of the Year 1/AS specification.

What it says in the spec	What you need to know
How the different modes and language associated with different media forms communicate multiple meanings.	• The different ways in which, for example, visual codes, written language and mode of address convey meaning in newspapers. For example, the use of puns and alliteration in headlines.
How the combination of elements of media language influence meaning.	• How elements of media language, such as the headline, caption and choice of central image in tabloid newspapers, work together to construct meaning.
How developing technologies affect media language.	• Developing technologies allow media organisations to combine different elements of media language, including images, video and written text, on one platform, for example on a newspaper website.
The codes and conventions of media forms and products, including the processes through which media language develops as genre.	• The generic format and style of newspapers has remained relatively unchanged; it has developed as a genre through digital convergence. • A repertoire of elements is used across different newspapers, for example the masthead which establishes a brand identity. Conventions are common to media forms (newspapers) and sub-genres (tabloids). • The predictable elements that belong to a specific media form, for example all newspapers, despite their differences, are recognisable as such due to media language elements, for example language and images.

(continued)

Link

Media Language in relation to newspapers is covered on pages 77–78 of the Year 1/AS student book.

Top Revision Tip

The newspaper form is covered in detail in Component 1; it appears in both sections A and B and is also studied in relation to all aspects of the theoretical framework: Media Language, Representation, Media Industries and Audiences. You will also be required to consider contexts in relation to this form, including social and cultural, economic and political. It is therefore important that you familiarise yourself with a range of newspapers as part of your revision. This should include front pages and a selection of inner pages.

Quickfire Revision

3.19 Why can newspapers not be described as a window on the world, despite the fact they give us information about what is occurring daily?

Take it Further

3.8 Explore a range of newspaper front pages and consider how media language is used to establish a brand identity.

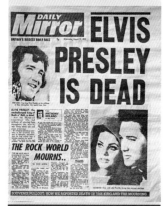

The codes and conventions of newspaper front pages have remained relatively unchanged over time. The front page has been used to chronicle national and global events.

Link

Chapter 9 of this revision guide will demonstrate how the statements from the specification relate to the examination questions.

Top Revision Tip

Although the Media Language question in the Component 1 examination will focus on an unseen product, for example a newspaper front page, your study of the set product will have prepared you to explore the features of media language used in any newspaper product.

What it says in the spec	What you need to know
The processes through which meanings are established through intertextuality.	• The way in which newspapers may create meanings by referencing another media product. For example, the use of the recognisable but manipulated image of the Statue of Liberty on the *Daily Mirror* (see page 99) to illustrate the paper's views about the USA Presidential election.
How audiences respond to and interpret the above aspects of media language.	• The different ways in which audiences may respond to the way in which media language is constructed to persuade them within newspapers. For example, at the time of a general election the tabloid newspapers in particular will seek to influence the result by their front pages. Newspaper readers will often accept the way in which a story is constructed by the newspaper, as it reflects their ideas and opinions. They will choose not to purchase the newspapers that offer contradictory views to their own.

Apply it!

3.31 Find as many examples of newspaper codes and conventions as you can in the newspaper front pages pictured below.

Apply it!

3.32 Match the following newspaper terms with the correct definition and their purpose and effect.

Newspaper term	Definition	Purpose and effect
A. The masthead	**1.** A block of text that introduces the story. It is usually in a different style from the body text.	**i.** This can signify the ethos and values of the paper, for example 'Daily Mirror' suggests that the newspaper reflects news truthfully.
B. The headline	**2.** The name of the paper and choice of typography.	**ii.** To broaden the target audience by suggesting stories in addition to, for example, political content. The focus may be on entertainment or the arts.
C. A standalone	**3.** A smaller headline placed below the main headline.	**iii.** To focus the reader on a key element of the story or to establish an enigma.
D. The plug/ puff	**4.** An extract from a story enlarged and placed in the text.	**iv.** To attract the audience. Some newspapers employ language devices such as hyperbole and alliteration to dramatise the story.
E. A splash	**5.** A picture story that exists on its own on the front page or links to a story inside the paper. It is usually only accompanied by a caption.	**v.** To draw attention to the story and to give a brief introduction to the key elements – 5 Ws.
F. The strapline	**6.** A banner which usually runs across the top of the front page and advertises what is in the newspaper or its supplements.	**vi.** Provides more information about the lead story or serves to anchor the meaning of the central image.
G. A pull quote	**7.** A line of words in larger letters, placed centrally and often incorporating language techniques.	**vii.** To suggest that the, often sensational, story is exclusive to the paper.
H. A standfirst	**8.** The prominent news story which is often the front page lead.	**viii.** Used usually by broadsheets whose aim is to break-up the front page copy and attract the readers' eyes.

Apply it!

3.33 Role of the expert

Working in groups, each member independently researches an example of a different newspaper front page. They then discuss how media language is used to communicate meaning.

The group should be active listeners considering:

- use of subject-specific terminology
- understanding of media language
- reference to specific examples from the chosen products
- application of theory, for example semiotics
- understanding of the codes and conventions of the newspaper form.

Give constructive feedback to the presenter, referring to the positive aspects and what could have been improved. To avoid giving unhelpful negative feedback, use the traffic light system:

Green: better then I could have done it.

Amber: the same as I would have done it.

Red: I could have done it better. Here you need to give specific suggestions as to what you would have said.

Apply it!

3.34 Consider how the combination of elements of media language communicates meaning in this front page from the *Daily Mirror* (1 April 2019). Use your knowledge of the set newspaper product to help you.

1. What **paradigmatic choices** have been made in the construction of this front page?

   Consider:
   - selection of stories
   - hierarchy of stories (news values)
   - choice and use of images.

5. How are the generic **codes** and **conventions** of the newspaper form used to construct meaning?

   Consider the:
   - headline
   - subheading and strapline – the language features used
   - standfirst
   - plug/puff – the messages this communicates about this newspaper and its readers
   - use of images.

2. How do **technical codes** convey messages?

   Consider:
   - layout and design decisions
   - choice and positioning of images
   - typography.

3. How does **language and mode of address** construct meaning?

   Consider the:
   - choice of language
   - use of the personal pronoun
   - use of hyperbole
   - notions of exclusivity.

4. How does the combination of elements of media language influence meaning?

   Consider:
   - how the use of language and the mode of address reflect the ideas and attitudes of this newspaper
   - how the narrative constructed in the lead story positions the audience.

6. How is **intertextuality** used in the Mick Jagger story? What is its purpose and effect?

Applying Theory and Theoretical Perspectives: Semiotics

Reminder

- Semiotics, including Roland Barthes, is the set theory for Media Language in Year 1/AS.
- You may also have studied other relevant theories and theorists related to semiotics.

Checklist of key points

Semiotics, Roland Barthes

⊘ **Statement**: The idea that texts communicate their meanings through a process of signification.

Application: *Newspapers regularly use signs and codes that signify multiple messages to audiences. The use of polysemic signs, for example the Union flag or Big Ben, will quickly resonate with an audience who will attach meanings to these signs.*

⊘ **Statement**: The idea that signs can function at the level of denotation, which involves the 'literal' or common-sense meaning of the sign, and at the level of connotation, which involves the meanings associated with or suggested by the sign.

Application: *In newspapers, colours and iconic signs are used to communicate messages. The denotation of Big Ben is a large clock face in central London, the connotations are related to the capital city and the seat of power, authority and tradition. The connotations of the Union flag will change according to the event being reported, for example a royal wedding, a sports event, or an English Defence League (EDF) rally.*

⊘ **Statement**: The idea that constructed meanings can come to seem self-evident, achieving the status of myth through a process of naturalisation.

Application: *Myths reflect the dominant ideology of the time and make certain social constructions appear natural. Myths function as extended metaphors and, for example, are often used by the more popular press to ridicule the opposition politicians. John Crace in the Guardian introduced the term 'The Maybot' in his political sketches, this came to then be used more universally as a way of describing the then Prime Minister, Theresa May. Political cartoonist, Steve Bell in the Guardian created a mythical representation of Theresa May, focusing on her leopard skin shoes. The Daily Mail's repetition and consequent naturalising of the term 'migrant' constructed a negative representation of this social group, many of whom were refugees. In doing so this reflected the dominant right-wing ideology of the newspaper and was largely accepted by the right-wing readership.*

Link

Structuralism, the additional Section A Media Language theory, will be explored in relation to the set and additional products in the Year 2/A Level revision guide.

Apply it!

3.35 Consider how you could use semiotics to develop your analysis of the set and additional newspaper products you have studied.

Take it Further

3.9 Consider how you can use semiotics to analyse the additional examples of newspapers you have studied independently and in class.

Consider how you can use semiotics to discuss political contexts in newspapers.

Link

Representation in newspapers is covered in more detail on pages 79–81 of the Year 1/AS student book.

Revising Representation: Newspapers

Reminder

- Representation is one of the key elements of the theoretical framework.
- It must be studied in relation to all the forms and products in Section A of Component 1.
- In Year 1/AS you will have explored how events, issues, social groups and individuals are represented in newspapers.
- You will have considered how representations in newspapers relate to social and cultural, political and economic media contexts.
- This aspect of the theoretical framework will be assessed in Component 1 Section A through comparison of a set and an unseen product in the same or different forms. For example, you may be required to compare representations in the set newspaper you have studied with a page from a different newspaper, or an advertisement.
- Your exploration of representation as a key concept and additional examples of the form will prepare you for the unseen resource.

Checklist of key points

☑ All newspapers have access to the same news stories; however, which stories they select and how they choose to re-present issues and events will differ.

Issues and events in newspapers

☑ The decisions made by a newspaper about how to construct representations will be influenced by its values, attitudes and beliefs.

☑ The way in which events and issues are represented will influence the reader.

☑ The stereotypes used in newspapers may reinforce rather than challenge preconceived ideas. The readers of the newspaper look to have their assumptions confirmed by the stories they read and will therefore choose to read newspapers that reflect their ideas and beliefs.

Quickfire Revision

3.20 What affects the way in which a newspaper represents a particular issue or event?

Newspapers may re-present the same event in different ways.

Revision Checklist: Representation in Newspapers

It is important to familiarise yourself with the key statements related to the different elements of the Year 1/AS specification.

What it says in the spec	What you need to know
The way events, issues, individuals (including self-representation) and social groups (including social identity) are represented through a process of selection and combination.	• Newspapers, in their reporting of issues, events and social groups, construct versions of reality. They make paradigmatic choices through the selection and combination of, for example, headlines, images and captions in order to communicate a viewpoint.
The way the media through re-presentation construct versions of reality.	• The producers of newspapers construct a representation of an event or social group which they present as the truth. All newspapers will re-present the same event differently, reflecting a different, mediated, view, when in fact it is a version of reality.
The processes which lead media producers to make choices about how to represent events, issues, individuals and social groups.	• The choices that newspaper producers make can be influenced by the media organisation (e.g., its political leaning or its corporate identity), the context, economic factors and the target readership.
The effect of social and cultural context on representations.	• The attitudes, beliefs and concerns of the society of the time will influence the construction of representations in media products. The *Daily Mirror*, as a left-wing newspaper, regularly reports on concerns about social inequalities and the effects of austerity using personal stories as a focus.
How and why stereotypes can be used positively or negatively.	• Stereotypes can be used as a cultural shortcut, but reinforcement over time can make them appear natural. For example, the negative representation of refugees in the *Daily Express* and *Daily Mail*.
How and why particular social groups, in a national and global context, may be under-represented or misrepresented.	• The dominant, powerful groups in society largely control what is produced. As a result, a **dominant ideology** is communicated and minority groups are often marginalised. Although many areas of the press have reflected social changes in the way in which they represent gender and ethnicity, there are still examples of the under- and misrepresentation of these groups.

Apply it!

3.36 Consider how the representations of social groups are constructed in the additional examples of newspapers you have studied. How can the representations be said to reflect the attitudes and values in society?

3.37 Consider how the way in which women politicians are represented on the following front page of the *Daily Mail* reflects society.

Quickfire Revision

3.21 What is meant by dominant ideology?

3.22 Why was Brexit, as an event, more problematic for some newspapers than others in the way that they constructed a representation and gave their viewpoint?

(continued)

Top Revision Tip

The work you have done exploring media language in relation to the set and additional products will help when analysing how representations are constructed, as these two aspects of the theoretical framework are related.

Take it Further

3.10 Look at the front pages of a range of newspapers from the same day. Consider the processes of selection that have taken place. What does this tell you about the different newspapers and their readers?

What it says in the spec	What you need to know
How media representations convey values, attitudes and beliefs about the world and how these may be systematically reinforced across a wide range of media representations.	• The dominant ideology of a patriarchal society is evident in some areas of the press and conveyed through the way in which certain issues, events and social groups are represented. The values and attitudes of the newspapers will influence the way in which representations are constructed, for example political leanings. More liberal newspapers aim to reflect a more diverse society in accordance with their liberal views.
How audiences respond to and interpret media representations.	• Newspapers can be said to be opinion leaders and as such are powerful in influencing their readers. They will construct representations of events and issues that reinforce the preconceived ideas of their audience. For example, some newspapers represent young people as feral and out of control. The readership who already hold this belief will agree.

Apply it!

3.38 Use the following questions to help you to focus your revision of the representation of issues and events in the set product and the additional newspaper pages you have studied.

1. How has an issue or event been re-presented by the newspaper? Consider: language and mode of address, visual, technical and audio codes, and anchorage.

2. What has influenced the decisions made by the media producers in how to represent the issue or event?

3. Are the values, attitudes and beliefs of the newspaper evident in their representation of the event? Is there evidence of political bias in the reporting of the issue or event? This may be evident in, for example, the headline or the choice of images?

4. What is the focus of the representation? How has the representation been mediated to encode ideas and messages?

5. What processes of selection and paradigmatic choices have been made in the construction of the representation? What decisions have been made about what to include and what to omit?

6. How has the representation of the issue or event been constructed to portray a version of reality? Consider how the re-presentation of the issue or event may reflect a viewpoint.

7. How will the representation affect the way in which different audiences may interpret the event or issue? Consider the role of newspapers as opinion leaders and advocates for social change. In 2018 the *Daily Mirror* ran a campaign to scrap parking charges in hospital car parks, urging its readers and the government to take action.

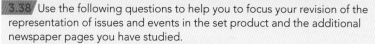

Consider how some newspapers can be agents of social change through the way in which they represent issues.

3.39 Use the following table to compare the choices that have been made in the representation of the events in the *Sun* front page and the front page of the *Daily Mirror* on the right.

Key point	The *Daily Mirror*	The *Sun*
How the event is represented through the processes of selection and combination	Headlines and subheadings Choice and use of images Use of language	Headlines and sub-headings Choice and use of images Use of language
The reasons for the choices made in representing the event	Political comment – choice of image linked to attitude of newspaper How the article reflects political leanings National implications of global event	The role of the newspaper as an opinion leader The pro-Brexit stance of the newspaper Negative representation of May is unusual for a right-wing newspaper
The similarities in the representations of the event	Use of a manipulated image with cultural significance to communicate meanings Construction of a negative representation of the event Use of hyperbolic language Use of a dramatic headline Use of recognisable cultural references to signify meaning Use of anchorage creating meaning	
The differences in the representations of the event	Global versus national events Political ethnocentricity of the *Sun* – link to how readers will interpret the story Specific detail of the *Sun* story. The *Daily Mirror* is more suggestive on the front page Different political leanings evident in treatment of the two events	
How far the representations of the event relate to relevant media contexts	Social context – global story with implications for Britain Political context – treatment of the Trump story reflects left-wing allegiance of paper to the Democrats This is reflected in the choice of images and copy in the set article	Social context – reflects what is happening at the time Political context – usually government supporting newspaper, but is pro-Brexit and doesn't want a delay in leaving. The newspaper urged its readers to vote 'leave' in the 2016 referendum

You will find tips on how to structure a comparison response in Chapter 9 of this revision guide.

Top Revision Tip

The key points in the table are similar to the bullet points that will be part of the representation question in Section A. This is an extended response question worth 25 marks. The bullet points will guide you in what you need to include in your response. You must address all the bullet points, although not necessarily equally.

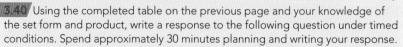

Apply it!

3.40 Using the completed table on the previous page and your knowledge of the set form and product, write a response to the following question under timed conditions. Spend approximately 30 minutes planning and writing your response.

Compare the choices that have been made in the representation of the events in the set *Daily Mirror* front page and article and the front page of the *Sun*. In your answer you must consider:

- how the events are represented through the processes of selection and combination
- reasons for choices made in the representation of the event
- the similarities and differences in the representation of the event
- how far the representations relate to relevant media contexts.   [25 marks]

Political Contexts in Newspapers

As you will have seen from the products you have studied in class and the examples contained in the Year 1/AS student book and this revision guide, newspapers offer a wealth of opportunities to study how the political contexts of newspapers reflect the political landscape at the time they were produced. When you are revising political contexts, consider the following questions:

- How do the newspapers you have studied reflect the political contexts in which they were made? Consider the choice of stories and how they are presented through, for example, headlines, the choice of images and the captions that anchor them.
- How does the way in the representations are constructed reflect the political contexts in which the newspaper was produced?
- How explicit are the political viewpoints of the newspaper? This will depend upon the style of the newspaper and its readers. The *Daily Mirror*, a tabloid newspaper with a left-wing orientation, will be more explicit in its criticism of the right-wing government than a quality broadsheet, where the political comment may be more implicit.
- How have political contexts shaped the newspaper? Is there evidence of mediation in the newspapers you have studied? How may this in turn shape the response of the readers to the news stories?

Applying Theory and Theoretical Perspectives: Representation

Reminder

- Theories of representation, including Stuart Hall, is the set representation theory for newspapers in Year 1/AS.
- You may have also studied other relevant theories and theorists related to Representation.

Checklist of key points

Stuart Hall, theories of representation

✓ **Statement**: The idea that representation is the production of meaning through language, with language defined in its broadest sense as a system of signs and that the relationship between concepts and signs is governed by codes.

Application: This is true of newspapers where media language is used to communicate messages through rapidly recognisable signs and codes that are interpreted by the audience. These signs and codes are used in constructing representations, for example codes of clothing lead to assumptions about behaviour and social standing (young people in hoodies and politicians in suits). Also, the way in which the Union and EU flags were used on newspaper front pages to represent the Brexit conflict.

✓ **Statement**: The idea that stereotyping, as a form of representation, reduces people to a few simple characteristics or traits.

Application: Newspapers use stereotypes as shortcuts to convey meaning. They isolate key characteristics that are recognisable to audiences, who will then predict behaviour and narrative. For example, the repeated stereotype of starving children in Africa, which excludes any positive representation of the region in the news and reinforces preconceived ideas.

✓ **Statement**: The idea that stereotyping tends to occur where there are inequalities of power, as subordinate or excluded groups are constructed as different or 'other'.

Application: This statement can be applied to the example of developing countries cited above and to the representation of the refugee crisis in some newspapers whose aim is to reinforce differences and to adopt an ethnocentric point of view. The owners of newspapers are powerful in their ability to influence their readers and to reinforce a particular stereotype, resulting in readers believing it is a true representation.

Apply it!

3.41 Produce a short podcast exploring **either**:

- How two of the newspapers you have studied reflect the political contexts in which they were made.

Or

- How you can apply Stuart Hall's theory of representation above to the newspaper set product and another example you have studied in class.

Share the podcasts with your peers.

Link

In Year 2/A Level, you will explore Stuart Hall's theory in relation to the additional set products. This will be covered in the Year 2/A Level revision guide. There are no additional theories for the newspaper representation form in Year 2/A Level.

Quickfire Revision

3.23 Which inner pages of the newspaper may help to reinforce the political viewpoint of the newspaper?

Newspapers are often responsible for constructing largely negative representations of some social groups.

Newspapers

Representation

» **Social groups**: e.g., gender, age, ethnicity

» **Events**: e.g., the election of President Trump, the Brexit referendum

» **Issues**: e.g., social issues, including poverty, the problems in the NHS, climate change

CONSIDER:

» How the representation is constructed through selection and combination of elements

» The processes that lead media producers to make choices about the representations

» How the re-presentation constructs a version of reality

» How the representation reflects the values, attitudes and beliefs of the newspaper and its readers

» How stereotypes are used

» How audiences may respond to and interpret the representations

CONTEXTS

» Political

» Economic

» Social and cultural

Points to Remember

» **Newspapers** are studied in Component 1 Section A in relation to Media Language and Representation

» You could be asked to respond to an unseen page/pages from a newspaper in a Media Language question. This is worth 10 marks and you must use your knowledge and understanding of the newspaper form

» Or, in a Representation question, you may be required to compare the set product with another newspaper page, or with a product in a different form. This is an extended response question worth 25 marks and requires you to refer to media contexts

» Use key terminology related to the form and semiotics

KEY THEORIES/THEORETICAL PERSPECTIVES

» Semiotics: Roland Barthes

» Representation: Stuart Hall

Media Language

CODES and CONVENTIONS of the form

The repertoire of elements of the newspaper form that are common to all examples:

» headlines

» central image

» straplines and subheadings

» puffs/plugs

Consider how these are used to construct the brand identity of the newspaper.

VISUAL CODES

Consider the connotations of:

» Clothing

» Colour

» Expression

» Gesture

» Signs and codes

TECHNICAL CODES

Consider the purpose and effect of:

» the layout and design

» the selection and combination of the chosen elements

» paradigmatic choices

» manipulation of images

LANGUAGE AND MODE OF ADDRESS

» Use of language devices, e.g. hyperbole

» Use of the personal pronoun to engage audiences

» Subject-specific lexis

» Lexical differences between newspapers, e.g. popular and quality

⌄ Section B: Investigating Media Industries and Audiences

Reminder

- Media Industries and Audiences are the focus for the exploration of the forms and products you will have studied for Section B.

- The focus of Section B is different from Section A; it is not the textual features of the products you will have studied, but the products as examples of the relevant industry and audience issues they illustrate.

- In preparing for this section you will have developed your knowledge and understanding of key elements of the set media industries, including ownership and funding, regulation, global production and distribution.

- You will have explored media audiences in relation to the set forms, considering targeting, categorisation and construction of audiences as well as how audiences consume, interact with and respond to the media.

- Advertising is only studied in relation to Audiences and film is only studied in relation to Media Industries.

- In investigating Media Industries and Audiences across the set products you will be aware that you need to cover the statements set out in the specification in relation to these elements of the theoretical framework. These statements will be referred to in the different sections of this revision guide.

Link

There is a reminder of the set products you are required to study in Chapter 1 of this revision guide.

Link

Section B of Component 1 is covered in detail on pages 82–119 of the Year 1/AS student book.

Exploring how audiences engage with media products is an integral aspect of the theoretical framework.

Revising Media Industries Statements

Apply it!

3.42 In the following table, tick to show that you understand the statement. An example has been given for you. Demonstrate your understanding by giving a different example of how you have applied the statement to an additional form or product you have studied in Section B.

Statement	✓	Example	Different example
Processes of production, distribution and circulation by organisations, groups and individuals in a global context.		Industry processes vary depending on the media form and type of product. Technology has had a significant impact on the way in which media products are produced, distributed and circulated. For example, news websites have changed the way in which newspapers distribute content (e.g., the *Daily Mirror*).	
The specialised and institutionalised nature of media production, distribution and circulation.		Some products have independent, niche production, distribution and circulation processes, and are therefore more specialised, while others are more mainstream. *Late Night Woman's Hour* (*LNWH*) can be termed a more specialised and niche product due to its production by the BBC, a public service broadcaster, its scheduling time and the distribution methods.	
The relationship of recent technological change and media production, distribution and circulation.		The importance of online media platforms to the distribution and circulation of media products (e.g., BBC iPlayer, BBC Sounds and podcast for *LNWH*). The importance of technologies to the marketing, for example viral and online campaigns (e.g., *Straight Outta Compton*), and the role social media plays in involving fans in marketing and promotion.	
The significance of patterns of ownership and control, including **conglomerate** ownership, **vertical integration** and **diversification**.		The patterns of ownership of different industries will have an impact upon what is produced, for example the political allegiance of the *Daily Mirror*. Media conglomerates can exert considerable power and control, for example the mainstream film industry.	

(continued)

Quickfire Revision

3.24 What is a conglomerate?

3.25 What is vertical integration?

3.26 What is meant by diversification?

Statement	✓	Example	Different example
The significance of economic factors, including commercial and not-for-profit public funding, to media industries and their products.		Funding has an impact upon what is produced. The BBC (not-for-profit) is required to produce diverse content for a more niche, specialised audience. Whereas, commercial media industries (gaming) are more profit-driven and must create products that are financially successful.	
How media organisations maintain, including through marketing, varieties of audiences both nationally and globally.		This will differ according to the media form and product. Technological developments have facilitated global audience reach through online distribution and circulation channels, for example the role of social media in the marketing of *Straight Outta Compton*.	
The regulatory framework of contemporary media in the UK.		Media industries in the UK are regulated in different ways. The regulatory framework can change (e.g., the press) and will have an impact upon the industry and its products.	

 Link

Chapter 2 of this revision guide gives an overview of Media Industries and further revision tasks.

 Link

The additional statements required for Media Industries in Year 2/A Level are covered in the Year 2/A Level revision guide.

 Top Revision Tip

In addition to the set products you should also have studied examples of the contemporary and **emerging media** related to these products.

 Top Revision Tip

Be clear about the focus of this section. You are not required to engage in textual analysis of the set products.

 Quickfire Revision

3.27 Define emerging media and give two examples.

Revising Audience Statements

3.43 In the following table, tick to show that you understand the statement. An example has been given for you. Demonstrate your understanding by giving a different example of how you have applied the statement to a set form or product you have studied in Section B.

Statement	✓	Example	Different example
How audiences are grouped and categorised by media industries, including by age, gender and social class, as well as by lifestyle and taste.		Media producers categorise audiences in order to target them more effectively. For example, advertisers will profile audiences to ensure that their product has the right reach. Audiences may be categorised in terms of demographics (age, gender, socio-economic group) and psychographics (values, attitudes, lifestyles).	
How media producers target, attract, reach, address and potentially construct audiences.		Media producers employ a range of strategies to market their products to audiences. The way in which specific products, for example newspapers, select and present their stories constructs the idea of their target audience.	
How media industries target audiences through the content and appeal of media products and through the ways in which they are marketed, distributed and circulated.		The appeal of the product will differ according to the media form. *Assassin's Creed III* appeals to the female gamer through the inclusion of the female protagonist. This was also a main focus of the marketing.	
The interrelationship between media technologies and patterns of consumption and response.		Media technologies allow audiences to consume the media in different ways (*LNWH* podcast). This also facilitates active audience responses through, for example, social media.	
How audiences interpret the media, including how and why audiences may interpret the same media in different ways.		A range of factors affect how an audience may interpret a media product, including gender, age and culture. A reader of a different political persuasion will respond differently to the *Daily Mirror* than a left-wing reader who agrees with the newspaper's viewpoint.	
How audiences interact with the media and can be actively involved in media production.		Audiences interact differently according to the media form and product. Video games are immersive forms actively involving the gamer at every stage. Audiences can also be prosumers creating their own media content, citizen journalists regularly contribute to news platforms, for example.	

Assassin's Creed III targets the female gamer. The related online community contribute to the marketing of the product.

Link

Chapter 2 of this revision guide gives an overview of Audiences and further revision tasks.

Link

The additional statements required for Audiences in Year 2/A Level are covered in the Year 2/A Level revision guide.

Quickfire Revision

3.28 How is the BBC funded?

3.29 Give an example of how a newspaper constructs its audience.

Take it Further

3.11 Research the ongoing debate about the role of social media in terms of self-regulation. Facebook, for example, asserts that it is not a publisher or a media company but a tech platform and therefore does not have the journalistic responsibilities that would apply to news websites. Read the following article online, which is useful in explaining the issue: Sam Levin (2018, 3 July) 'Is Facebook a Publisher? In Public it Says No, but in Court it Says Yes', the *Guardian*, www.theguardian.com/technology/2018/jul/02/facebook-mark-zuckerberg-platform-publisher-lawsuit.

The ordinary person can create their own media content. Newspapers will often publish images taken by citizen journalists.

Revising the Set Forms and Products: Radio

Link

Radio is covered in more detail on pages 83–89 of the Year 1/AS revision guide.

Revising Terminology

- Commercial broadcaster
- Cross-platform marketing
- Music-led radio
- Public service broadcaster
- Speech-led radio
- Station profile
- Stripping
- Syndicated output

For assessment from 2021 you will be required to study extracts from at least one *LNHW* podcast selected by your teacher. 'Home' can remain the episode for study if your teacher so chooses. As you will still be studying *LNWH*, the information and tasks included in this revision guide are still relevant and can be adapted if a different episode is chosen.

Reminder

- Radio is studied in Component 1 Section B in relation to Media Industries and Audiences.
- The product you will have studied at the time of writing is *Late Night Woman's Hour*, 'Home', 28 October 2016.
- In order to inform your study of this programme you will also have explored the links with *Woman's Hour* and the profile of Radio 4.
- Radio as a form has subject-specific terminology that you should use in your discussion of the industry and audiences.
- There is also terminology related to Media Industries and Audiences, which will enhance your examination responses.
- The set theory/theorist for Media Industries in Year 1/AS and Year 2/A Level is power and media industries, including Curran and Seaton.
- The set theory/theorists for audiences in Year 1/AS is reception theory including Stuart Hall.
- These theories remain the same in Year 2/A Level. In addition, in Year 2/A Level you will study regulation (Livingstone and Lunt) for Media Industries. For Audiences you will explore fandom, including Jenkins, and 'end of audience', including Shirky.

Checklist of key points

- ⊘ The radio industry is one of the oldest and most traditional media forms. It has changed and developed as technology has progressed.
- ⊘ Despite predictions that this form would not survive in the digital age, it has reinvented itself to take on the competition from digital platforms and other media products.
- ⊘ Each radio station, whether commercial or not-for-profit, has a distinct profile characterised by, for example, its content, the presenters and their marketing strategies.
- ⊘ This channel identity has been established over time; however, the branding may be regularly updated, for example the logo.
- ⊘ There are over 300 commercial radio stations in the UK, including national **commercial radio**, independent local radio and community radio.
- ⊘ The BBC is a public service broadcaster funded by the licence fee. It is both national and regional. This funding arrangement allows the stations some aspect of freedom as they are less driven by ratings and profit.
- ⊘ Each year the BBC produces a very detailed Annual Report, commenting on the past year's successes and concerns, and setting out its vision for the coming year.
- ⊘ Every 11 years the government sets out its aims for the BBC in a Royal Charter.
- ⊘ BBC Radio 4, like other BBC stations, is specialised and distinctive in its output. As a response to audience research, the station has attempted to widen its appeal and embrace digital opportunities.

The radio industry has responded to changes in technology by offering audiences the opportunity to access content in different ways.

Revision Checklist: The Radio Industry

It is important to familiarise yourself with the key statements related to the different elements of the Year 1/AS specification.

What it says in the spec	What you need to know
Processes of production, distribution and circulation by organisations, groups and individuals in a global context.	• Technology has had a significant impact on the way in which radio products are produced, distributed and circulated by the BBC. *LNWH* and other radio programmes are available globally across different platforms to appeal to a range of audiences.
The specialised and institutionalised nature of media production, distribution and circulation.	• *LNWH* reflects the remit of the BBC as a media institution to offer content to a range of audiences, some of which are specialised. The fact that the BBC is a public service broadcaster, largely funded by the licence fee, allows it the freedom to produce more niche content.
The relationship of recent technological change and media production, distribution and circulation.	• The importance of online media platforms to the distribution and circulation of media products both nationally and globally (e.g., BBC iPlayer, app and podcast for *LNWH*). Listeners are also still able to access the programme live.
The significance of patterns of ownership and control, including conglomerate ownership, vertical integration and **diversification**.	• The importance of ownership, including the values and beliefs of an organisation. The BBC, as a public service broadcaster, has a remit to offer diverse content that appeals to a range of audiences. It is an industry model that is not driven by ratings and profit. There is, however, a level of control exerted by the government through the Royal Charter, which has caused some recent controversy.
The significance of economic factors including commercial and not-for-profit public funding, to media industries and their products.	• The way in which an industry is funded influences what is produced. The public service remit of the BBC has an impact on the diversity of products in its schedule, for example *LNWH*.

(continued)

Link

Media Industry in relation to radio is covered on pages 83–87 of the Year 1/AS student book.

Quickfire Revision

3.30 What characterises a commercial radio station?

3.31 Give an example of how radio has responded to technological change in the way that it distributes its content.

Apply it!

3.44 Look again at the published Radio 4 schedule of programmes. Using this information and what you have learned about the station, write a short profile of Radio 4.

3.45 **Hot-seating**

Work in pairs. One person researches the BBC as a broadcaster and the second person BBC Radio 4 in particular. Take it in turns to be in the 'hot seat' and answer questions about your research.

Take it Further

3.12 Look at the BBC's Annual Report, which includes its mission statement, its responsibilities as a public service broadcaster and makes specific reference to Radio 4. It can be found online at: https://assets.publishing.service.gov.uk/government/uploads/system/uploads/attachment_data/file/724568/bbc_annualreport_201718.pdf.

Take it Further

3.13 Research the responses to the 2016 Royal Charter, when the government was perceived to be interfering and threatening the autonomous nature of the BBC as an institution.

What it says in the spec	What you need to know
How media organisations maintain, including through marketing, varieties of audiences nationally and globally.	• BBC Radio engages in a range of marketing strategies, including cross-platform marketing, the BBC website, trailers and more traditional forms, for example billboards. It recently launched BBC Sounds. • iPlayer, as an online distribution platform, reaches a global audience.
The regulatory framework of contemporary media in the UK.	• BBC Radio is regulated by Ofcom, which is accountable to Parliament, publishes standards and deals with complaints.
The impact of 'new' digital technologies on media regulation, including the role of individual producers.	• The BBC must adhere to the rules and regulations laid out by Ofcom in relation to its content across all platforms.

LISTEN WITHOUT LIMITS

Screenshots from the TV advertisement for BBC Sounds – a recent example of how BBC Radio is responding to technological change in the way in which it distributes its content.

Apply it!

3.46 Fill in the missing words and phrases:

The BBC is a _____ _____ _____, meaning that it caters for a diverse range of tastes and audiences and produces content that is not dictated by _____ interests. The BBC does not sell advertising and is not _____ driven; it is mainly funded by the _____ _____, making it accountable to its audience.

BBC Radio engages in _____ _____ marketing, whereby its radio stations and specific programmes are advertised on BBC television and on the BBC website.

BBC Radio has addressed changes in technology by making its content available on _____ and _____, so making it a viable digital option for the audience.

BBC Sounds

BBC Sounds is a personalised audio app combining live and on-demand radio, music and podcasts. It incorporates new features, making it a development from BBC iPlayer, including a 'Recommends' facility which learns from listening habits. The slogan 'listen without limits' reinforces the fact that the BBC is changing in order to address changes in digital technologies.

Take it Further

3.14 Find out more about BBC Sounds in the online article 'What is the BBC Sounds App?' at: www.bbc.co.uk/sounds/help/sounds-intro.

Watch the BBC Sounds trailer, 'Get the BBC Sounds App for Personalised Music, Radio and Podcasts', on YouTube: www.youtube.com/watch?v=t9GFeeqwY7E.

Revising the Set Product: *Late Night Woman's Hour*

Apply it!

3.47 Consider the following questions when you are revising the set radio product.

1. How does *LNWH* demonstrate the **codes** and **conventions** of speech-based radio?

Consider:

- format, style and mode of address.

2. How typical is *LNWH* of Radio 4 output?

Consider:

- other programmes produced by the station
- the concern of Radio 4 to widen its audience base
- why this programme may be less likely to appear on a commercial radio station.

3. How has recent **technological change** had an impact on the **distribution** and **circulation** of *LNWH*?

Consider:

- the different platforms through which listeners can access the programme
- the introduction of BBC Sounds.

4. How does *LNWH* adhere to **Ofcom regulations**?

Consider:

- plurality in broadcasting
- a wide range of appeal
- the protection of audiences.

5. How does *LNWH* reflect the **ethos** of **public service broadcasting**?

Consider:

- the specialised nature of the programme and the topics it covers
- if it educates, informs and entertains (Lord Reith)
- if it caters for a range of audiences and tastes.

6. How does the BBC maintain varieties of audiences for *LNWH*?

Consider:

- if the aim of the programme is appeal to a wide or niche audience
- the choice of Lauren Laverne as a presenter
- the ways in which the programme is marketed.

Top Revision Tip

The focus of the examination questions for this section of Component 1 Section B is industry. The questions will be designed to allow you to show your understanding of the set industry, using the set product to illustrate your points. You will not be required to analyse the product in isolation.

Some of the questions will be shorter, assessing your knowledge or knowledge and understanding of aspects of the radio industry.

Understanding the format of this section will help you to focus your revision.

Link

Regulation (Livingstone and Lunt), the additional Section B Media Industries theory, will be explored in relation to the radio industry in the Year 2/A Level revision guide.

Applying Theories and Theoretical Perspectives: Power and Media Industries

Reminder

- Power and media industries, including James Curran and Jean Seaton, is the set theory for Media Industries in Year 1/AS.
- You may also have studied other relevant theories and theorists related to media industries that could enhance your response.

Checklist of key points

Power and media industries, Curran and Seaton

☑ **Statement**: The idea that the media is controlled by a small number of companies primarily driven by the logic of profit and power.

Application: The BBC is a major deliverer of radio and television content across a range of platforms. As a company it can be more flexible because it is not focused on profit and does not have to sell advertising. This gives it more freedom to create programmes that appeal to niche/minority audiences (LNWH).

☑ **Statement**: The idea that media concentration generally limits or inhibits variety, creativity and quality.

Application: The ethos of the BBC as a public service broadcaster is to be diverse in its output and to appeal to a wide range of audiences. While it does have to create successful programmes to justify the licence fee, this freedom from commercial interests allows the BBC to deliver more creative content.

☑ **Statement**: The idea that more socially diverse patterns of ownership help to create the conditions for more varied and adventurous media productions.

Application: Late Night Woman's Hour is a good example of the creative and innovative programming delivered by BBC Radio 4. It also illustrates its ability to adapt its content and commission programmes to address the under-representation of some social groups in their schedule.

Apply it!

3.48 Try to predict the shorter knowledge and understanding questions that may be asked in relation to the radio industry. These usually have a low mark tariff and require short answers.

Apply it!

3.49 Consider how you could use this theory and the theoretical perspective related to Media Industries and notions of power and control to develop your analysis of the radio industry and *LNWH*.

Radio: Audience

Reminder

- You will use the set product *LNWH* to explore issues related to Audience, considering aspects such as targeting, categorisation and how audiences are constructed.
- You will also consider how audiences consume radio and the opportunities they have to interact and respond.
- *LNWH* is an evolving media product created in response to audience demand.
- The production of the programme illustrates the BBC's aim to broaden audience reach.

Checklist of key points

The radio as a media form has surprisingly managed to survive and develop, despite competition. It has a range of different audience appeals that make it unique. It is a medium that offers different audience experiences:

- ⊘ **The blind medium**: There are no visual images, which encourages the use of the imagination. The programme style is different from those on television, as radio must paint the picture through words, sounds and music.
- ⊘ **The companion medium**: There is a personal link, established through the mode of address, between the broadcaster and the listener. There are interactive opportunities for the listener to become involved in the programme.
- ⊘ **The intimate medium**: Radio is very personal; the listener can feel as if the presenter is speaking directly to them.
- ⊘ **The undemanding medium**: The listener can engage in other activities while listening to the radio, it does not demand the attention as television does.
- ⊘ Recent technological changes have impacted upon the way in which audiences access and listen to radio output. A major development was the arrival of DAB (digital audio broadcasting).
- ⊘ The competition has been strong but the creation of listen again facilities, station websites and podcasts have been instrumental in the survival of the form. **Audio streaming** has also broadened the global audience.

Quickfire Revision

3.32 Give an example of how a listener can interact with a radio programme.

3.33 How has audio streaming had an impact on the global audience?

Top Revision Tip

The focus of Section B is not the products themselves, but how they illustrate relevant audience issues. It is therefore important to understand the radio audience and then apply this understanding to the set product.

Apply it!

3.50 Write at least two paragraphs explaining the impact of media technologies on the patterns of consumption in radio.

Revision Checklist: Radio Audience

It is important to familiarise yourself with the key statements related to the different elements of the Year 1/AS specification.

What it says in the spec	What you need to know
How audiences are grouped and categorised by media industries, including by age, gender and social class, as well as by lifestyle and taste.	• The Radio 4 audience can be clearly categorised in terms of demographics, for example age and class. *LNWH* is an example of audience grouping that challenges the more typical profile. The content relates to lifestyle and taste and illustrates the station's aim to appeal to a different audience group.

(continued)

What it says in the spec	What you need to know
How media producers target, attract, reach, address and potentially construct audiences.	• This is evident through the choices made by media producers in the construction of the product and the listener, for example, in the case of *LNWH*, the scheduling time, presenter, guests, themes and topics. The developments in technology have had an impact on the reach of the programme.
How media industries target audiences through the content and appeal of media products and through the ways in which they are marketed, distributed and circulated.	• Specific appeals differ according to the form and the product. For example, in *LNWH* the persona of Lauren Laverne will appeal to a younger female audience. The distribution of the programme across a range of digital platforms also targets the younger demographic.
The interrelationship between media technologies and patterns of consumption and response.	• Advances in media technology have changed the patterns of audience consumption. Radio programmes can be accessed in different ways, giving audiences flexibility and control. Technological advancements also have given audiences the means to respond through, for example, social media and the programme's website.
How audiences interpret the media, including how and why audiences may interpret the same media in different ways.	• In terms of *LNWH*, consider a possible male response to a programme with a specifically female target. The programme initially had some criticism for its subject matter and mode of address, so consider the responses from a more traditional Radio 4 demographic. Social media allows the responses to be widely aired and could be said to contribute to the marketing of the programme.
How audiences interact with the media and can be actively involved in media production.	• This differs according to the form and product but has been made easier for all media forms due to advances in digital technology. Social media and websites offering interactive opportunities are widely used by audiences.

Ease of access targets the *LNWH* demographic.

Apply it!

3.51 *Late Night Woman's Hour*: Audience

Consider the following audience questions in relation to the set product.

> For assessment from 2021, these questions can be adapted to suit the episode you are studying in your centre.

1. How does *LNWH* construct its audience?

Consider:

- the choice of topic for the set episode 'Home'
- the selection of guests: how they appeal to the perceived audience
- scheduling time
- the style of programme, for example language and mode of address.

2. What are the **demographic** and **psychographic** groupings for this programme?

Consider:

- age, class, gender and income
- values, attitudes and lifestyles.

3. How have the producers of *Late Night Woman's Hour* **targeted** and **attracted** the audience?

Consider:

- who the target audience is and how you know this
- the choice of presenter and her diverse radio profile, for example *Six Music*, *Desert Island Discs*
- how the topics discussed in the programme and the choice of intellectual, female guests appeal to a more specialised audience
- the scheduling time
- the focus on women only – there are no male guests
- the duration of the programme
- the speech-led style.

4. How **technological** developments have impacted upon BBC Radio and this programme.

Consider:

- the different ways *LNWH* and other radio content can be distributed and circulated
- the ways that the audience can access this programme and how this relates to the target audience.

Apply it!

3.52 Plan a response to the following Section B Question 4 question, using your knowledge and understanding of radio audiences and the set product:

> Explain how the producers of radio programmes attract audiences? Refer to *Late Night Woman's Hour* to support your points.
>
> [10 marks]

Spend approximately 10 minutes answering this question.

Top Revision Tip

Although you are not engaging in textual analysis of the set product, you will need to use specific examples from the set episode to support the points you want to make about audience.

Apply it!

3.53 **Economic contexts**

Consider how various organisations have different patterns of funding.

How does the BBC's not-for-profit, publicly funded model affect the content, distribution and circulation of its products?

Social and cultural contexts

How does the BBC's decision to commission *LNWH* and the style and content of the programme reflect the time in which it was produced?

Link

Fandom (Jenkins) and 'end of audience' (Shirky), the additional Section B Media Industries theories, will be explored in relation to the radio industry in the Year 2/A Level revision guide.

Quickfire Revision

3.34 How will cultural experience have an impact upon the way an audience may respond to *LNWH*?

Applying Theories and Theoretical Perspectives: Reception Theory

Reminder

- Reception theory, including Stuart Hall, is the set theory for Audiences in Year 1/AS.
- You may also have studied other relevant theories and theorists related to Media Industries that could enhance your response.

Checklist of key points

Reception theory, Stuart Hall

☑ **Statement**: The idea that communication is a process involving encoding by producers and decoding by audiences.

Application: The choice of presenter, guests and subject matter of this and other episodes encodes messages about the ethos of the BBC and the perceived audience for LNWH. This will be decoded differently by diverse audiences according to factors, including age, gender and cultural experience.

☑ **Statement**: The idea that there are three hypothetical positions from which messages and meanings may be decoded.

Application: Answer Apply it! 3.54.

Apply it!

3.54 Match the following theory positions with the correct definition and then apply them to *LNWH*.

Theory position	Definition	Application to *LNWH*
A. The dominant-hegemonic position	**1.** The encoder's message is understood but the decoder disagrees with it, reading it in an oppositional way.	**A.**
B. The oppositional position	**2.** The legitimacy of the encoder's message is acknowledged in general terms, although is adapted to fit the experiences or context of the decoder.	**B.**
C. The negotiated position	**3.** The encoder's intended meaning (the preferred meaning) is fully understood and accepted.	**C.**

Points to Remember

» Radio is studied in Component 1 Section B in relation to Media Industries and Audiences.

» You need to study the set podcast of *Late Night Woman's Hour*, 'Home'.

» The focus of this section of the examination paper is media industries and audiences, you will not be required to engage in textual analysis of the set products but use them to highlight issues related to the radio industry and audiences.

» You will need to learn and apply subject-specific terminology in your discussion of the industry, audiences and radio.

Radio

Audiences

» Radio audiences are targeted through content, mode of address, genre, themes, marketing and distribution

» Developments in technology have had a significant impact on the ways in which the radio audience can engage with the product, including on different devices and across a range of platforms. A major development was the arrival of DAB (digital audio broadcasting)

» Radio stations have a distinctive identity and their output will appeal specifically to their target audience

» Certain stations, e.g. Radio 4, have tried to broaden their audience appeal by producing programmes to target a less typical audience demographic (LNWH)

» Social media and interactive opportunities on the BBC Sounds website offer opportunities for social interaction and audience input and comment, and are an important marketing and circulation platform for the producers

SET PRODUCT: *LATE NIGHT WOMAN'S HOUR*

» This programme targets a younger female audience with the choice of presenter, scheduling time and topics

» The topics discussed in the programme and the choice of intellectual, female guests appeal to a more specialised audience indicative of a public service broadcaster

» The intimate style of the programme and the inclusion of high-brow, academic guests reinforce the idea of the audience demographic

» The target audience is reached through the distribution of the programme across a range of platforms including the new BBC Sounds

CONTEXTS

» Social and cultural
» Economic

KEY THEORIES/THEORETICAL PERSPECTIVES

» Industry: Power and media industries, including Curran and Seaton

» Audience: Reception theory, including Stuart Hall

Industry

» The radio industry is one of the oldest and most traditional media forms. It has changed and developed as technology has progressed

» Despite predictions that the radio form would not survive in the digital age, it has re-invented itself to take on the competition from digital platforms and other media products

» There are over 300 commercial radio stations in the UK including national commercial radio, independent local radio and community radio

» The BBC is a public service broadcaster, mainly funded by the licence fee. It is both national and regional. The funding arrangement allows the stations some aspect of freedom as they are less driven by ratings and profit

» Each year the BBC produces a very detailed Annual Report commenting on the past year's successes and concerns and setting out its vision for the next year

» Every 11 years the government sets out its aims for the BBC in a Royal Charter

» The way in which an industry is funded influences what is produced. The public service remit of the BBC has an impact on the diversity of products in its schedule

» The BBC is regulated by Ofcom and must adhere to the rules and regulations laid out in relation to its content across all platforms

Set Product: *Late Night Woman's Hour*

» It was launched in 2015 in response to the demands of the industry and to fulfill the remit of the BBC to cater for diverse audiences

» It is linked to the long-running *Woman's Hour*, a Radio 4 programme which also produces content aimed at women

» *LNWH* reflects the ethos of public service broadcasting through the specialised nature of the programme and the topics it covers

» The BBC can produce a programme like *LNWH* as it has some freedom from commercial pressures and has funding from the licence fee allowing it to commission more specialised content

Link

Film is covered in relation to Section B on pages 90–97 of the Year 1/AS student book.

Link

I, Daniel Blake, the additional Year 2/A Level film product, will be covered in the Year 2/A Level revision guide.

For assessment for 2021 the AS/Year 1 set film product will be: *Black Panther* (2018). Although this set product is different, the mainstream film form remains the same and the information and revision tasks included in this guide will still be relevant.

Quickfire Revision

3.35 Which extracts from the film will help in exploring aspects of the film industry?

Top Revision Tip

Straight Outta Compton should be studied as a product through which aspects of the film industry can be explored, not textually analysed as you would for a Section A product.

Quickfire Revision

3.36 What is meant by synergy?

Revising the Set Forms and Products: The Film Industry

Reminder

- Film is studied in Component 1 Section B in relation to Media Industries only. You are not required to study film in relation to Audiences.
- The film industry is a cross-media study, including film marketing.
- The set product you will have studied at the time of writing is: *Straight Outta Compton* (2015).
- Film as a form has subject-specific terminology that you need to use in your discussion of the industry.
- There is also terminology related to Media Industries that will enhance your examination responses.
- The set theory/theorists for Media Industries in Year 1/AS and Year 2/A Level is power and media industries, including Curran and Seaton.
- This theory remains the same in Year 2/A Level. In addition, the Year 2/A Level Media Industries theories you will study are regulation (Livingstone and Lunt) and cultural industries (Hesmondhalgh).

Checklist of key points

- ☑ You will have studied the set film product and the marketing strategies employed across various media platforms, exploring how convergence has an impact on the promotion of the film.
- ☑ As this is a cross-media study exploring the set film as a contemporary example of the film industry, you will also have studied at least one trailer and one poster from the film and online marketing.
- ☑ Selected extracts from the set film product will exemplify specific industry elements.
- ☑ How films are produced and distributed is an important element of the film industry and differs between mainstream and independent films. It is important to understand the economic contexts related to the film industry that define the products that are made.
- ☑ Films are categorised by their genre, but the production context is also relevant, including the star actors, film company and production values.
- ☑ Mainstream high-concept films are produced by film studios that are part of media conglomerates. These are financially powerful companies with the means to back films in return for profit.
- ☑ These companies operate a **synergy** model and have the means to promote, distribute and exhibit the films they make.
- ☑ Independent films are made by companies that are outside the mainstream and may be privately funded. They are usually made by smaller film companies.

Apply it!

3.55 Match the following film terms with the correct definition.

Film term	Definition
A. Distribution	**1.** All the opportunities available to the audience to view a film, including at multiplex cinemas, independent and arthouse cinemas, film festivals and online.
B. High-concept film	**2.** A company that owns other companies across a range of media platforms. This increases their market domination and facilitates their ability to distribute and exhibit the product.
C. Exhibition	**3.** A rating given to a film, informing the audience of its suitability according to a range of criteria, including levels of violence, sexual content and bad language.
D. Convergence	**4.** A film that can be encapsulated in a sentence or two. The genre is recognisable to audiences making it easily marketable. It is high budget.
E. Horizontal integration	**5.** The link between the producer and the audience. This term refers to all the processes involved in the release, marketing and promotion of the film.
F. Media conglomerate	**6.** When different companies that produce and sell similar products, for example films, merge in order to facilitate production and distribution and increase profits.
G. Vertical integration	**7.** The process through which different media industries and forms merge. This has been facilitated by developments in digital technology.
H. Classification	**8.** A process whereby one company acquires another involved at a different level of the industry.

Revising Terminology

- Classification
- **Convergence**
- Distribution
- Exhibition
- High-concept film
- **Horizontal integration**
- Media conglomerate
- Regulation
- **Vertical integration**

Quickfire Revision

3.37 Give two examples of how convergence works in the film industry.

3.38 Give an example of vertical integration in the film industry.

3.39 Give an example of horizontal integration in the film industry.

Cineworld IMAX Cinema, Telford, Shropshire

Take it Further

3.15 Visit the BBFC website and research the criteria used to classify films and the recent decisions that have been made (www.bbfc.co.uk).

The film industry operates a range of different production and distribution models, largely determined by style, genre and budget.

Take it Further

3.16 Read 'How is the Watershed Changing in the Modern TV World?' by Ben Dowell (2018, 4 May), on the *Radio Times* website, about the regulation of media service providers:

www.radiotimes.com/news/2018-05-04/how-is-the-watershed-changing-in-the-modern-tv-world/.

Revision Checklist: The Film Industry

It is important to familiarise yourself with the key statements related to the different elements of the Year 1/AS specification.

What it says in the spec	What you need to know
Processes of production, distribution and circulation by organisations, groups and individuals in a global context.	• Technology has had a significant impact on the way in which film products are produced, distributed and circulated. Films are no longer only available in cinemas, but also through other digital platforms, including Netflix and Amazon.
The specialised and institutionalised nature of media production, distribution and circulation.	• The film industry operates different production and distribution models, which are largely determined by ownership and funding. For example, more specialised, independent films demonstrate different production values to those of mainstream films.
The relationship of recent technological change and media production, distribution and circulation.	• The impact of technological developments on media production processes, for example CGI in film production. The importance of online media platforms to the distribution and circulation of films both nationally and globally. The significance of 'new' technologies to film marketing, for example viral marketing campaigns, the use of social media and the involvement of fans in the promotion of a film.
The significance of patterns of ownership and control, including conglomerate ownership, vertical integration and diversification.	• The importance of ownership, including the values and beliefs of an organisation. In the film industry media conglomerates and vertical and horizontal integration can lead to the creation of powerful monopolies. In contrast, the more niche, independent media companies demonstrate greater diversification in the ways that they produce, market and distribute films.
The significance of economic factors, including commercial and not-for-profit public funding, to media industries and their products.	• The way in which an industry is funded influences what is produced. Multi-national conglomerates in the film industry aim to create products that are financially successful, this may mean that they are less experimental and rely on staple genres, re-makes and sequels. More independent companies have the scope to be more creative and innovative in what they produce.

(continued)

What it says in the spec	What you need to know
How media organisations maintain, including through marketing, varieties of audiences nationally and globally.	• Film distribution companies engage in a range of marketing strategies, including viral campaigns, trailers and more traditional forms, for example billboards and posters. The aim is to reach multi-national audiences; to do so campaigns will be adapted for different countries.
The regulatory framework of contemporary media in the UK.	• The UK film industry is regulated by the BBFC. It classifies films using a set of criteria and sets the age certificate of films (theatrical and DVD as well as digital/streaming). In the USA the regulatory body is the Motion Picture Association of America (MPAA). A film may be awarded a different classification in different countries.
The impact of 'new' digital technologies on media regulation, including the role of individual producers.	• Internet service providers are subject to regulation; however, there is much debate about the extent to which online content can and/or should be regulated. The regulation of providers such as Amazon and Netflix is more complex. Netflix falls within the jurisdiction of Holland, but it still has to abide by the terms of the European Union's Audio Visual Media Services (AVMS) Directive, which sets rules and standards for on-demand services. Amazon Prime does come under the jurisdiction of the AVMS, which is enforced by Ofcom.

Netflix and other media service providers have changed the way in which films are distributed.

Independent or Mainstream?

3.56 In the following table, decide which of the statements describes a mainstream, high-concept film and which applies to an independent film.

Statement	Mainstream, high concept or independent?
1. Includes clearly defined characters which may be stereotypes or archetypes.	
2. The film may have a limited release and might rely on initial screenings at independent film festivals as part of the marketing.	
3. Has visual appeal including, for example, lavish sets and high-budget action scenes.	
4. The narrative is central and is often the key selling point in the absence of stars.	
5. It is aesthetically different, for example using obvious hand-held cameras, filmed in black and white or employs low-key lighting to establish realism.	
6. Has a straightforward narrative with universal themes, ensuring broad audience appeal.	
7. The theme of the film may be related to a social issue.	
8. There is evidence of the film maker and their artistic vision.	
9. Contains marketable elements, including a recognisable soundtrack and iconic images.	
10. May be distributed through independent and art-house cinemas.	
11. Features high-profile stars synonymous with the film genre.	
12. There is a lack of recognisable stars and less elaborate settings, suggesting a lower budget.	
13. The content and style may be unique and distinguishable to the sub-genre or director.	
14. High production values are evident through cinematography, sets, costumes and special effects.	

Link

If you have also studied *I, Daniel Blake* in Year 1/AS, you will be able to apply the relevant statements relating to independent films to this set product. This film will be discussed in detail in the Year 2/A Level revision guide.

The Everyman Cinema, London is an independent cinema.

Revising the Set Product: *Straight Outta Compton*

Apply it!

3.57 Answer the following questions about *Straight Outta Compton*.

1. Who directed *Straight Outta Compton*?
2. Which company made the film?
3. What is interesting about the film's distribution company, from an industry perspective?
4. In what year was the film released?
5. What is the sub-genre of the film?
6. Which stars featured in the film and what was their significance? How were they used in the film's marketing?
7. What was distinctive about the viral marketing campaign for the film? What was the related product?
8. What was the slogan for this viral campaign?
9. How were celebrities, including Eminem, involved in the marketing?
10. Give two examples from one of the trailers illustrating how audiences were targeted.
11. What classification was given to the film and the trailers?
12. How did the film posters help to establish the brand identity of the film?
13. How important was social media in the marketing of the film?
14. The film was nominated for an Oscar. In what category?

Apply it!

3.58 Consider how you can apply the criteria for a mainstream film to *Straight Outta Compton*.

Link

If you need help with this task, refer to pages 94–97 of the Year 1/AS student book.

The members of NWA co-produced the film and were important to its marketing and economic success.

Top Revision Tip

Make sure that you can refer to specific examples from the trailers, posters and online marketing from the film in your examination response, where relevant.

Top Revision Tip

Some of the questions in this section will be shorter, lower-tariff questions, assessing your specific knowledge or knowledge and understanding of aspects of the film industry.

Top Revision Tip

Try to predict the shorter knowledge and understanding questions that may be asked in relation to the film industry. These usually have a low mark tariff and require short answers.

Link

Regulation (Livingstone and Lunt) and cultural industries (Hesmondhalgh), the additional Section B Media Industries theories, will be explored in relation to the film industry in the Year 2/A Level revision guide.

Applying Theories and Theoretical Perspectives: Power and Media Industries

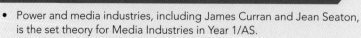

Reminder

* Power and media industries, including James Curran and Jean Seaton, is the set theory for Media Industries in Year 1/AS.
* You may also have studied other relevant theories and theorists related to media industries that could enhance your response.

Checklist of key points

Power and media industries, James Curran and Jean Seaton

⊘ **Statement**: The idea that the media is controlled by a small number of companies primarily driven by the logic of profit and power.

Application: Straight Outta Compton was co-produced by influential members of NWA and Legendary Pictures, and distributed by Universal Pictures, a vertically integrated subsidiary of NBC Universal, which is owned by Comcast, a media conglomerate. Financial success was therefore assured, with the film making over $200 million.

⊘ **Statement**: The idea that media concentration generally limits or inhibits variety, creativity and quality.

Application: Films made by the mainstream production companies and distributed by media conglomerates try to ensure financial success by producing more of the same, for example films in the same franchise, or in genres that are popular at the time. Independent film companies, however, have greater freedom from commercial interests, allowing them to deliver more creative content.

⊘ **Statement**: The idea that more socially diverse patterns of ownership help to create the conditions for more varied and adventurous media productions.

Application: Many films are now made as part of a collaborative experience with global input in terms of concepts and finance, this allows film makers to be more adventurous. Where the focus remains on financial success such as with the big film companies, there is less scope for innovation and creativity.

Revising Contexts: Film

Economic	*Straight Outta Compton* was a commercial success. This was facilitated by the fact that it was co-produced by members of NWA. Ice Cube and Dr Dre were used in the marketing rather than the film actors, as they were more recognisable to fans, thus limiting the financial risk. The film was distributed by Universal Pictures, a vertically integrated subsidiary of NBC Universal, which is owned by Comcast, a financially powerful media conglomerate. Synergy was also instrumental in the success of the film.
Political	The film's narrative reflects the political situation at the time, dealing with racial tension and the resulting violence brought about by the declining relationship between black youth and the establishment. The band itself and its name carry a controversial political message. Political statements are contained in the film and its marketing materials.

Set Product: Straight Outta Compton

» Straight Outta Compton is a biopic and was released in 2015. The film was a commercial and critical success, making over $200 million

» Straight Outta Compton was co-produced by influential members of NWA and Legendary Pictures and distributed by Universal Pictures, a vertically integrated subsidiary of NBC Universal, which is owned by Comcast, a media conglomerate.

» The film was marketed in range of ways, including traditional methods of global trailers and film posters. Digital marketing was also used, Beats by Dr Dre launched a campaign to promote the film, including the posting of memes around the topic of 'everyone is straight outta somewhere'

» The stars, Ice Cube and Dr Dre, were the focus of the biopic and were central to the marketing, appealing to the gangster/rap fan community

» The film was rated 15 by the BBFC, but the video release and the Director's Cut were rated 18

Points to Remember

» Film is studied in Component 1 Section B in relation to industry only

» The film industry is a cross-media study, including film marketing

» The set product you will have studied at the time of writing is Straight Outta Compton (2015)

» The focus of this section of the examination paper is Media Industries, you will not be required to engage in textual analysis of the set products but use them to highlight issues related to the film industry

» You will need to learn and apply subject-specific terminology in your discussion of the industry and film products

Key Terminology

» Classification
» Convergence
» Distribution
» Exhibition

» High-concept film
» Media conglomerate
» Vertical integration
» Regulation

Film

KEY THEORIES/THEORETICAL PERSPECTIVES

» Industry: Power and media industries, including James Curran and Jean Seaton

Industry

» Films are categorised by their genre, but the production context is also relevant including the stars, the film company and the production values

» Technological developments have had an impact on film processes, e.g. CGI

» How films are produced and distributed is an important element of the film industry and differs between mainstream and independent films. It is important to understand the economic contexts related to the film industry which defines the products that are made

» Online media platforms are also important to the distribution and circulation of films both nationally and globally. 'New' technologies play a significant role in film marketing, e.g. viral marketing campaigns, the use of social media and the involvement of fans in the promotion of a film

» Mainstream high-concept films are produced by film studios that are part of media conglomerates. These are financially powerful companies with the means to back films in return for profit

» These companies operate a synergy model and have the means to promote, distribute and exhibit the films they make

» Independent films are made by companies that are outside the mainstream and may be privately funded. They are usually made by smaller film companies

» Social media platforms and fan communities are important in the distribution and circulation of films

CONTEXTS

» Economic
» Political

Link

Newspapers are covered in more detail on pages 98–105 of the Year 1/AS student book.

Link

The Times, the additional Year 2/A Level newspaper product, will be covered in the Year 2/A Level revision guide.

Revising Terminology

- Broadsheet
- Circulation
- Ethnocentricity
- Gatekeepers
- Left wing
- News agenda
- News values
- Political bias
- Readership
- Right wing
- Tabloid

Quickfire Revision

3.40 Give an example of a newspaper in each of the three categories: a quality broadsheet, a mid-market and a tabloid or red top.

3.41 Give two advantages of newspaper websites for readers.

Top Revision Tip

The *Daily Mirror* must be studied as a product through which aspects of the newspaper industry and audiences can be explored, not textually analysed as you would for a Section A product.

Revising the Set Forms and Products: Newspapers

Reminder

- Newspapers are studied in Component 1 Section B in relation to Media Industries and Audiences. This form is the in depth study and you will have explored the newspaper products in relation to all areas of the theoretical framework.
- The product you will have studied at the time of writing is the *Daily Mirror*.
- In order to inform your study of this newspaper you will also have explored its role as an evolving media product and the relevant industry and audience issues it highlights.
- You will have explored one complete issue of the *Daily Mirror* chosen by your teacher as well as pages from the newspaper's website, including the homepage and one other page.
- The newspaper form has subject-specific terminology that you should use in your discussion of the industry and audiences.
- You will also have been taught terminology related generally to media industries and audiences that will enhance your examination responses.
- The set theory/theorist for media industries in Year 1/AS level and Year 2/A Level is power and media industries, including Curran and Seaton.
- The set theory/theorists for Audiences in Year 1/AS is reception theory, including Hall, and cultivation theory, including Gerbner.
- These theories remain the same in Year 2/A Level. In addition, in Year 2/A Level, in relation to Media Industries, you will study regulation (Livingstone and Lunt) and cultural industries, including Hesmondhalgh. For Audiences you will also explore 'end of audience' theory, including Shirky.

Newspapers: Industry

Checklist of key points

- ☑ Print newspapers are divided into three clear categories defined by the style of the publication and the way in which they present news: quality broadsheets, mid-markets and tabloids or red tops.
- ☑ The print newspaper industry is in decline and newspapers have introduced a range of different strategies to cope with this, including changing their size and reducing the number of pages they produce.
- ☑ The newspaper industry is very powerful and ownership is in the hands of a few groups and individuals. These patterns of ownership have an impact upon the production and distribution of newspapers.
- ☑ Most newspapers have a political leaning, this may be explicit or less obvious, depending on the style of the newspaper. The political affiliation will affect the stories that are chosen and how they are represented in the newspaper.
- ☑ Newspapers have had to adapt to technological change and the changing way in which audiences access news. All national newspapers and most local publications now have an online presence. The newspaper's website offers a more rolling news programme that can be regularly updated and has interactive features.
- ☑ Changes in technology also have had an effect on how news is gathered. News channels now frequently use citizen journalism, particularly when a story is unexpected or in a remote area.

Print newspapers can be categorised according to size, style and political allegiance.

The political leanings of the paper may be more explicit when they are covering politically important stories, for example Brexit.

News Values

Apply it!

3.59 Complete the following table about **news values**.

News value	Definition	Example
	An event that is a shock or out of the ordinary, which will take precedent over other news items.	
Personalisation		A first-hand account/ interview about what it is like to use a foodbank.
	Stories that are already in the news and continue to run or are updated as new elements appear.	
Elite nations/ elite persons		Stories about the USA and President Trump will be higher up the **news agenda** than those from other countries.
	For some newspapers, the closer to home the story is, the more interesting to the reader.	

Quickfire Revision

3.42 What are news values?

3.43 What is the news agenda?

Top Revision Tip

For Section B you need to study key pages from a whole edition of the newspaper. This edition of the *Daily Mirror* **must be different** from the set product you studied for Section A.

Link

If you need help to complete this table, refer to pages 100–101 of the Year 1/AS student book.

Link

If you need help with this task, refer to pages 93–103 of the Year 1/AS student book.

Apply it!

3.60 Match the following newspaper terms with the correct definition.

Newspaper term	Definition
A. Tabloid	**1.** An estimate of how many people read the newspaper. Most newspapers have more than one reader per copy, so this number is bigger than the amount of papers produced.
B. Broadsheet	**2.** Describes newspapers that tend to support political parties that believe in the free market and oppose socialist ideas, for example the Conservative Party and UKIP.
C. Circulation	**3.** The list of stories that may appear in a particular newspaper and will reflect the ideas and ethos of the paper.
D. Readership	**4.** The newspaper's size. This size newspaper is more compact and smaller. The focus of the content is lighter news, for example celebrity gossip.
E. Right wing	**5.** The people in control at the newspaper, for example the owner, editors and journalists, who select and construct the news for the reader.
F. Left wing	**6.** Describes a larger, better quality newspaper that focuses on more serious news. The lighter, non-news elements are often contained in supplements. These newspapers are more expensive as they have more content.
G. News agenda	**7.** Describes those newspapers that tend to support political parties such as the Labour Party that campaign for social equality.
H. News values	**8.** When a newspaper may show support for a particular political party. This will be evident through the choice of stories, the treatment of certain issues and the political cartoons. It may be subtle or more obvious when newspapers think they can affect major decisions, for example in an election.
I. Gatekeepers	**9.** The count of how many copies of the newspaper are distributed.
J. Political bias	**10.** The criteria that will influence the decisions made by those in control of the newspaper regarding what will appear in the newspaper and why.

Revision Checklist: Newspapers (Industry)

It is important to familiarise yourself with the key statements related to the different elements of the Year 1/AS specification.

What it says in the spec	What you need to know
Processes of production, distribution and circulation by organisations, groups and individuals in a global context.	• Technology has had a significant impact on the way in which newspapers are produced, distributed and circulated. Newspapers are no longer only available in print form but are accessible on websites and as apps. Individuals can also produce the news as **citizen journalists**.
The specialised and institutionalised nature of media production, distribution and circulation.	• The ownership and funding models operated by different newspapers will affect what is selected for coverage in the paper and what is rejected. Some newspapers are more financially secure as they are part of big conglomerates, others are struggling and exploring means of surviving financially.
The relationship of recent technological change and media production, distribution and circulation.	• The impact of technological developments on media production processes, for example the ability to have 'live news' updates on newspaper websites and the speed at which news can be gathered and reported globally. The importance of online media platforms to the distribution and circulation of newspapers both nationally and locally.
The significance of patterns of ownership and control, including conglomerate ownership, vertical integration and diversification.	• The importance of ownership and the values and beliefs of an organisation. In the newspaper industry, media conglomerates and vertical and horizontal integration can lead to the creation of powerful monopolies. Media organisations such as newspapers are controlled by powerful groups in society, which may lead to a lack of diversity in what is produced and the messages disseminated.

Take it Further

3.17 *Our mission is to make sense of a rapidly changing world for our readers. To challenge wrongs where we see them. To stand up for the underdog against authority. And to entertain.*

Read more about the values of the *Daily Mirror* and how it see its place in the industry in the 'Letter From the Editor', on the Mirror website:

www.mirror.co.uk/about-us/#mission.

Quickfire Revision

3.44 What is meant by citizen journalism?

3.45 What advantages does citizen journalism have for newspapers?

(continued)

Newspapers are distributed and circulated through traditional print and via digital platforms.

What it says in the spec	What you need to know
The significance of economic factors, including commercial and not-for-profit public funding, to media industries and their products.	• The way in which an industry is funded influences what is produced. Multi-national conglomerates that own newspapers as part of their empire have the flexibility to make a loss, as this will be offset by their other interests. Newspapers with smaller, more independent owners are more economically vulnerable.
How media organisations maintain, including through marketing, varieties of audiences nationally and globally.	• This will differ depending on the industry. In relation to the newspaper industry, online distribution and circulation platforms help organisations to maintain varieties of audiences both nationally and globally. Newspaper websites present the news in bite-sized chunks, unlike the print version. This may be more attractive to a younger audience who are digital natives.
The regulatory framework of contemporary media in the UK.	• IPSO is the press-funded regulator of newspapers and magazines. Impress is the state-approved press regulator. Both have been set up following the **Leveson Report**. Most newspapers are currently members of IPSO.
The impact of 'new' digital technologies on media regulation, including the role of individual producers.	• Internet service providers are subject to regulation; however, there is much debate about the extent to which online content can and/or should be regulated. With the rise of fake news and the distrust of news platforms, newspapers have to be more vigilant when they are accepting news stories from the public.

Revising the Set Product (Industry): The *Daily Mirror*

Apply it!

3.61 Answer the following revision questions about the industry elements of the *Daily Mirror*.

1. Who owns the *Daily Mirror*? How has this changed recently and why?

   Consider:

   - the newspaper group that was bought by the *Daily Mirror* in 2018
   - what was unusual about this merger
   - the advantages of this deal
   - the rebranding of the newspaper group.

2. What is the **political stance** of the *Daily Mirror*? Give an example of how this is evident in the edition of the newspaper you have studied.

   Consider:

   - how the ownership shapes the publication
   - the ways in which stories are selected and constructed
   - the choice of front-page stories, headlines and use of language
   - elements from inside the newspaper, for example the editorial, letters pages and other stories and features covered that reinforce the political leaning of the newspaper.

3. How has recent **technological change** had an impact on the distribution and circulation of the *Daily Mirror*?

   Consider:

   - the availability of the product across a range of digital platforms facilitating ease of use and immediacy
   - how the changes to distribution and circulation have targeted a new audience.

Top Revision Tip

The focus of the examination questions for this section of Component 1 Section B is industry. The questions will be designed to allow you to show your understanding of the set industry, using the set product to illustrate your points. You will not be required to analyse the product in isolation.

Some of the questions will be shorter, assessing your knowledge or knowledge and understanding of aspects of the newspaper industry.

You may also be required to discuss contexts related to the set product.

Understanding the format of this section will help to focus your revision.

Apply it!

3.62 Try to predict the shorter knowledge and understanding questions that may be asked in relation to the newspaper industry. These usually have a low mark tariff and require briefer answers.

The newspaper industry has had to adapt to changes in technology in order to continue to exist as a form.

Mirror Online: The intelligent t...

www.mirror.co.uk

Mirror NEWS ▾ POLITICS SPORT ▾

Link

Regulation (Livingstone and Lunt) and cultural industries (Hesmondhalgh), the additional Section B Media Industries theories, will be explored in relation to the newspaper industry in the Year 2/A Level revision guide.

The concentrated ownership of the newspaper industry directly affects the content, ideas and messages.

Apply it!

3.63 Consider how you could apply the points made in the quote below to enhance your analysis of the newspaper industry and your set product.

It is equally mistaken to believe that the press and broadcasting simply reflect political forces. In the first place, some groups – stronger, richer, and with better access – are always able to secure more attention than others. Secondly, the media do have some political autonomy. (James Curran and Jean Seaton (1991)Power Without Responsibility: Press, Broadcasting and the Internet in Britain (4th edition), page 1)

Applying Theories and Theoretical Perspectives: Power and Media Industries

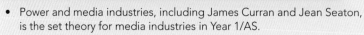

Reminder

- Power and media industries, including James Curran and Jean Seaton, is the set theory for media industries in Year 1/AS.
- You may also have studied other relevant theories and theorists related to Media Industries that may enhance your response.

Checklist of key points

Power and media industries, James Curran and Jean Seaton

☑ **Statement**: The idea that the media is controlled by a small number of companies primarily driven by the logic of profit and power.

Application: *The newspaper industry is largely run by a small number of large conglomerates that dominate the market. This is a capitalist model whereby ownership is concentrated. The Daily Mirror's 2018 deal to buy the Express and Star newspaper group, Northern and Shell, was undertaken in order to maximise profits in a struggling industry. There were concerns about this merger which were investigated by the Competition and Markets Authority and Ofcom. Reach plc is now one of Britain's biggest newspaper groups.*

☑ **Statement**: The idea that media concentration generally limits or inhibits variety, creativity and quality.

Application: *Where the ownership of the press is concentrated within a few powerful companies, this then inevitably inhibits access to a range of viewpoints. The press has greater freedom to communicate ideas and opinions than, for example, broadcast media. This becomes a topic for discussion when the largely right-wing bias of the press means that the same messages appear across different newspapers and there is a lack of a range of diverse views.*

☑ **Statement**: The idea that more socially diverse patterns of ownership help to create the conditions for more varied and adventurous media productions.

Application: *Curran and Seaton argue that the quality of the press has suffered as their focus is on the need to make a profit in a competitive marketplace, resulting in an aversion to risk. Where ownership is concentrated and where the purpose of the product is to communicate a particular message to the reader, then the creative potential of the product is restricted – this is true of the tabloid press. The broadsheet press, with their less explicit bias, is seen to produce more varied content, this is particularly the case with, for example, the Guardian and the i, where the ownership is less restrictive.*

Newspapers: Audience

Reminder

- In Section B you are studying the set product in terms of the audience issues that are highlighted.
- You will have looked at pages from a full edition of the set product and sections of the website to broaden your understanding of the brand as an evolving product.
- The edition of the *Daily Mirror* you will refer to in Section B is different from the issue set in Section A.

Checklist of key points

☑ Newspapers in their print and digital form employ a range of strategies to attract, reach, address and potentially construct audiences.

☑ Audiences are targeted through content, layout and design, mode of address, ideas and messages, marketing and distribution.

☑ The newspaper is aware of its target audience and will produce content that will appeal to them and is in line with their ideas and political allegiance.

☑ The newspaper will attract a range of audience responses according to whether the reader accepts the preferred reading or has an oppositional response to the newspaper.

☑ The newspaper form has had to adapt and change to maintain its audience in the face of competition from new digital platforms.

☑ Audiences can access the *Daily Mirror* across a range of digital platforms as well as through the more traditional print version. In June 2019, Mirror Online received its highest monthly audience of 25.49 million UK **unique viewers**.

☑ Online newspaper sites have a range of advantages for readers: they are immediate and updated regularly, they offer interactive opportunities, combine print, audio and audio-visual experiences, are easy to navigate, are available on portable devices for the 'on the go' audience and often contain an easily accessible archive facility.

Revision Checklist: Newspapers (Audience)

It is important to familiarise yourself with the key statements related to the different elements of the Year 1/AS specification.

What it says in the spec	What you need to know
How audiences are grouped and categorised by media industries, including by age, gender and social class, as well as by lifestyle and taste.	• Newspapers categorise audiences for targeting and appeal purposes. Reaching the intended audience is important for both the newspaper and its potential advertisers. Each newspaper has a specific target audience and the content and ethos of the publication will be constructed to attract that audience. • Audiences may be categorised in terms of demographics (age, gender, socio-economic group, etc.) and psychographics (values, attitudes, lifestyles, etc.).

(continued)

Quickfire Revision

3.48 What is meant by a unique viewer?

3.49 Which theorist discusses the three hypothetical positions from which messages and meanings may be decoded? What is the name of this theory?

Take it Further

3.19 Read more information about the *Daily Mirror*'s online audience, '*Daily Mirror*'s Online Traffic Hits Record Highs', on the Newsworks website:

www.newsworks.org.uk/news-and-opinion/daily-mirrors-online-traffic-hits-record-highs

This site can also provide you with up-to-date audience figures for the various news brands.

Apply it!

3.64 Look at some of the news stories on Mirror Online and the comments related to them. What do they tell you about the audience on this platform?

One of the interactive opportunities offered on the Mirror Online is the ability to comment on stories and to see and comment on the responses of other readers.

What it says in the spec	What you need to know
How media producers target, attract, reach, address and potentially construct audiences.	• This is evident through the choices made by media producers in the construction of the product and the reader. In the case of the *Daily Mirror* this includes the selection of hard and soft news relevant to the audience, the front page and the political standpoint. The developments in technology have had an impact on the reach of the product.
How media industries target audiences through the content and appeal of media products and through the ways in which they are marketed, distributed and circulated.	• Specific appeals differ according to the form and the product. The newspaper will select the content appropriate to its target audience. The distribution of the newspaper across a range of digital platforms also targets the younger demographic who may not access the print product.
The interrelationship between media technologies and patterns of consumption and response.	• Advances in media technology have changed the patterns of audience consumption. Newspapers can be accessed in different ways, including online and through Twitter feeds, giving audiences flexibility and control. • Technological advancements also have given audiences the means, to respond through, for example, social media and the newspaper's website.
How audiences interpret the media, including how and why audiences may interpret the same media in different ways.	• Many factors, social and personal, affect the way in which audiences may respond to newspapers, including their age, gender, situated culture, background, values, etc. In terms of the *Daily Mirror*, consider the response of a right-wing audience to the newspaper in comparison to a left-wing reader.
How audiences interact with the media and can be actively involved in media production.	• This differs according to the form and product, but it has been made easier for all media forms due to advances in digital technology. • Social media and websites offering interactive opportunities, including the opportunity to comment on the newspaper's content, are widely used by audiences.

The *Daily Mirror* is the fourth most famous newspaper and the tenth most popular.

The newspaper is most popular with Baby Boomers and Generation X.

The *Daily Mirror*: Audience Facts

In December 2019, the multi-platform audience was 5,110,000 of which 1,005,000 were print readers and 3,997,000 were accessing the title via a mobile device.

It is more popular with women than men.

The age of the main readers of the newspaper in print and online is 35+.

Fans of the newspaper said the newspaper:
'Stands up for ordinary people.'
'In touch with ordinary people.'
'Informative and helps me keep in touch.'

(Source: YouGov, 2018, Daily Mail, https://yougov.co.uk/topics/media/explore/newspaper/Daily_Mail)

(Source: data from www.newsworks.org.uk/daily-mirror)

Analysing the Mirror Online

The political news illustrates the leaning of the newspaper, with the negative representation of Boris Johnson. This is reinforced through the selection of images that use visual codes to communicate messages and the choice of hyperbolic language.

The font style and colour palette reinforce the brand and establish links to the print newspaper.

The navigation bar suggests the less formal mode of address of the online newspaper, for example 'Weird News', and targets an audience who want to be entertained as well as informed. The fact that 'Sport' is the third heading suggests the target audience.

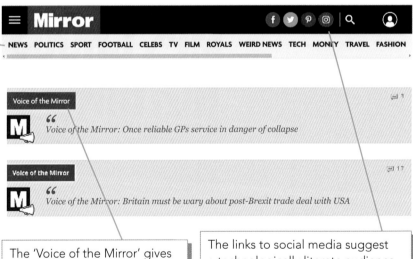

The 'Voice of the Mirror' gives the audience access to the opinions of the paper.

The links to social media suggest a technologically literate audience who access the website across different platforms.

Take it Further ➕

3.20 Place yourself in the role of a *Daily Mirror* reader. Revise the edition of the newspaper your teacher has chosen by responding as a preferred reader of the paper. Choose some of the pages and explain how they relate to you as the target audience.

Top Revision Tip 💡

Analysing the full edition of the set product

The following inner pages are useful in establishing the target audience of the newspaper, whichever edition you are studying:

- the editorial
- the letters page
- opinion pieces
- hard news stories
- soft news features.

Revising the Set Product (Audience): *The Daily Mirror*

Apply it!

3.66 Answer the following questions about the *Daily Mirror*'s audience.

1. How does the *Daily Mirror* target and attract its audience?

   Consider:
   - who the target audience is and how you know this
   - the style of the newspaper, including the layout and design and use of language
   - the choice of content
   - the left-wing political bias evident in the editorial, front page and letters page.

2. How does the *Daily Mirror* construct its audience?

   Consider:
   - the selection of stories and the front-page splash that suggest the left-wing reader with a social conscience
   - the selection of non-news content, suggesting what the newspaper considers to be the interests of the reader, for example reality television
   - the style of the newspaper, for example layout and design features and use of language
   - the mode of address, suggesting the reader will share the opinion of the paper.

3. How have **technological** developments impacted upon the *Daily Mirror*?

   Consider:
   - the different ways the *Daily Mirror* can be distributed and circulated
   - how the audience can access and interact with this newspaper and the way this relates to this target audience.

4. What are the **demographic** and **psychographic** groupings for this newspaper?

   Consider:
   - age, class, gender and income
   - values, attitudes and lifestyles
   - how you can establish this from the selected pages.

Apply it!

3.67 Using one of the 'Audiences' statements from the specification, write your own 8 mark Question 4 question related to the *Daily Mirror*.

Write a list of points you would expect to see in the response.

Link

'End of audience' (Shirky), the additional Section B Audiences theory, will be explored in relation to newspapers in the Year 2/A Level revision guide.

Apply it!

3.68 Stuart Hall's reception theory

Choose two pages from the edition of the *Daily Mirror* you are studying in class.

Consider:

- how they have been encoded by the creators of the product
- the ideas and messages the newspaper wants to communicate to its readers.

Using Hall's theory, explain how audiences may decode these pages differently.

Applying Theories and Theoretical Perspectives: Reception Theory and Cultivation Theory

Reminder

- Reception theory, including Stuart Hall, and cultivation theory, including George Gerbner, are the set theories for Audiences in Year 1/AS.
- You may also have studied other relevant theories and theorists related to media industries and newspapers that could enhance your response.

Checklist of key points

Reception theory, including Hall

Ⓢ **Statement**: The idea that communication is a process involving encoding by producers and decoding by audiences.

Application: The choice of headline, images, and news and non-news content encodes messages about the ethos of the Daily Mirror owners and editor, and the perceived audience for the newspaper. The newspaper contents will be decoded differently by diverse audiences, according to factors including age, gender and cultural experience.

Ⓢ **Statement**: The idea that there are three hypothetical positions from which messages and meanings may be decoded: dominant-hegemonic, negotiated and oppositional.

Application: This theoretical perspective can also allow you to discuss passive and active audiences in relation to the newspapers – to what extent do audiences 'accept' the messages in the products? What evidence is there of audiences actively responding or interacting with these products, for example comments on the websites, social media feeds or letters to the print newspaper?

Cultivation theory, including Gerbner

Ⓢ **Statement**: The idea that exposure to repeated patterns of representation over long periods of time can shape and influence the way in which people perceive the world around them (i.e. cultivating particular views and opinions).

Ⓢ **Application**: *Consider the political messages and values of the Daily Mirror and how they affect the way stories are represented. Consider how the newspaper constructs its readers through the repetition of the left-wing perspective of the newspaper, which may influence what the audience think about the issues of the time. To what extent may audience views be shaped by the newspapers that they read? This in turn reinforces the dominant ideologies of the newspaper in relation to politics and social issues.*

Revising Contexts: The *Daily Mirror*

Social and cultural	Newspapers reflect the society and culture in which they were produced. The *Daily Mirror* is one of the few left-wing publications in a largely right-wing dominated press. Its readers are from the lower-middle/working class demographic and consequently it communicates messages about key social issues that relate to the audience. As well as covering political stories, it also runs stories on its website and in print editions that highlight social inequalities and is often the voice of under- and misrepresented groups in society.
Economic	Newspapers have faced severe economic challenges recently, as fewer people are buying print copies and instead are accessing news on digital formats. Some newspapers that are part of big conglomerates are more protected, but those run by smaller companies are in danger. Some titles have introduced subscriptions for their websites in an attempt to recoup losses from print sales and paywalls. Patterns of ownership and control, funding and regulation are hugely significant when discussing the political contexts of newspapers.
Political	Newspapers reflect the political contexts in which they are made through their representations, values and messages, and through aspects of their ownership and political orientation, which may be implicit or explicit. The political leaning of the newspaper will influence the representations and messages that they construct. The audience will have expectations of the way in which the newspaper will treat certain political issues. The *Daily Mirror*, as a left-wing publication, will reflect the political situation of the time in a way that will reflect the ethos of the paper.

 Apply it!

3.69 Revise the selected pages from the edition of the *Daily Mirror* you have studied in detail, then consider how these pages reflect the social and cultural, economic and political contexts.

 Top Revision Tip

Ensure that you understand where on the examination paper you may be asked to refer to contexts.

 Top Revision Tip

Although your teacher will have selected a specific issue of the *Daily Mirror* for you to study as your set product, looking at other editions of the newspaper will help to broaden your understanding of the publication.

 Apply it!

3.70 **Create a podcast**

Working in small groups and using the issue of the *Daily Mirror* you have studied in class, produce a short podcast discussing how different contexts are evident in the newspaper. Each member of the group should focus on a different context.

 Apply it!

3.71 Consider how social and cultural and political contexts are evident on the front cover of this edition of the *Daily Mirror*.

Newspapers

Points to Remember

» Newspapers are studied in Component 1 Section B in relation to Media Industries and Audiences.

» This form is the in depth study and is studied in relation to all areas of the theoretical framework

» You must study one complete issue of the Daily Mirror and pages from the newspaper's website, including the homepage and one other page

» This edition of the Daily Mirror must be different from the one studied for Section A

» The focus of this section of the examination paper is Industry and Audiences; you will not be required to engage in textual analysis of the Daily Mirror

» You will need to learn and apply subject-specific terminology in your discussion of Industry and Audiences

Audiences

» Newspapers in their print and digital form employ a range of strategies to attract, reach, address and potentially construct audiences

» Newspapers will produce content that appeals to their target audience and is in line with their ideas and political allegiance

» The way in which the newspaper constructs the stories will influence the audience response

» Digital platforms offer different opportunities for active audiences

» Newspaper audiences may be categorised in terms of demographics (age, gender, socio-economic group, etc.) and psychographics (values, attitudes, lifestyles, etc.)

SET PRODUCT: THE DAILY MIRROR

» Its slogan 'the intelligent tabloid' is an attempt to distance it from other less serious tabloids. However, it does have an aim to entertain readers as well as inform them

» It has a social conscience and its stories appeal to working class, left-wing readers

» The age of the main readers of the newspaper in print and online is 35+ and it is read by men and women

» In December 2019 the multi-platform audience was 5,110,000, of which 1,005,000 were print readers and 3,997,000 were accessing the title via a mobile device (Source: data from www.newsworks.org.uk/daily-mirror)

CONTEXTS

» Social and cultural

» Political

» Economic

Industry

» The newspaper industry is very powerful and ownership is in the hands of a few groups and individuals

» Print newspapers are divided into three clear categories, defined by the style of the publication and the way in which they present news

» The print newspaper industry is in decline and newspapers have introduced a range of different strategies to cope with this, e.g. creating websites and apps

» Most newspapers have a political leaning that will affect which stories are chosen and how they are represented in the newspaper

» Newspapers have had to adapt to technological change and the changing ways in which audiences access news. This has also affected how news is gathered

SET PRODUCT: THE DAILY MIRROR

» In 2018 the Daily Mirror bought the Express and Star newspaper group in order to save money through the pooling of resources. The group became known as Reach plc (previously Trinity Mirror). Reach plc is the UK's second largest newspaper group. Its print and online portfolio reaches 38.6 million people per month

» The Daily Mirror is a left-wing newspaper which supports the Labour Party and campaigns against social injustice

» Its political allegiance is evident in the front-page stories, editorial, political cartoons, opinion pieces and letters page

» The newspaper is distributed across a range of digital platforms. Mirror Online does not have a paywall and is available free to readers both on the web and as an app

KEY THEORIES/THEORETICAL PERSPECTIVES

» Industry: Power and media industries, including James Curran and Jean Seaton

» Audience: Reception theory, including Stuart Hall and cultivation theory including George Gerbner

Revising the Set Forms and Products: Advertising

Reminder

- Advertising is studied in Component 1 Section B in relation to Audiences only. You are not required to study advertising in relation to Media Industries.
- The set products you will have studied, at the time of writing, are:
  - *Tide* print advertisement (1950s) and
  - *WaterAid* audio-visual advert (2016).
- Advertising as a form has subject-specific terminology that you need to use in your discussion of audiences.
- There is also terminology related specifically to audiences that will enhance your examination responses.
- The set theories/theorists for Audiences in Year 1/AS are media effects, including Bandura, cultivation theory, including Gerbner, and reception theory, including Hall.
- These theories remain the same in Year 2/A Level; there are no additional Audience theories.

Checklist of key points

- ⊘ Advertising is a powerful media industry. All media forms use advertising as a means of promoting their products and services to potential audiences.
- ⊘ There are different sub-genres of advertising, with different aims and purposes and different strategies for targeting audiences. For example, advertisements that may communicate information, raise awareness or promote products.
- ⊘ The advertising industry reflects the sociological, cultural and historical contexts of the time in which the product was made. The form adapts according to changes in society, for example in terms of gender representation.
- ⊘ The producers of advertisements have a very clear idea about their target audience, collated from market research data. Advertising agencies construct databases about audiences so they are able to appeal to the target one. Targeting the right audience is the key to success, regardless of what is being 'sold'.
- ⊘ The aim of the producers of advertisements is to create a brand identity which will resonate with the target audience, communicate a message about the product or organisation and be memorable.
- ⊘ Audiences are organised into categories by the producers of adverts so that they can be reached more effectively.
- ⊘ Due to changes in technology, the advertising industry has had to address how it reaches audiences. As a result, it has moved away from advertising on more traditional platforms and has experimented with newer, digital platforms.

" *. . . no-one shall take it away*"

Those who smoke Craven 'A' seldom care for other cigarettes

Link

Advertising is covered in relation to Section B on pages 107–114 of the Year 1/AS student book.

Link

There are no additional advertising products to be studied in Year 2/A Level. The additional elements of advertising required for study in Year 2/A Level will be covered in the relevant revision guide.

Top Revision Tip

The focus of Section B is not on the products themselves, but how they illustrate relevant audience issues. It is therefore important to understand audiences in relation to the advertising form and then apply this understanding to the set products.

Quickfire Revision

3.50 Give an example of a traditional and a digital advertising platform.

3.51 How have the representations of gender in advertising changed to reflect changes in society?

Advertisements reflect society. The promotion of cigarettes is no longer permitted but was acceptable when this 1950s advert was made. The promotion of tobacco products in the press and on billboards was banned in 2003.

141

Top Revision Tip

The way you approach your revision of the advertising products for Section B will be different from how you studied the same products for Section A. You need to be clear about this different focus.

Quickfire Revision

3.52 What is meant by the click-through rate and why is it helpful to advertisers?

Apply it!

3.72 Write at least two paragraphs explaining the impact of media technologies on the ways in which audiences are targeted by advertisers.

Top Revision Tip

Using the language of the theoretical framework and the form being assessed will enhance your examination response.

Revision Checklist: Advertising: Audiences

It is important to familiarise yourself with the key statements related to the different elements of the Year 1/AS specification.

What it says in the spec	What you need to know
How audiences are grouped and categorised by media industries, including by age, gender and social class, as well as by lifestyle and taste.	• Advertising agencies group audiences in order to make them easier to target. They categorise them in terms of demographics (age, gender and social status) and also by psychographics (values, attitudes and lifestyles).
How media producers target, attract, reach, address and potentially construct audiences.	• This is evident through the choices made by media producers in the construction of the product and the consumer, for example through media language and the construction of representations. • Advertising agencies gather data to allow them to target audiences more directly. The developments in technology also have had an impact on how audiences can be reached.
How media industries target audiences through the content and appeal of media products and through the ways in which they are marketed, distributed and circulated.	• Specific appeals differ according to the form and the product, for example charity campaigns may appeal to audiences with a social conscience. The use of celebrity endorsers may also appeal to sections of the audience. The promotion of brands and services across a range of digital platforms also targets the younger demographic.
The interrelationship between media technologies and patterns of consumption and response.	• Advances in media technology have changed the patterns of audience consumption. Audiences can be targeted more easily through digital platforms and can interact with campaigns online. Purchases can be made and donations given through the click of a button. Technology also enables data to be used to specifically target audiences through their search and purchase history. Social media platforms, including Facebook, also help advertisers target and reach audiences by way of the **click-through rate**.
How audiences interpret the media, including how and why audiences may interpret the same media in different ways.	• Many factors, social and personal, affect the way in which audiences may respond to advertisements, including their age, gender, situated culture, background, values, etc. The way in which audiences interpret advertisements may also change over time, for example a modern reading of the *Tide* advert will be very different from that of the 1950s consumer. (continued)

What it says in the spec	What you need to know
How audiences interact with the media and can be actively involved in media production.	• This differs according to the form and product but has been made easier for all media forms due to advances in digital technology. Social media and websites offer interactive opportunities and are widely used by audiences to 'talk back' to advertisers.

Top Revision Tip

Consider how you could use your knowledge and understanding of the strategies used in the *WaterAid* advertisement to answer a Section B Question 4 about how the advertising industry attracts audiences.

Apply it!

3.73 Complete the following table.

Term	Definition	Application to *Tide* and/or *WaterAid*
Categorisation		
Demographic		
Psychographic	A category of audiences based on values, opinions, attitudes and lifestyles.	
Target audience	The specific group at whom the advert is aimed.	
Response		Modern audiences may have an oppositional response to the *Tide* advert due to the representation of women evident.
Appeal		The *WaterAid* advert appeals to the social and moral conscience of the audience through the personal story of Claudia.
Consumer		
Brand identity	The image created by the product that becomes recognisable to an audience over time.	
Unique selling point		The *WaterAid* advert employs a unique positive perspective that is unusual for a charity advert.
Mode of address	The way in which adverts 'speak' to audiences will directly affect their response, for example the use of personal pronouns and hyberbole.	

Apply it!

3.74 *WaterAid*: **Audiences**

Consider the following Audiences questions in relation to the *WaterAid* set product.

1. How have the producers of *WaterAid* targeted and attracted the audience?

Consider:

- who the target audience is
- how you know this
- how the choice of Claudia encourages personal identification
- the unconventional use of visual and audio codes that may encourage the audience to engage and donate
- the message that appeals to an audience with a sense of social responsibility.

2. How have the producers of the *WaterAid* advert constructed audiences?

Consider:

- the choice of audio track
- the use of media language, including technical and visual codes
- the focus on Claudia
- the distribution of the advert through YouTube and social networks
- the appeal at the end of the advert

3. What are the demographic and psychographic groupings for this advertisement?

Consider:

- age, class, gender and income
- values, attitudes and lifestyles.

4. How have technological developments impacted upon the advertising industry?

Consider:

- the different ways the set product and other advertisements can be distributed and circulated
- how the audience can access this advertisement and related content and how this relates to the target audience.

Apply it!

3.75 How could you use the images here from the *WaterAid* advert to support your points in an Audience examination question?

650 million people still don't have access to clean drinking water

Reg charity no: 288701 England & Wales and SC039479 Scotland.

Revising the Set Product: *Tide*

Apply it!

3.76 Consider the following Audiences questions in relation to the *Tide* set product.

1. How does the *Tide* advert target and appeal to the 1950s female audience?

Consider:

- the use of colour and font styles
- the use of visual codes, including clothing, gesture and expression
- the use of hyperbole and other language devices in establishing the brand
- the choices made about how the woman has been represented
- the creation of the narrative encouraging identification
- the intertextuality between the woman featured and star icons.

2. How does this advert construct the idea of the audience?

Consider:

- how true a representation this is of a 1950s wash day
- how the construction of domestic perfection targets aspirers
- the advert's use of women with whom the target audience may personally identify
- the perceived importance of clean washing related to the role and responsibility of the woman.

3. What does this advert tell us about audiences of the time?

Consider:

- the link between domestic cleaning products and appliances and social status
- the importance of advances in technologies for the average housewife.

4. What are the **demographic** and **psychographic** groupings for this advert?

Consider:

- age, class, gender and income
- values, attitudes and lifestyles
- how these can be established from the advert.

Quickfire Revision

3.53 What was the purpose of the convention in adverts of the time of including two women having a conversation?

Apply it!

3.77 Role play revision

Place yourself in the role of a 1950s advertising agency executive. Write a pen profile aimed at the target audience for the *Tide* advertising campaign.

Apply it!

3.78 Write a response to the following Section B Question 4 question using your knowledge and understanding of advertising audiences and the set product. You should spend no more than 10 minutes on this:

Explain how the producers of advertisements target audiences. Refer to the *Tide* advert to support your points. [8 marks]

Take it Further

3.21 Contexts

Research the social and cultural context of the time and consider how the *Tide* advert exemplifies these contexts.

Consider:

- the role of women in a post-war world
- the targeting of domestic products and appliances at women
- the social and cultural context of the 1950s and how this had an impact on advertising strategies.

Take it Further

3.22 What might the theorist say?

In groups of three, each person takes responsibility for one of the three hypothetical audience positions suggested by Hall. Each person then speaks as the theorist about the set advertising products.

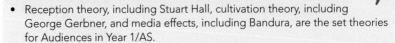

Applying Theories and Theoretical Perspectives: Reception Theory

Reminder

- Reception theory, including Stuart Hall, cultivation theory, including George Gerbner, and media effects, including Bandura, are the set theories for Audiences in Year 1/AS.
- You may also have studied other relevant theories and theorists related to advertising that could enhance your response.

Checklist of key points

Reception theory, Stuart Hall

⊘ **Statement**: The idea that communication is a process involving encoding by producers and decoding by audiences.

Application: With regard to the two advertising set products, you will need to consider their different sub-genres and the time in which they were produced. The two adverts have a different purpose but both use language, narrative, visual and technical codes to communicate messages about the product being promoted to the audience.

⊘ **Statement**: The idea that there are three hypothetical positions from which messages and meanings may be decoded: dominant-hegemonic, negotiated and oppositional.

Application: This theoretical perspective can also allow you to discuss passive and active audiences in relation to advertising – to what extent do audiences 'accept' the messages in the products? In charity adverts, for example, what evidence is there of audiences actively responding or interacting with these products, for example comments on the websites, social media feeds or actual donations? What are the different ways in which the 1950s woman may have responded to the Tide advert?

Cultivation theory, including Gerbner

⊘ **Statement**: The idea that exposure to repeated patterns of representation over long periods of time can shape and influence the way in which people perceive the world around them (i.e. cultivating particular views and opinions).

Application: Consider the messages and values encoded in the set products. Consider how the Tide advertisement constructs its readers through the reinforcement of the idea of domestic perfection. To what extent may audience values be shaped by the dominant ideologies encoded in advertisements? With regard to charity adverts, some of the more typical conventions used have made audiences desensitised and, as such, less willing to interact with the product.

⊘ **Statement**: The idea that cultivation reinforces mainstream values (dominant ideologies).

Application: Consider how the WaterAid advertisement may challenge Gerbner's theory in the way in which it addresses the audience and the messages it communicates about developing countries.

Media effects, including Bandura

⊘ **Statement**: The idea that the media can implant ideas into the mind of the audience directly.

Application: This can be said to be true in relation to some forms of advertising. Consider the ideas encoded in the Tide advert and the impact these may have had on women of the time. Also consider how this theoretical perspective can be applied to the WaterAid advertisement where alternative representations of developing countries are presented which may elicit a different response from the audience and change their views and behaviour.

Top Revision Tip

When revising the *Tide* advertisement, you should always bear in mind the historical context and avoid analysing a 1950's product from a 21st-century perspective.

✏️ **Apply it!**

3.79 Consider how you could use Gerbner's theory in analysing the *WaterAid* advertisement. Can you find points that both support and challenge Gerbner's theoretical perspective?

Quickfire Revision

3.54 Give two examples of the ideas encoded in the *Tide* advert that may have shaped how women perceived the world around them.

Charity donation service texts cost £3 and one standard network rate message. WaterAid receives 100% of donations.

Top Revision Tip

As you will not have a copy of the *Tide* advert in the examination with you, you should ensure that you are able to support the points you want to make about aspects of audience with specific examples from the set product. If you have studied other examples of similar adverts, you should ensure that you do not confuse these with the set product.

Adverts in the 1950s implanted ideas into the minds of women (and men) about what it meant to be a successful housewife.

Take it Further

3.23 What might the theorist say?

Imagine that you are Stuart Hall. What would he say about the two set products in relation to his theoretical perspective?

What might Stuart Hall say?

The producer of the advert encodes meaning in the product. The dominant-hegemonic audience position will accept that meaning; for example, it is my responsibility to donate money to help people like Claudia.

STUART HALL

Take it Further

3.24 What might the theorist say?

Imagine that you are George Gerbner. What would you say about the two set products in relation to his theoretical perspective?

What might George Gerbner say?

The exposure of repeated patterns of representation of developing countries in charity adverts influences audience perceptions of the country, its people and issues.

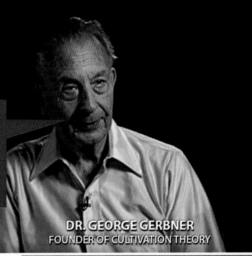

DR. GEORGE GERBNER
FOUNDER OF CULTIVATION THEORY

Take it Further

3.25 What might the theorist say?

Imagine that you are Albert Bandura. What would you say about the two set products in relation to his theoretical perspective?

What might Albert Bandura say?

Advertisements directly implant ideas into the minds of audiences about the world in which we live and what we need to be successful. This may result in direct action from the audience, for example buying the product or supporting the cause.

Apply it!

3.80 Contexts

Consider how you could apply the relevant contexts to these set advertising products:

Political contexts

Charity advertisements reflect the society that produces them and this will include global and political issues. Consider how the *WaterAid* advert is making a political comment about global inequalities.

Social and cultural

The *WaterAid* advert addresses the issues of the misrepresentation of developing countries at the same time as highlighting the social injustice of a specific cultural group.

Link

Young and Rubicam's theory is covered in more detail on page 108 of the Year 1/AS student book.

Quickfire Revision

3.55 What sort of audience categorisation did Young and Rubicam advocate?

Apply it!

3.81 Additional theories

Another useful additional theory you may have studied in relation to the advertising set products is Young and Rubicam's research into how cross-cultural consumer characteristics group audiences through motivational needs. Consider which of the main groups are relevant to the set advertising products you have studied: Mainstreamers, Aspirers, Explorers, Succeeders or Reformers.

Advertising: Audiences

How media forms target, reach and address audiences, how audiences interpret and respond to them and how audience members become producers

Audience Responses

» How audiences interpret and respond to advertisements
» How audiences may respond to and interpret the same advertisements in different ways
» What affects the way in which an audience interprets and responds to advertisements, e.g. gender, age, culture

KEY TERMINOLOGY

» Active
» Appeal
» Attract
» Brand identity
» Consumer
» Demographic
» Passive
» Positioning
» Psychographic
» Reach
» Target
» Unique selling point

SET PRODUCT: WATERAID

» 2016 charity advert created by Atomic London and shot in Zambia
» The aim is to show a positive representation of how communities benefit from what we take for granted
» The advert challenges the way in which charities usually address audiences

CONTEXTS

» *Tide*: Historical, social and cultural
» *WaterAid*: Social and cultural, economic, political

Where is it Assessed?

» Component 1 Section B Question 4
» Component 3 through knowledge and understanding of the TF

Points to Remember

» Advertising is studied in Component 1 Section B in relation to audiences only
» You need to study two advertising products: a print product, *Tide* (1950s), and an audio-visual product, *WaterAid* (2016)
» These products are the same as those studied for Section A, but the focus has changed
» The focus of this section of the examination paper is audience, you will not be required to engage in textual analysis of the set products but use them to highlight issues related to audiences
» You will need to learn and apply subject-specific terminology in your discussion audiences and advertising

KEY THEORIES/THEORETICAL PERSPECTIVES

» Media effects: Albert Bandura
» Cultivation theory: George Gerbner
» Reception theory: Stuart Hall

Audience Categorisation

» Demographic: age, gender, class, income
» Psychographic: values, attitudes and lifestyles (Young and Rubicam)
» Tribes
» How grouping helps the industry to effectively target the audience

AUDIENCE APPEAL STRATEGIES

» What is meant by the target audience?
» The techniques used by advertisers to target audiences, e.g. content, appeal, marketing, distribution and circulation of products
» How media producers reach, attract and address audiences
» How audiences are positioned by advertisements
» The ways in which media producers construct audiences

SET PRODUCT: TIDE

» 1950s advert produced by Proctor & Gamble
» Target audience was 1950s women with responsibility for the home. The aim was to make the women feel valued
» The advert uses a range of persuasive strategies typical of adverts of the time to target the audience
» The advert constructs an audience striving for domestic perfection

AUDIENCE INTERACTION

» Passive and active audiences
» The impact of technology in facilitating audience consumption of and response to advertisements

Revising the Set Forms and Products: Video Games

Reminder

- The Video Games form is studied only in Component 1 Section B and in relation to Media Industries and Audiences.
- The product you will have studied, at the time of writing, is: *Assassin's Creed III: Liberation* (2012).
- In order to inform your study of this product you will have explored at least one age-appropriate extract from the game.
- The video games form has subject-specific terminology that you need to use in your discussion of the media industry and audiences.
- There is also terminology related to media industries and audiences that will enhance your examination responses.
- The set theory/theorist for Media Industries in Year 1/AS and Year 2/A Level is power and media industries, including Curran and Seaton.
- The set theories/theorists for audiences in Year 1/AS are reception theory, including Stuart Hall, and media effects, including Bandura.
- These theories remain the same in Year 2/A Level. In addition, in Year 2/A Level you will study regulation, including Livingstone and Lunt, for Media Industries and cultural industries, including Hesmondhalgh. For Audiences you will explore fandom, including Jenkins, and 'end of audience', including Shirky.

Link

The Video Games form is explored in more detail on pages 115–119 of the Year 1/AS student book.

Revising Terminology

- Augmented reality
- Avatar
- Computer role-playing game (CRPG)
- Massively multi-player online role-playing game (MMORPG)
- Open World play
- Persistent worlds
- Virtual costuming
- Virtual reality

Checklist of key points

☑ Video games are a relatively new media form and as such the video games industry has seen a rapid growth in recent years.

☑ Developments in technology have allowed for more and more sophisticated games to be created and marketed to audiences.

☑ The playing of computer games is now taken more seriously, so the products are accepted as valid for study in the same way as other media products.

☑ Many games are complex and challenging for the player and the form is interactive and demanding in ways that other media products are not.

☑ This form raises different issues compared with other media industries, for example in terms of regulation and the suitability of the content of some games that are easily accessed by young people.

☑ How video games are produced and distributed is an important element of the industry. It is necessary to understand the economic contexts related to the video games industry which define the products that are made.

☑ In addition to the production elements of the form, there also have been developments in how products can be marketed and distributed and the way in which audiences can be maintained through innovative marketing strategies.

☑ Video games sales are very competitive across platforms and producers. Many games are distributed across a range of consoles and platforms to ensure economic success.

Top Revision Tip

Using relevant media terminology will demonstrate your knowledge and understanding, and will enhance your examination response.

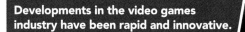

Developments in the video games industry have been rapid and innovative.

Top Revision Tip

Assassin's Creed III: Liberation has to be studied as a product through which aspects of the video games industry can be explored, not textually analysed as you would for a Section A product.

Quickfire Revision

3.56 Why is regulation problematic for the video games industry?

Top Revision Tip

The video games industry is constantly developing and changing. Engage in regular research that will keep you up to date with advances in the industry.

Take it Further

3.26 Read Kevin Anderton's (2019, 26 June) 'The Business of Video Games: Market Share for Gaming Platforms in 2019', *Forbes*, www.forbes.com/sites/kevinanderton/2019/06/26/the-business-of-video-games-market-share-for-gaming-platforms-in-2019-infographic/#9c11ad77b254, which explores the recent research made into the video gaming market.

Revision Checklist: Video Games: Industry

It is important to familiarise yourself with the key statements related to the different elements of the Year 1/AS specification.

What it says in the spec	What you need to know
Processes of production, distribution and circulation by organisations, groups and individuals in a global context.	• Technology has had a significant impact on the way in which video games are produced, distributed and circulated. Video games are distributed and circulated across a range of different platforms to expand audiences. These platforms ensure that a global audience is reached, contributing to the economic success of the product.
The specialised and institutionalised nature of media production, distribution and circulation.	• The video games industry operates different production and distribution models, which are largely determined by ownership and funding. Games developers and publishers are large, independent, multi-national conglomerates with a lot of power within the industry.
The relationship of recent technological change and media production, distribution and circulation.	• The impact of technological developments on media production processes, for example virtual reality headsets. The importance of a range of media platforms to the distribution and circulation of video games globally. The significance of social media and fan communities in the circulation of video games.
The significance of patterns of ownership and control, including conglomerate ownership, vertical integration and diversification.	• The importance of ownership, including the values and beliefs of an organisation. In the video games industry, multi-nation media conglomerates can lead to the creation of powerful monopolies with high revenues.
The significance of economic factors including commercial and not-for-profit public funding, to media industries and their products.	• The way in which an industry is funded influences what is produced. Multi-national conglomerates in the video games industry aim to create products that are financially successful, this may mean that they are less experimental and rely on staple genres and franchises, for example *Assassin's Creed* and *Grand Theft Auto*. These commercial models are driven by profit, with economic success as their key aim.

(continued)

What it says in the spec	What you need to know
How media organisations maintain, including through marketing, varieties of audiences nationally and globally.	• Video games publishers and distributors engage in a range of marketing strategies, including viral campaigns, trailers and more traditional forms, for example billboards and posters. The aim is to reach global audiences and campaigns may be adapted for use in different countries. • Games producers may also introduce marketing devices during the life of the game, for example the buying of skins for virtual characters.
The regulatory framework of contemporary media in the UK.	• The regulation of video games is difficult and controversial. • The UK games industry uses the PEGI system; however, this only applies to the physical copies of the games being bought. • The VSC (Video Standards Council) is the statutory body responsible for age-rating video games using the PEGI system.
The impact of 'new' digital technologies on media regulation, including the role of individual producers.	• Internet service providers are subject to regulation; however, there is much debate about the extent to which online content can and/or should be regulated. This is particularly relevant to the video games industry where, due to the advances in technology, games can be accessed by children through downloads and streaming.

The VSC age-rates video games in the UK using the PEGI system.

Apply it!

3.82 Economic contexts

Consider how you could use the information in this section to answer a question focusing on economic contexts in the video games industry.

Give three points that you would make in the first part of an industry question focusing on this context.

Take it Further

3.27 Visit the VSC website where you will find more information about the regulation of video games in the UK: https://videostandards.org.uk/RatingBoard/.

The VSC 'Annual Report and Accounts 2018' details decisions made and concerns raised about specific games, see, for example, page 13 of the 2018 Report, which discusses *Fortnite*, https://videostandards.org.uk/MzCms/ContentImage.ashx?cpath=000%5c000%5c948%5c950%5cVSC+Annual+Report+2018.pdf.

The global market for video games will reach $137.9 billion in 2018 and is estimated to reach $180.1 billion by 2021.

The Asia-Pacific region leads the global market and is the fastest growing with 52% of the total global market.

Video Games Industry: Interesting Facts

All segments of the games market are growing steadily. Mobile revenues are the largest segment.

The Virtual, Augmented and Mixed Reality games market will be worth $8.8 billion by the end of 2020 with VR as the dominant form.

By 2022 it is estimated that 175.2 million VR headsets will be bought by consumers across ten major markets.

(Source: adapted from https://ukie.org.uk/research#fact_sheet)

Apply it!

3.83 Match the following video games terms with the correct definition.

Video games term	Definition
A. Augmented reality	**1.** Where skins can be bought for characters in the virtual world of the game and allows the gamer to make choices about how to represent characters. It also allows the game's publishers to make money.
B. Virtual reality	**2.** The player's representation of themselves within the game.
C. Persistent worlds	**3.** A computer-generated three-dimensional simulation of a world that can be interacted with in a seemingly physical way through the use of specific digital equipment. This allows the gamer to feel immersed in the environment.
D. Avatar	**4.** A narrative-driven video game that allows a large number of players to interact in the game's evolving world at the same time.
E. Open World Play	**5.** Computer-generated content overlaid on a real-world environment. The content is engaged with through portable devices and devices that can be worn, for example headsets and glasses.
F. Virtual costuming	**6.** A game in which the player controls the actions of a character and is able to move freely through the game's fantasy world.
G. MMORPG	**7.** A game where the player is given the freedom to explore a virtual world and make choices that determine the next moves, giving a feeling of control.
H. CRPG	**8.** This is a feature of MMORPG games, whereby the game world continues even when the gamer is not engaged with it, so replicating real life.

 Top Revision Tip

Remember that the focus of Section B Question 3 is industry. You will be required to demonstrate your knowledge and understanding of the video games industry and to apply that to the set product.

Using relevant terminology will help you to show your understanding of the form.

 Link

If you need help with this task refer to pages 116–117 of the Year 1/AS student book.

Top Revision Tip

Some of the questions in Section B will be shorter, lower tariff questions, assessing your specific knowledge or knowledge and understanding of aspects of the video games industry.

Top Revision Tip

Some of the questions in Section B will be shorter, lower tariff questions, assessing your specific knowledge or knowledge and understanding of aspects of the video games industry.

As well as looking at extracts from the game, it is important to explore the other marketing devices used by the game's publisher, including trailers.

Revising the Set Product: *Assassin's Creed III: Liberation*

Apply it!

3.84 Answer the following questions about *Assassin's Creed III: Liberation*.

1. In what year was the game released?
2. What is the game's sub-genre?
3. For which games console was the product originally designed?
4. What was distinctive about the features of this console at the time of the game's release?
5. Which company developed the game?
6. What marketing ploy was used by this company for the game's release to tap into the existing market?
7. What is the PEGI rating for the game?
8. Name the three major territories for video game distribution.
9. Give an example of one of the additional opportunities offered to gamers through the initial choice of video game console.
10. What technical process did the game undergo in 2019?
11. Who is the regulator of the video games industry in the UK?

Applying Theories and Theoretical Perspectives: Power and Media Industries

Link

Regulation (Livingstone and Lunt) and cultural industries (Hesmondhalgh), the additional Section B Media Industries theories, will be explored in relation to the film industry in the Year 2/A Level revision guide.

Reminder

- Power and media industries, including James Curran and Jean Seaton, is the set theory for Media Industries in Year 1/AS.
- You may also have studied other relevant theories and theorists related to media industries that could enhance your response.

 ## Checklist of key points

Power and media industries, James Curran and Jean Seaton

⊘ **Statement**: The idea that the media is controlled by a small number of companies primarily driven by the logic of profit and power.

Application: Ubisoft (software producer) and Sony (hardware producer) created Assassin's Creed III: Liberation. The game was a key development in the well-established franchise that offered elements of the familiar and new elements aiming to achieve commercial success.

⊘ **Statement**: The idea that media concentration generally limits or inhibits variety, creativity and quality.

Application: Video games made by games publishers and distributed by powerful companies, for example Ubisoft, try to ensure financial success by producing more of the same, for example games in the same franchise, or in genres that are popular at the time. Assassin's Creed III: Liberation is part of a successful games franchise and was launched alongside the latest version to ensure maximum marketing reach. However, in producing a version of the game featuring a female protagonist and aimed at the female gamer, the publisher was demonstrating variety and creativity in its output.

⊘ **Statement**: The idea that more socially diverse patterns of ownership help to create the conditions for more varied and adventurous media productions.

Application: Video games are economically significant across the three major territories of Japan, Europe and the USA. Many video games are now made by global computer games publishers, for example Ubisoft, this economic stability allows companies to be more adventurous. The release of new gaming technology and games from popular franchises can be major economic events. As the market is so competitive and is expanding yearly, the publishers must be adventurous in the production, marketing and distribution of their products.

Rayman Adventures (left) was developed by Ubisoft.

Quickfire Revision

3.57 What defines a casual gamer?

3.58 What is a core gamer?

Video Games: Audience

Checklist of key points

- ⊘ Video games employ a range of strategies to attract, reach, address and potentially construct audiences.

- ⊘ Audiences are targeted through content, gameplay, mode of address, genre, themes, and marketing and distribution strategies.

- ⊘ Developments in technology have had a significant impact on the ways in which the gaming audience can engage with the product, including on different consoles and across a range of platforms.

- ⊘ Different games appeal to a diverse range of gamers, for example hand-held consoles appeal to the 'on the go', more **casual gamer**, while more traditional consoles are marketed at **core gamers**.

- ⊘ The games publishers are aware of their target audience, particularly if the game is part of a franchise, and will produce content that may appeal to them and their expectations.

- ⊘ Video games offer a range of interactive opportunities not offered by other media forms that make them attractive to a particular demographic. These include multi-playing online experiences, the unique experience of playing in persistent worlds and the appeal of role-playing.

- ⊘ Video games also appeal to their audience through the use of intertextuality. Games are often derived from other media forms, for example comics, books and films.

- ⊘ Video games appeal to and are targeted at different audiences. Different games position audiences in different ways, for example single- or multi-player or in the role of an avatar.

- ⊘ There are some misconceptions about gamers: they are not all young, nor are they all men. The gaming community is very diverse and the profile of the gamer is broad.

- ⊘ As well as the interactive opportunities offered by gameplay, fan communities offer opportunities for social interaction and are an important marketing and circulation platform for the game producers.

- ⊘ The perceived effects of video games on audiences is an ongoing and often controversial topic of discussion. Violent games come under criticism regarding the effect over-exposure to gaming worlds may have on young people's behaviour. Other research suggests that the more serious video games have positive effects on the player, including the development of technical and social skills.

Contrary to popular belief, a diverse range of people play video games.

(Source: ukie, 'UK Video Games Fact Sheet',https://ukie. org.uk/sites/default/ files/UK%20Games%20 Industry%20Fact%20 Sheet%20October%20 2018.pdf, page 48)

THE U.K. GAMER
KEY CONSUMER INSIGHTS

NUMBER OF GAMERS
32.4M

TOTAL GAME REVENUES
$4.2BN

#5
MARKET IN THE WORLD

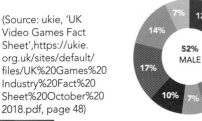

AGE/GENDER
ACTIVE MOBILE PLAYERS*

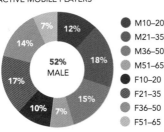

52% MALE

- ● M10–20
- ● M21–35
- ● M36–50
- ● M51–65
- ● F10–20
- ● F21–35
- ● F36–50
- ● F51–65

7% / 12% / 14% / 18% / 17% / 15% / 10% / 7%

* Plays more than once a month

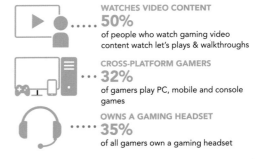

WATCHES VIDEO CONTENT
50%
of people who watch gaming video content watch let's plays & walkthroughs

CROSS-PLATFORM GAMERS
32%
of gamers play PC, mobile and console games

OWNS A GAMING HEADSET
35%
of all gamers own a gaming headset

Revision Checklist: Video Games: Audiences

It is important to familiarise yourself with the key statements related to the different elements of the Year 1/AS specification.

What it says in the spec	What you need to know
How audiences are grouped and categorised by media industries, including by age, gender and social class, as well as by lifestyle and taste.	• Games producers group audiences in order to make them easier to target. They categorise them in terms of demographics (age, gender and social status) and also by psychographics (values, attitudes and lifestyles). The female gamer and the 'on the go' player were relatively new audience demographics targeted in the marketing for *Assassin's Creed III: Liberation*.
How media producers target, attract, reach, address and potentially construct audiences.	• This is evident through the choices made by media producers in the construction of the product and the consumer, for example in video games through elements of media language and the construction of representations. The existence of the female protagonist in games, including *Assassin's Creed III: Liberation*, can be said to construct a female audience by offering a platform for female identification in a largely male domain. • A range of data about gaming audiences is available to allow publishers to target audiences more directly. The developments in technology, including consoles and platforms, has also had an impact on how audiences can be reached.
How media industries target audiences through the content and appeal of media products and through the ways in which they are marketed, distributed and circulated.	• Specific appeals differ according to the form and the product. The gaming industry often uses the power and appeal of the franchise to target loyal audiences. Many games also have unique selling points related to the opportunity to download exclusive content. • The interactivity of the form also has obvious appeal and the ability to interact with other gamers as part of a multi-player global community.

(continued)

Apply it!

3.85 Write a short profile of the *Assassin's Creed III: Liberation* audience.

Quickfire Revision

3.59 Give another example of how video games audiences may interact with the product.

Top Revision Tip

Although you are not engaging in textual analysis of the set product, you will need to use specific examples from the video game to support the points you want to make about audience.

Top Revision Tip

Remember that in the Section B examination questions, the first part of the question will focus on Audiences. The second part will then usually ask you to show your knowledge and understanding by referring to the set product.

What it says in the spec	What you need to know
The interrelationship between media technologies and patterns of consumption and response.	• Advances in media technology have changed the patterns of audience consumption, this is particularly true of the video game form. The way in which games are distributed gives an audience choice and control over how they play, what they play and who they play with. • Fan communities allow audiences to interact and share experiences, while fan responses may have a direct impact on the development of a game. Digitally convergent media platforms offer a unique experience to the gamer.
How audiences interpret the media, including how and why audiences may interpret the same media in different ways.	• Many factors, both social and personal, affect the way in which audiences may respond to video games, including their age, gender, situated culture, background, values, etc. Some video games have received negative responses from audiences regarding the perceived effects on young people's behaviour. However, other research suggests that video games can improve both motor and social skills.
How audiences interact with the media and can be actively involved in media production	• This differs according to the form and product but has been made easier for all media forms due to advances in digital technology. Video games involve direct interactivity with the product through role play.

The game constructs an idea of the female audience through their perceived identification with Aveline.

Assassin's Creed III: Liberation: Audience

Apply it!

3.86 Consider the following Audience questions in relation to the set product *Assassin's Creed III: Liberation*.

1. How have the producers of *Assassin's Creed III: Liberation* targeted, attracted and reached their audience?

Consider:

- who the target audience is for the game
- the initial launch of the game on a specific, niche platform
- the subsequent expansion of the game onto more platforms and consoles to broaden the audience reach
- the decisions made about characters and narrative
- the opportunities to gain extras related to the game.

2. How does the content and appeal of the game target the potential audience?

Consider:

- the role-playing format of the game
- the links with the Assassin's Creed franchise used in the marketing
- the cultural significance of the female protagonist in terms of addressing the under-/misrepresentation of women in video games
- the appeal of buying extra elements of the game
- the appeal of the remastered version of the game and the additional features for the target audience.

3. How have the producers of *Assassin's Creed III: Liberation* advertisement constructed audiences?

Consider:

- the focus on the female protagonist
- the active role of Aveline in the narrative related to the role-playing potential
- the game as a platform for female identification
- that the product initially was launched for a hand-held device aimed at the 'on the go' gamer.

4. How may different audiences respond to the game?

Consider:

- if Aveline subverts or reinforces expectations of female characters in video games
- the significance of the 18 PEGI rating to audience responses
- the possible response of the male gamer/player of the existing *Assassin's Creed* games.

5. What are the **demographic** and **psychographic** groupings for this programme?

Consider:

- age, class, gender and income
- values, attitudes and lifestyles.

Apply it!

3.87 How could immersion in video games potentially change behaviours?

3.88 What might the theorist say?

Imagine that you are Albert Bandura. What would you say about the set video game product in relation to his theoretical perspective?

Take it Further

3.28 Read 'Do Video Games Encourage Violent Acts?' (Tom Faber (2019, 14 August) *Financial Times*, www.ft.com/content/1c5914b6-bdb7-11e9-9381-78bab8a70848) and consider how you could apply the points made to support or challenge Bandura's theory.

Quickfire Revision

3.60 What is meant by transgressive behaviour?

Link

Fandom, including Jenkins, and 'end of audience', including Shirky, the additional Section B Audience theories, will be explored in relation to the video games industry in the Year 2/A Level revision guide.

Applying Theories and Theoretical Perspectives

Reminder

- Reception theory, including Stuart Hall and media effects, including Albert Bandura are the set theories for audiences in Year 1/AS.
- You may also have studied other relevant theories and theorists related to audiences and video games that could enhance your response.

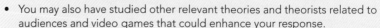

Checklist of key points

Media effects, including Albert Bandura

⊘ **Statement**: The idea that the media can implant ideas into the mind of the audience directly.

Application: This can be said to be true in relation to some video games. Consider how this theoretical perspective can be applied to Assassin's Creed III: Liberation where the role-playing and interactive elements of the game suggest the acceptable nature of violent action, and how this may change audience behaviours.

⊘ **Statement**: The idea that media representations of **transgressive behaviour**, such as violence or physical aggression, can lead audience members to imitate those forms of behaviour.

Application: The game received an 18 rating from PEGI due to the violent content. Consider Bandura's arguments, focusing on observation and imitation in relation to the set product. Are gamers likely to imitate the behaviours evident in the game?

Consider if Bandura's theory can be effectively applied when the gamer is choosing to be actively involved in the violent actions of a game, rather than passively watching them.

Reception theory, including Stuart Hall

⊘ **Statement**: The idea that there are three hypothetical positions from which messages and meanings may be decoded: the dominant-hegemonic position; the negotiated position; and the oppositional position.

Application: Answer Apply it! 3.89 on the next page.

Apply it!

3.89 **Stuart Hall – reception theory statement**

The idea that there are three hypothetical positions from which messages and meanings may be decoded.

Apply Hall's reception theory to *Assassin's Creed III: Liberation*.

Position	Definition	Application to *Assassin's Creed III: Liberation*
The dominant-hegemonic position	The encoder's intended meaning (the preferred meaning) is fully understood and accepted.	
The oppositional position	The encoder's message is understood but the decoder disagrees with it, reading it in an oppositional way.	
The negotiated position	The legitimacy of the encoder's message is acknowledged in general terms, although is adapted to fit the experiences or context of the decoder.	

Revising Contexts

Social and cultural	As video games are a relatively new media form, consider what they tell us about society. There is an obvious topic of discussion in terms of gender issues. Females are largely under-represented in games or appear as stereotypes. Female gamers, although a very relevant audience, are still in the minority.
Economic	The video games industry is very powerful and the launches of new games, consoles and gaming technology are huge economic events. Money is invested in the games industry in hard- and software. The global software market is expected to grow to $180.1 billion by the end of 2021. (Source: www.ukie.org.uk)

Apply it!

3.90 Consider how you could apply these contexts specifically to *Assassin's Creed III: Liberation*.

Points to Remember

» Video games is studied in Component 1 Section B in relation to audiences only

» You need to study at least one extract from the game Assassin's Creed III: Liberation (2012), which can be accessed online. It will also help to consider other marketing materials, e.g. the trailer for the existing and re-mastered edition

» The focus of this section of the examination paper is media industries and audiences, you will not be required to engage in textual analysis of the set products but use them to highlight issues related to the video game industry and audiences

» You will need to learn and apply subject-specific terminology in your discussion of the industry, audiences and video games

Video Games

Audience

» Gaming audiences are targeted through content, gameplay, mode of address, genre, themes, marketing and distribution

» Developments in technology have had a significant impact on the ways in which the gaming audience can engage with the product, including on different consoles and across a range of platforms

» Different games appeal to a diverse range of gamers, e.g. hand-held consoles appeal to the 'on the go', more casual gamer, while more traditional consoles are marketed at core gamers

» The interactive, role-playing elements of video games means that audiences are largely active and can create their own narratives within the world of the game

» Fan communities offer opportunities for social interaction and are an important marketing and circulation platform for the game producers

SET PRODUCT: ASSASSIN'S CREED III: LIBERATION

» This game targets the female gamer with the strong protagonist Aveline, an avatar, as well as the male gamer through the inclusion of recognisable elements of the franchise

» The role-playing, interactive element is part of the game's appeal. There are single- and multi-player modes

» The game was launched alongside the latest version of the film Assassin's Creed to clearly establish it as part of the franchise

» The target audience was initially reached through the launch on PlayStation Vita, a unique selling point, before being developed on other platforms and consoles

CONTEXTS

» Social and cultural

» Economic

Industry

» The video games industry has seen a rapid growth in recent years and this is projected to rise steadily

» Games developers and publishers are large independent, multi-national conglomerates with a lot of power within the industry. Their aim is to create products that are financially successful globally

» Developments in technology have allowed for more sophisticated games to be created and marketed to audiences across a range of consoles and digital platforms

» Other technological developments have had an impact on media production processes, e.g. virtual reality headsets and portable consoles for 'on the go' gaming

» Video games publishers and distributors employ a range of marketing strategies, including viral campaigns, trailers and more traditional forms, e.g. billboards and posters, in order to reach global audiences

» Social media platforms and fan communities are important in the distribution and circulation of video games

» The regulation of this industry raises issues related to the suitability of the content of some games that are easily accessed by young people

SET PRODUCT: ASSASSIN'S CREED III: LIBERATION

» Developed by Ubisoft, a French global computer developer and publisher whose aim is to 'work with passionate people and make fun games'. (Source: www.ubisoftgroup.com)

» Launched in 2012 on PlayStation Vita, the Sony hand-held device, which was innovative at the time

» A trailer was also released and other marketing included 'walk-throughs' on YouTube and additional content, e.g. character skins

» In 2014 it was re-released as a high-definition re-work and was made available across a range of consoles and platforms

KEY THEORIES/THEORETICAL PERSPECTIVES

» Industry:
Power and media industries, including James Curran and Jean Seaton

» Audience:
Reception theory, including Stuart Hall, and media effects theory, including Albert Bandura

Component 1: Investigating the Media: Assessment

4

How Will I Be Assessed?

The Component 1 examination assesses the theoretical framework: Media Language, Representation, Media Industries, Audiences and Media contexts. It consists of two sections:

Section	Forms	Questions
Section A: Investigating Media Language and Representation	Advertising and marketing Music video Newspapers	One question assesses Media Language in relation to an unseen audio-visual or print resource. One question assesses Representation and is an extended response comparing a set product with an unseen audio-visual or print resource in the same or a different form.
Section B: Investigating Media Industries and Audiences	Advertising Film Newspapers Radio Video games	One stepped question assessing knowledge and understanding of Media Industries in relation to one of the forms you have studied. One stepped question assessing knowledge and understanding of Audiences in relation to a different form.

Link

A quick guide to the key aspects of the theories and theoretical perspectives you are required to study is in Chapter 10 of the Year 1/AS student book.

Top Revision Tip

In Section A there will always be one print and one audio-visual unseen product.

What Theories and Contexts Do I Need to Revise?

	Section A	Media Language theories	Representation theories	Contexts
Advertising and marketing	*Tide*	Semiotics (including Hall)	Theories of representation (including Hall) Theories of identity (including Gauntlett)	Historical Social and cultural
	WaterAid			Social and cultural Economic Political
	The Kiss of the Vampire			Historical Social and cultural
Music video	*Dream*	Semiotics	Theories of representation (including Hall) Theories of identity (including Gauntlett)	Social and cultural
	Formation			
Newspapers	The *Daily Mirror*	Semiotics	Theories of representation (including Hall)	Social and cultural Economic Political

Top Revision Tip

Depending on how the course has been structured in your centre, you may have studied some Year 2/A Level products in Year 1. However, if you are taking the AS examination, only the Year 1 products will be assessed on this examination paper.

Top Revision Tip

You must study the set theorists and theoretical perspectives for this component, but you can also refer to other relevant theories to enhance your examination responses and show your broad understanding of the subject.

	Section B	Media Industries	Audiences	Contexts
Advertising	*Tide*	N/A	Theories of media effects (including Bandura) Cultivation theories (including Gerbner) Reception theories (including Hall)	Historical Social and cultural
	WaterAid			Social and cultural Economic Political
Newspapers	The *Daily Mirror* Complete edition chosen by your centre; related social and online media products	Power and media industries (including Curran and Seaton)	Cultivation theories (including Gerbner) Reception theories (including Hall)	Social and cultural Economic Political
Film	*Straight Outta Compton* Cross-media study	Power and media industries (including Curran and Seaton)	N/A	Economic Political
Radio	*Late Night Woman's Hour* Related online and social media content	Power and media industries (including Curran and Seaton)	Reception theories (including Hall)	Social and cultural Economic
Video games	*Assassin's Creed III: Liberation* Related online and social media content	Power and media industries (including Curran and Seaton)	Media effects (including Bandura) Reception theories (including Hall)	Social and cultural Economic

 Top Revision Tip

Reading around the set theories and theoretical perspectives will give you a better understanding of them, allowing you to apply them more effectively to the set products.

5

Component 2: Investigating Media Forms and Products

⊻ Section A: Television

Set Product Options

> **Reminder**
>
> - For Section A of Component 2, you will have studied **one** of the three set television products shown below.

Option 1	Option 2	Option 3

Life on Mars	**Humans**	**The Jinx**
Series 1, Episode 1	Series 1, Episode 1	Episode 1: 'A Body in the Bay'
BBC	Channel 4/AMC	HBO

- You will have looked at all four areas of the theoretical framework – Media Language, Representation, Media Industries and Audiences.
- You will have studied Neale's theory of genre, Todorov's theory of narratology, Hall's theory of representation and Hall's reception theory, exploring how each of these theories can be applied to your set television product.
- You will also have considered the influence of relevant contexts on your set television product.

Revising Your Set Television Product

In this section, you will find revision checklists for each of the four areas of the theoretical framework, along with tips and suggestions about how to revise key topics.

Media Language

Revision Checklist: Media Language

Quickfire Revision

5.1 What does the term polysemic mean?

The following checklist outlines the key aspects of Media Language that you need to know for the Television section of Component 2.

What it says in the spec	What you need to know
How the different modes and language associated with different media forms communicate multiple meanings.	• How images, sound and speech convey meanings in television products. • The **polysemic** nature of television products.
How the combination of elements of media language influence meaning.	• How elements of media language such as camerawork, editing and sound work together to convey meaning in your set television product.
The codes and conventions of media forms and products, including the processes through which media language develops as a genre.	• The audio, technical and visual codes used in television products. • The particular ways in which audio, technical and visual codes are used in your set television product. • The genre conventions that your set television product uses.
The dynamic and historically relative nature of genre.	• The way in which genres change over time. • How your set television product reflects the development of the genre to which it belongs.
The processes through which meanings are established through intertextuality.	• The way in which direct or indirect references to other texts communicate meanings in your set television product.
How audiences respond to and interpret the above aspects of media language.	• The different ways in which audiences may respond to the codes, conventions and intertextual references used in your set television product.

Quickfire Revision

5.2 What term is used to describe visual elements that appear in audio-visual products such as television programmes or films?

5.3 What is the difference between diegetic and non-diegetic sound? What is the difference between diegetic and non-diegetic sound?

Top Revision Tip

Remember that it is important to discuss *how* and *why* particular codes and conventions have been used rather than simply identifying or describing them. Considering the purpose and effect of relevant codes and conventions will give your answers greater analytical depth.

Apply it!

5.2 Analyse a specific sequence from your set television product, making notes on the codes and conventions that have been used, and the way in which they convey meanings.

Revising Television Codes and Conventions

Here is a reminder of some of the main codes and conventions used in television products:

Visual codes	Settings, props, clothing/costumes, colours, graphics, facial expressions, gestural codes
Audio codes	Dialogue, music, sound effects, voice-over
Technical codes	Camera shots, movements and angles, editing

Apply it!

5.1 Focusing specifically on technical codes, make a note of as many different camera shots, movements and angles as you can think of, completing the table below.

Technical code	Examples
Camera shots	
Camera angles	
Camera movements	

Visual codes such as settings, costumes and props play an important role in establishing the two different timeframes in *Life on Mars*.

Revising Genre

When revising your set television product, you will need to make sure that you have a good understanding of the genre it draws on. Here is a reminder of some of the conventions most commonly associated with crime dramas, science fiction and documentaries:

Crime drama conventions	Science-fiction conventions	Documentary conventions

• Narratives concerned with crime and investigation • Stock characters such as criminals, investigators, suspects, witnesses, etc. • The iconography of crime – crime scene tape/markers, forensic equipment, police cars, interview rooms, etc.	• Narratives concerned with time or space travel, different worlds or alternative realities • Stock characters such as scientists, robots, androids or aliens • Futuristic iconography – science labs, artificial intelligence, futuristic/alien landscapes, etc.	• Narratives concerned with real people and real events • Interviews, fly-on-the-wall footage, voice-over narration • Reconstructions, archive footage, still images

Apply it!

5.3 Which of these genre conventions can you identify in the set television product you have studied? Find a particular sequence in the set episode that illustrates the way in which they have been used.

How to Revise Neale's Theory of Genre

One of the required theories that you will need to revise for your set television product is Steve Neale's theory of genre.

KEY THEORY: Steve Neale's Theory of Genre

- The idea that genres may be dominated by repetition, but they are also marked by difference, variation and change.
- The idea that genres change, develop and vary as they borrow from and overlap with one another.
- The idea that genres exist within specific economic, institutional and industrial contexts.

Link

For an explanation of Neale's theory of genre see page 127 of the Year 1/AS student book.

When revising Neale's theory of genre, you should make sure that you understand what each of the three bullet points in the box above means and that you can apply them to your set television product. Try using the questions in the table on the following page as a basis for your revision.

Aspect of Neale's theory	Questions to consider
• The idea that genres may be dominated by repetition, but they are also marked by difference, variation and change.	• In what ways is your set television product similar to other products in the same genre? Which genre conventions does it use? • How does your set television product differ or vary from other products in the same genre?
• The idea that genres change, develop and vary as they borrow from and overlap with one another.	• How does your set television product differ from *earlier* products in the same genre? How does it show the way in which the genre has developed or evolved over time? • Does your set television product show any evidence of **genre hybridity**? Does it borrow conventions from more than one genre?
• The idea that genres exist within specific economic, institutional and industrial contexts.	• Why would programmes in this genre be attractive to television companies and broadcasters? Do they have ready-made audiences? How might they be used to generate revenue? Is there an international market for this type of programme? • How might products in this genre fit with the broadcaster's ethos, remit or brand identity?

Quickfire Revision

5.4 What does the term genre hybridity mean?

Link

For an introduction to narrative concepts and a summary of Todorov's theory of narratology see pages 139–142 of the Year 1/AS student book.

Revising Narrative

As well as revising the genre conventions of your set television product, you will also need to think about its narrative structure and the narrative devices it uses.

Apply it!

5.4 The following table shows a number of terms and concepts that are useful when exploring the narratives of television products. Match the following narrative terms and concepts with the correct definition.

Link

If you need a reminder of what any of the narrative terms mean, look at the information on pages 139–141 of the Year 1/AS student book.

Narrative term/ concept	Definition
A. Enigma code	**1.** A narrative structure that combines aspects of the series and the serial (e.g., individual episodes may feature self-contained narratives but there are also broader story arcs that run across multiple episodes).
B. Flashback	**2.** A television product in which each individual episode is a self-contained narrative.
C. Restricted narrative	**3.** A narrative device that disrupts chronological order by showing the viewer something that occurred at an earlier point in time.
D. Unrestricted narrative	**4.** A narrative device that is conventionally used at the end of an episode or prior to an advert break in order to create suspense.
E. Cliffhanger	**5.** A narrative in which the story arc runs over multiple episodes.
F. Serial	**6.** A narrative where the viewer knows more than the characters within the diegetic world of the text, providing them with a privileged spectator position.
G. Series	**7.** A question or mystery that a narrative sets up in order to create audience interest. Also known as the hermeneutic code.
H. Flexi-narrative	**8.** A narrative in which information is withheld from the viewer so that they only know as much as characters within the diegetic world of the text.

How to Revise Todorov's Theory of Narratology

The key narrative theory that you will need to revise for your set television product is Todorov's theory of narratology.

KEY THEORY: Tzvetan Todorov's Theory of Narratology

- The idea that all narratives share a basic structure that involves a movement from one state of **equilibrium** to another.
- The idea that these two states of equilibrium are separated by a period of imbalance or disequilibrium.
- The idea that the way in which narratives are resolved can have particular ideological significance.

Quickfire Revision

5.5 What does the term equilibrium mean?

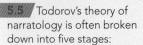

Apply it!

5.5 Todorov's theory of narratology is often broken down into five stages:

1. Equilibrium
2. Disequilibrium
3. A recognition that equilibrium has been disrupted
4. Attempt to repair the disruption
5. New equilibrium

Which of these five stages can you identify in the set episode you have studied?

Top Revision Tip

Remember that a single episode of a television programme may not necessarily culminate in the restoration of equilibrium, particularly if that episode is part of a serial. Similarly, some television programmes may begin with disequilibrium or a recognition that equilibrium has been disrupted.

Take it Further

5.1 In order to build audience interest, television products often use particular narrative strategies and devices to prolong the period of imbalance or disequilibrium. Consider whether your set product does this. Does it use enigma codes to create suspense, for example?

When revising Todorov's theory, you may find it useful to consider the following questions:

- How does the set episode of the television product you have studied begin?
  - Is there an initial state of equilibrium? If so, what is the nature of this equilibrium?
  - If the narrative skips the initial state of equilibrium and begins with disequilibrium or a recognition that the equilibrium has already been disrupted, why do you think this has been done? Is there still an implied state of equilibrium prior to the point at which the set episode begins?
- How is disequilibrium or a sense of imbalance introduced into the narrative?
  - What happens to disrupt the initial state of equilibrium?
  - How is this disruption signified?
- How does the set episode end?
  - Is there any sense of narrative resolution?
  - Is a new state of equilibrium established? If not, consider what the reason for this might be. Is the set episode part of a broader narrative, for example?

The set episode of _The Jinx_ opens with the discovery of Morris Black's body in Galveston, Texas.

Apply it!

5.6 **Create your own narrative timeline**

As a revision aid, you may find it useful to create a timeline showing the key narrative events that occur in the set episode of the television product you have studied, similar to the one shown at the top of the following page. When creating your timeline, add details of the opening and ending of the episode and each of the key narrative events that occurs. You should also try to make a note of the narrative function that these actions or events perform. Do any of them disrupt the initial state of equilibrium or set up an enigma code, for example?

A key narrative event in the set episode of _Humans_ is Joe's decision to introduce a synth, Mia/Anita, into the Hawkins' household.

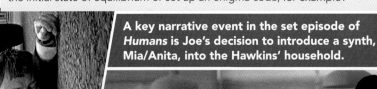

One of the most significant narrative events in the set episode of _Life on Mars_ is the car accident that precipitates Sam's journey back into the 1970s.

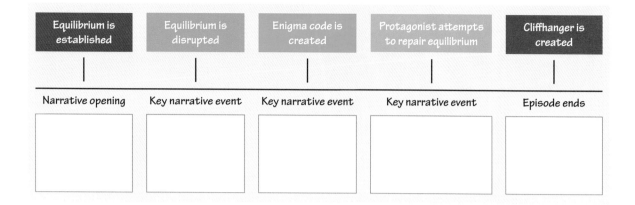

Equilibrium is established	Equilibrium is disrupted	Enigma code is created	Protagonist attempts to repair equilibrium	Cliffhanger is created
Narrative opening	Key narrative event	Key narrative event	Key narrative event	Episode ends

Revising Intertextuality

One of the ways in which television products communicate meanings is through intertextuality. This can take the form of direct references to specific texts or indirect allusions to other products in the same genre.

When revising your set television product, try to identify at least two uses of intertextuality in the set episode you have studied (some examples you could consider are provided below). In each case, think about the *purpose* and *effect* of the intertextual allusion.

- Does it invite the viewer to read a character, subject or situation in a particular way?
- Does it have thematic significance? In other words, does it relate to a particular theme or idea that the programme explores?
- Does it help to convey a sense of authenticity or **verisimilitude**?
- What pleasures does it offer the audience? (E.g., does it offer a sense of nostalgia or the pleasure of recognising and understanding the reference?)

Quickfire Revision

5.6   What does the term verisimilitude mean?

Examples of intertextuality in *Life on Mars*: David Bowie's song 'Life on Mars' playing on Sam's iPod (left), and a poster of Gary Cooper in the western *High Noon* on the wall of Gene Hunt's office (right).

Examples of intertextuality in *Humans*: the opening title sequence that features images of robots drawn from popular culture (above left), and a fake Channel 4 News interview with scientist Dr Ji Dae-Sun (above right).

Examples of intertextuality in *The Jinx*: newspaper report about the disappearance of Durst's first wife (above left), and a clip from home movie footage showing Robert Durst and his brother Douglas as children (above right).

Representation

Revision Checklist: Representation

The following checklist outlines the key aspects of representation that you need to know for the Television section of Component 2.

What it says in the spec	What you need to know
The way events, issues, individuals and social groups (including social identity) are represented through processes of selection and combination.	• How the representations in your set television product (e.g., of individuals or social groups such as men or women) are constructed through the combination of different elements of media language and the choices made by the programme-makers.
The effect of social and cultural context on representations.	• How the representations in your set television product have been shaped by the social and cultural contexts in which they have been produced (e.g., how they reflect particular social norms or cultural values).

(continued)

What it says in the spec	What you need to know
How and why stereotypes can be used positively and negatively.	• The extent to which the representations in your set television product reinforce or challenge stereotypes. • The reason for any stereotypical representations that feature in your set television product.
How and why particular social groups, in a national and global context, may be under-represented or misrepresented.	• The extent to which your set television product reflects the under-representation or misrepresentation of particular social groups (such as women or ethnic minorities) in the media, and the reasons for this.
How media representations convey values, attitudes and beliefs about the world and how these may be systematically reinforced across a wide range of media representations.	• The way in which the representations in your set television product can be seen to express particular ideas or values, and how these representations relate to broader patterns within the media.
How audiences respond to and interpret media representations.	• The different ways in which audiences may read and respond to the representations in your set television product.

For an explanation of Hall's theory of representation see pages 142–143 of the Year 1/AS student book.

How to Revise Hall's Theory of Representation

One of the theories that you will have looked at in preparation for Section A of Component 2 is Hall's theory of representation.

KEY THEORY: Stuart Hall's Theory of Representation

• The idea that representation is the production of meaning through language, with language defined in its broadest sense as a system of signs.

• The idea that the relationship between concepts and signs is governed by codes.

• The idea that stereotyping, as a form of representation, reduces people to a few simple characteristics or traits.

• The idea that stereotyping tends to occur where there are inequalities of power, as subordinate or excluded groups are constructed as different or 'other' (e.g., through **ethnocentrism**).

Quickfire Revision

5.7 What is ethnocentrism?

When revising Hall's theory, you may find it useful to consider the following questions:

Aspect of Hall's theory	Questions to consider
• The idea that representation is the production of meaning through language, with language defined in its broadest sense as a system of signs. • The idea that the relationship between concepts and signs is governed by codes.	• How are the representations in your set television product constructed through media language? • What role do visual, technical or audio codes play in constructing representations of individuals, social groups and (where relevant) issues or events in the set episode?
• The idea that stereotyping, as a form of representation, reduces people to a few simple characteristics or traits. • The idea that stereotyping tends to occur where there are inequalities of power, as subordinate or excluded groups are constructed as different or 'other' (e.g., through ethnocentrism).	• Are there any examples of stereotyping in your set television product? (E.g., does it reinforce or challenge particular stereotypes of gender or ethnicity?) • Do the representations in the set product reflect inequalities of power between different social groups? Do they reinforce **patriarchy** for instance? Are there any examples of ethnocentrism or othering?

Quickfire Revision

5.8 What does the term patriarchy mean?

Revising Representations of Gender

As part of your revision, you should re-familiarise yourself with the representations of gender in your set television product.

In order to do this, you may find it useful to either:

• Create a separate flashcard, poster or mind map for each of the main characters/people who appear in the set episode.

Or

• Create one poster or mind map focusing on the representation of men in the set episode and another focusing on the representation of women.

If you are studying *The Jinx*, you could create flashcards summarising the way in which female figures such as Debrah Lee Charatan and Jeanine Pirro are represented in the set episode.

DEBRAH LEE CHARATAN
ROBERT DURST'S CURRENT WIFE

JEANINE PIRRO
WESTCHESTER DISTRICT ATTORNEY

When creating your flashcards, posters or mind maps, make a note of the following:

- Any stereotypical traits that are exhibited.
- Any ways in which gender stereotypes are challenged or subverted.
- The roles and contexts in which men and women are represented (e.g., boss, investigator, authority figure, wife, mother, victim, love interest, etc.).
- Any instances in which men or women are sexually objectified.

Revising Representations of Ethnicity

As well as revising the representations of gender that feature in your set television product, you should also think about representations of race and ethnicity. The under-representation and **misrepresentation** of particular social groups is an important issue to consider here. As part of your revision, try to answer the following questions:

- Are there any racial or ethnic groups that appear to be under-represented in your set television product?
- If so, does this reflect broader power inequalities in the social or institutional contexts in which the programme was produced?
- Is there any evidence of **tokenism** in your set television product?
- Is there any evidence of racial or ethnic stereotyping in your set product?

If you are studying *Life on Mars* (above top), think about what the programme says about gender roles in the 1970s. If you are studying *Humans*, consider the extent to which female characters such as Niska (above bottom) and Mia are constructed as objects of a male gaze.

If you are studying *Life on Mars*, consider the extent to which the representation of Nelson the barman reinforces or challenges racial stereotypes.

Quickfire Revision

5.9 What is meant by misrepresentation?
5.10 What does the term tokenism mean?

If you are studying *Humans* (near right), consider how the programme could be seen to offer a commentary on racial politics (e.g., through allusions to slavery).
If you are studying *The Jinx* (far right), consider whether the representations of race and ethnicity in the programme could be seen as ethnocentric.

Industry

Revision Checklist for Industry

The following checklist outlines the key aspects of Industry that you need to know for the Television section of Component 2.

What it says in the spec	What you need to know
Processes of production, distribution and circulation by organisations, groups and individuals in a global context.	• How your set television product was produced, distributed and broadcast.
The specialised and institutionalised nature of media production, distribution and circulation.	• The industrial and institutional context in which your set television product was made and distributed and the particular organisations involved.
The significance of patterns of ownership and control, including conglomerate ownership, vertical integration and diversification.	• Whether the television company responsible for making and/or showing your set television product is privately or publicly owned and whether it is part of a larger conglomerate. • Whether the relevant television company is vertically integrated (i.e. does it have the means to both produce and distribute products?). • Whether the relevant television company has diversified into other media industries such as film or radio.
The significance of economic factors, including commercial and not-for-profit public funding, to media industries and their products.	• Whether the television company is funded through advertising, subscription, sponsorship or a licence fee, and how this impacts on the programmes it produces or broadcasts.
How media organisations maintain, including through marketing, varieties of audiences, nationally and globally.	• The ways in which your set television product was marketed and the particular audiences it targeted.
The regulatory framework of contemporary media in the UK.	• The role of Ofcom in regulating the UK television industry and its impact on your set television product.

Key Industry Information

When revising your set television product, you should make sure that you know about the industry contexts in which it was produced, distributed and broadcast. The two tables on the following page provide some basic factual information that should help you with this aspect of your revision.

Revising Production and Distribution

Production, distribution and broadcast contexts

	Life on Mars	Humans	The Jinx
Broadcaster/network	BBC	Channel 4/AMC	HBO
Production company	Kudos	Kudos (for Channel 4 and AMC Studios)	HBO Documentaries Hit the Ground Running Films Blumhouse Productions
Distributor	BBC Worldwide	Endemol Shine International	HBO and Sky

Ownership, funding and vertical integration

	BBC	Channel 4	HBO
Ownership	**Publicly owned**	Publicly owned	**Privately owned**
Main source of funding	Licence fee	Advertising	Subscription fees
Public service broadcaster?	✓	✓	✗
Vertically integrated?	✓ The BBC has its own distribution arm (BBC Worldwide) and some of its programmes are made by its own in-house production unit	✗ Channel 4 is a publisher-broadcaster, so its programmes are made by independent production companies rather than being produced in-house	✓ HBO has the means to produce and distribute its own programmes

Link

For a more detailed discussion of relevant aspects of the television industry, including ownership, funding, vertical integration, regulation and marketing, see pages 148–155 of the Year 1/AS student book.

Quickfire Revision

5.11 What is the difference between a publicly owned television company and one that is privately owned?

5.12 What is a public service broadcaster?

Top Revision Tip

The information provided here should be regarded as a starting point for your revision. It is not enough just to learn *facts* about the industry contexts in which your set television product was produced; you need to consider their *significance*. How have economic factors and institutional contexts had an impact on the set product, for example?

Revising Marketing

As part of your revision of the television industry, you should refamiliarise yourself with the marketing strategies used to promote your set television product.

5.7 The following table shows some of the marketing methods commonly used to promote television products. Put a tick in the box next to those you looked at when studying your set television product, adding notes on how they were used to target and appeal to particular audiences.

Marketing methods	✓	Notes on audience targeting
Trailers		
Posters/billboards		
Viral marketing campaigns		
Marketing stunts		
Websites		
Preview screenings and/or Q&A sessions		
Press and publicity		

Marketing *Life on Mars*

A useful overview of one of the marketing campaigns created to promote *Life on Mars* can be found on the website of Amanda Kirke and Paul Hodgson – the media creatives who produced the campaign on behalf of Red Bee Media. If you are studying *Life on Mars*, try to watch their case study video as part of your revision.

We used the original BBC globe and announcers from the 1970s

BBC**1** COLOUR

Apply it!

5.8 Here is one of the posters that was used to promote the second series of *Life on Mars*. Consider how it creates audience interest and appeal, using the questions below to help you.

1. Analyse the language used here. In what ways could 'in the nick' be seen as polysemic?

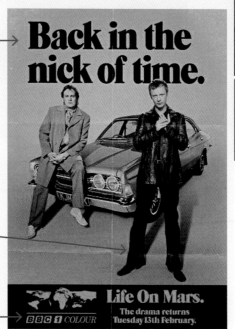

Back in the nick of time.

Life On Mars.
BBC**1** COLOUR
The drama returns
Tuesday 13th February.

A viral teaser in the style of Camberwick Green

BBC**1** COLOUR

'Life on Mars – Case Study – Amanda and Paul', available online at: amanda-paul.co.uk/life-on-mars/ or vimeo.com/87862346

2. How is iconography used to market the programme and create audience appeal?

3. How might this use of a BBC ident from the 1970s create audience appeal?

Marketing *Humans*

A video providing an overview of the 'Persona Synthetics' campaign (see below), which was used to build audience interest ahead of the launch of *Humans*, can be found on YouTube. If you are studying *Humans*, try to watch this as part of your revision.

'Persona Synthetics: Behind Channel 4's "Humans" Campaign', www.youtube.com/watch?v=qMxNoVxlWA4

James Walker
Head of Marketing, Channel 4

Channel 4 ad

5.9 Below is one of the posters used to promote the American launch of the show on AMC. Consider how it creates audience interest and appeal by answering the questions below.

1. What are the connotations of the typographical style used?

2. How does this tagline establish the genre of the programme and its main thematic concerns?

3. How does the layout and design of the poster convey meaning?

Marketing *The Jinx*

Many of the trailers and TV spots used to promote *The Jinx* can be found on the Matthew Cohen Marketing Creative website. If you are studying *The Jinx*, try to watch some of these as part of your revision.

5.10 On the right is one of the posters that was used to promote *The Jinx*. Consider how it creates audience interest and appeal, using the questions below to help you.

1. How does this tagline create audience interest and appeal?

2. Why does the poster include a reference to *Capturing the Friedmans*?

3. How does the layout and design of the poster create audience interest? Consider how design elements help to construct a particular representation of Robert Durst, for example.

Revising Regulation

When revising the regulatory framework of the UK television industry, you will need to make sure you understand:

1. Ofcom's role as the main UK regulator of communication services.

2. The purpose and function of the Broadcasting Code.

3. The impact of regulation on your set television product.

According to its website, Ofcom has to make sure:

- A range of companies provide quality radio and television programmes that appeal to diverse audiences.
- Viewers and listeners are protected from harmful or offensive material on TV, radio and on-demand.

Therefore, as part of your revision, you should consider how these aspects of Ofcom's role could be seen to impact on the UK broadcasters of your set television product.

For example, in the case of the BBC and Channel 4, the requirement to produce quality television programmes that appeal to diverse audiences is included in each of their remits, as they are both public service broadcasters (PSBs).

While Sky (the UK broadcaster of *The Jinx*) is not a PSB, 21st Century Fox's bid for the company was investigated by Ofcom in 2017. This is because part of Ofcom's role is to look at mergers and acquisitions that pose a threat to **media plurality**.

 Apply it!

5.11 The following table shows some of the issues covered by the Broadcasting Code, which determine whether or not a programme can be shown before the **watershed**. Consider which of these would be applicable to the programme you have studied, making notes on relevant aspects of the set episode.

Regulatory issue	Relevant aspects of the set episode
Violence (including its after-effects and descriptions of violence) and dangerous behaviour	
Offensive language	
Sex and nudity	
Drugs, smoking and alcohol	

 Take it Further

5.2 Further information about the aspects of the Broadcasting Code shown in the table below can be found on the Ofcom website in 'Section One: Protecting the Under-eighteens'.

 Quickfire Revision

5.13 What is meant by media plurality?

5.14 What is the watershed?

 Take it Further

5.3 If you are studying *Life on Mars* or *Humans*, look at the specific public service requirements set out in the remits of the BBC or Channel 4. If you are studying *The Jinx*, look at Ofcom's report on 21st Century Fox's proposed acquisition of Sky in 2017.

Audiences

Revision Checklist for Audiences

The following checklist outlines the key aspects of Audiences that you need to know for the Television section of Component 2.

What it says in the spec	What you need to know
How media producers target, attract, reach, address, and potentially construct audiences.	• The particular audiences that your set television product targets and attracts (e.g., particular demographics or psychographics, fans of certain genres or stars). • The strategies used by the producers of your set television product to target, reach and attract particular audiences. • The way in which the producers of your set television product construct their audiences (e.g., cultivating particular attitudes, values and beliefs in their viewers).
How media industries target audiences through the content and appeal of media products, and through the ways in which they are marketed, distributed and circulated.	• The way in which the genre, narrative, representations, aesthetics and mode of address of your set television product create appeal for the target audience. • The strategies used to market your set television product (e.g., poster/billboard campaigns, trailers, marketing stunts, press and publicity, websites, viral marketing and social media). • How your set television product was distributed (e.g., the different international territories in which it was shown, the channel(s) it was shown on, when it was scheduled and whether it was made available through catch-up/on-demand services).
How audiences interpret the media, including how they may interpret the same media in different ways.	• The different readings that audiences might make of the set television product, and the factors that might lead audiences to make different interpretations.

Link

For a discussion of television audiences and an introduction to Hall's reception theory see pages 155–156 of the Year 1/AS student book.

Revising Audience Targeting and Audience Appeal

As part of your revision of the television industry, you will already have looked at some of the ways in which media producers target and attract audiences. This means that the revision tasks on marketing on the previous pages can also be used for audience revision.

 Apply it!

5.12 In order to consolidate your understanding of this area of the theoretical framework, complete the following table, identifying at least two different audiences that the producers of your set television product have targeted, along with notes on the strategies that the producers have used to target and attract those audiences.

Target audience	Strategies used to target and attract the audience
(e.g., men, women, Gen X-ers, millennials, fans of a particular genre/star/director, etc.)	(e.g., representations, codes, conventions and narrative devices in posters, trailers and other marketing materials)

Thinking more specifically about the content and appeal of the set episode itself rather than the marketing materials used to promote it, complete the table below.

Aspect of the set episode	How and why it creates audience appeal
Narrative	
Representations	
Aesthetic	
Mode of address	

 Top Revision Tip

Aesthetics are to do with the look, feel or style of a programme. For example, some programmes might use a realist aesthetic, whereas others might be more stylised. A programme using a retro aesthetic would have the look or feel of an earlier era. There are also various ways in which a programme's mode of address might be described – it could be humorous, ironic, knowing, frightening, thrilling, dramatic, sensationalist or emotive, for example.

How to Revise Hall's Reception Theory

The key audience theory that you need to revise in preparation for Section A of Component 2 is Stuart Hall's reception theory.

KEY THEORY: Stuart Hall's Reception Theory

- The idea that communication is a process involving encoding by producers and decoding by audiences.
- The idea that there are three hypothetical positions from which messages and meanings may be decoded:
  - the dominant-hegemonic position: the encoder's intended meaning (the preferred reading) is fully understood and accepted
  - the negotiated position: the legitimacy of the encoder's message is acknowledged in general terms, although the message is adapted or negotiated to better fit the decoder's own individual experiences or context
  - the oppositional position: the encoder's message is understood, but the decoder disagrees with it, reading it in a contrary or oppositional way.

Take it Further

5.4 Read some of the reviews of your set television product in online newspapers, magazines or on entertainment websites, and look at the responses in fan forums. In each case, consider whether the viewer is assuming what Hall refers to as the dominant-hegemonic position, the negotiated position or the oppositional position.

In order to ensure that you can apply Hall's theory to your set television product, consider the following questions:

- What is the preferred reading of the television product?
  - How are we meant to respond to the representations of issues, events, individuals or social groups that we see?
- How is the audience encouraged to make a preferred reading of the television product?
  - What techniques do the programme-makers use to position the audience and align them with particular characters, values, attitudes or beliefs?
- How might the television product be read in an oppositional way?
  - What particular aspects of the programme might audiences object to? Why might some viewers make an oppositional reading of the television product?

Apply it!

5.13 Here are some hypothetical audience responses to the set television products. In each case, make a note of whether the response or position adopted would be dominant-hegemonic, negotiated or oppositional.

Life on Mars

Audience response	Audience position (dominant-hegemonic, oppositional or negotiated)
1. The 1970s music and cultural references were enjoyable but I found some of the sexism in the programme problematic.	
2. By constructing Gene Hunt as some sort of cult hero, the BBC is legitimising racism, misogyny and violence.	
3. As well as being hugely entertaining, the programme provided a fascinating insight into the culture and policing of the 1970s.	

Humans

Audience response	Audience position (dominant-hegemonic, oppositional or negotiated)
1. Not only was the narrative utterly gripping, its exploration of the cultural impact of AI was both fascinating and thought-provoking.	
2. The programme was full of clichés and its representations of women were sexist and two-dimensional.	
3. Overall, the programme was enjoyable, but some aspects of the narrative were a little far-fetched and difficult to believe.	

The Jinx

Audience response	Audience position (dominant-hegemonic, oppositional or negotiated)
1. To use real-life victims of crime as a source of voyeuristic entertainment in this way is distasteful and unethical.	
2. Overall, I found the programme interesting, although the narrative manipulation seemed a little heavy-handed at times.	
3. The programme provides a fascinating insight into one of the most disturbing and enigmatic figures in American criminal history.	

Revising Relevant Contexts

As part of your revision, you will need to make sure you can discuss the influence of relevant contexts on your set television product. The following table provides some examples of the kind of contextual factors that you may wish to consider.

Context	Life on Mars	Humans	The Jinx
Social and cultural context	• Debates regarding policing in the past and today. • The effect of social and cultural contexts on representations of gender and ethnicity. • The way in which audience responses to *Life on Mars* may reflect social and cultural circumstances.	• Debates regarding the role of AI in contemporary culture. • The effect of social and cultural contexts on representations of gender and ethnicity. • The way in which audience responses to *Humans* may reflect social and cultural circumstances.	• Debates regarding crime and violence in American society. • The effect of social and cultural contexts on representations of gender, ethnicity and social class. • The way in which audience responses to *The Jinx* may reflect social and cultural circumstances.
Historical context	• The idea that the conventions of the crime drama genre are historically relative. • The way in which audience interpretations of *Life on Mars* may reflect historical circumstances.	• The idea that the conventions of the science-fiction genre are historically relative. • The way in which audience interpretations of *Humans* may reflect historical circumstances.	• The idea that the conventions of the documentary genre are historically relative. • The way in which audience interpretations of *The Jinx* may reflect historical circumstances.
Economic context	• The BBC's status as a not-for-profit, public service broadcaster, funded by the licence fee. • The marketability of the crime drama genre.	• Channel 4's status as a not-for-profit, commercial public service broadcaster, funded by advertising and sponsorship. • The marketability of the science-fiction genre.	• HBO's status as a privately owned subsidiary of WarnerMedia, funded by subscription. • The marketability of the true crime documentary sub-genre.

Top Revision Tip

In preparation for Section B of the Component 2 exam, you should make sure you are familiar with the selected parts of your set magazine that have been specified for study. Digital copies of the set pages you are required to study can be found on the Eduqas website.

⩗ Section B: Magazines

Set Product Options

Reminder

Option 1	Option 2	Option 3
Woman	**Woman's Realm**	**Vogue**
29 August 1964	13 February 1965	July 1965
IPC	IPC	Condé Nast

- For Section B of Component 2, you will have studied one of the three set magazine products shown above.
- You will have looked at all four areas of the theoretical framework – Media Language, Representation, Media Industries and Audiences.
- You will have studied Barthes' theory of semiotics, Gauntlett's theory of identity, Curran and Seaton's theory of power and media industries, Gerbner's cultivation theory, and Hall's reception theory, exploring how each of these theories can be applied to your set magazine product.
- You will also have considered the influence of relevant contexts on your set magazine product.

Revising Your Set Magazine Product

In this section, you will find revision checklists for each of the four areas of the theoretical framework, along with tips and suggestions about how to revise key topics.

Top Revision Tip

While the approach taken here is to look at each area of the theoretical framework in turn, you may prefer to take a more synoptic approach when you are revising. For example, you could take a particular article, feature or advertisement from your set magazine, looking not only at its use of media language but also at the representations it offers and its relationship to relevant audiences. Once you have revised that particular article, feature or advertisement, you could then do the same thing again with another. Bear in mind that this text-led approach may not be as suitable for revising industry contexts, though, so you may need to look at this topic separately.

Media Language

Revision Checklist for Media Language

The following checklist outlines the key aspects of Media Language that you need to know for the Magazine section of Component 2.

What it says in the spec	What you need to know
How the different modes and language associated with different media forms communicate multiple meanings.	• The different ways in which images and text convey meaning in your set magazine product.
How the combination of elements of media language influence meaning.	• How elements of media language, such as photographs/illustrations and lexis, work together in your set magazine product to convey meaning (e.g., how captions or headlines provide anchorage for the images in the magazine).
The codes and conventions of media forms and products, including the processes through which media language develops as a genre.	• Magazine codes and conventions, and the way in which these codes and conventions are used in your set magazine product. • The genre conventions that your set magazine product uses.
The dynamic and historically relative nature of genre.	• The way in which magazine genres change over time. • How your set magazine product reflects changes in the genre to which it belongs.
How audiences respond to and interpret the above aspects of media language.	• The different ways in which audiences may respond to the codes and conventions used in your set magazine product.

Revising Magazine Codes and Conventions

In preparation for the Component 2 exam, you will need to make sure that you are familiar with the codes and conventions used in magazines.

Link

If you need a reminder of the purpose or function of any of these magazine conventions, look at the information on pages 160 and 164 of the Year 1/AS student book.

Take it Further

5.5 Consider the connotations of your magazine's title and the style of typography that is used for the masthead.

Apply it!

5.14 Some of the most commonly used magazine conventions are listed in the table below. In each case, make a note in the second column of the *purpose* of the convention or the *function* that it typically performs.

Magazine convention	Purpose or function
Masthead	
Cover lines	
Main cover image	
Stand-first	
Pull quote	
Caption	

Revising Genre

When revising your set magazine product, you will need to think about its use of genre conventions.

Apply it!

5.15 Here are some of the conventions commonly found in women's magazines. Using the contents page to help you, identify which of these conventions feature in the magazine you have studied and make a note of the titles of any relevant examples you find.

Genre convention	Examples from the set magazine
Beauty tips and features	
Fashion spreads	
Cookery items/recipes	
Sewing and knitting patterns	
Articles on love and relationships	
Problem pages	
Fictional stories	

Remember that you need to be aware of the dynamic and historically relative nature of genre and the way in which women's magazines have changed over time. Therefore, as part of your revision, you should consider the extent to which the set magazine you have studied differs from women's magazines today as well as from earlier women's magazines. Try answering the following questions:

- Have any of the genre conventions that featured in your set magazine gone out of fashion or become less commonplace?
- Have any new genre conventions emerged since your set magazine was originally published?
- Are the conventions of the women's magazine genre used differently today compared with the past? Have they had to adapt to social and cultural changes, for example?
- How, and to what extent, did the women's magazine genre change or evolve during the 1960s?

Top Revision Tip

Remember that general interest women's magazines such as *Woman* and *Woman's Realm* are likely to feature a broader range of genre conventions compared with more specialist women's magazines such as *Vogue*.

Take it Further

5.6 Think about the broader ideological significance of the genre conventions that the women's magazine you have studied uses. What messages do these conventions convey about female identity? What do you notice about the topics and interests that the women's magazine typically covers, for example?

Link

For an explanation of Barthes' theory of semiotics see pages 162–163 of the Year 1/AS student book.

Quickfire Revision

5.15 In semiotic theory, what is a myth?

Top Revision Tip

Analysing these advertisements from the set magazines will also help you develop the skills you need for the Media Language question in Section A of the Component 1 exam.

How to Revise Barthes' Theory of Semiotics

An important media language theory that you will need to revise in preparation for Section B of Component 2 is Roland Barthes' theory of semiotics.

KEY THEORY: Roland Barthes' Theory of Semiotics

- The idea that texts communicate their meanings through a process of signification.
- The idea that signs can function at the level of denotation, which involves the 'literal' or common-sense meaning of the sign, and at the level of connotation, which involves the meanings associated with or suggested by the sign.
- The idea that constructed meanings can come to seem self-evident, achieving the status of myth through a process of naturalisation.

Apply it!

5.16 Shown here are three advertisements from the set magazines. The denotative meaning of each advertisement is provided in the following table. Practise applying Barthes' semiotic theory by completing the statements relating to:

(a) the **connotations** of the signs that have been used (i.e. their *associated* meanings)

(b) the **myths** that the advertisements construct or reinforce (e.g., regarding gender roles and female identity).

Magazine advert	Denotative meaning	Connotative meaning	Myth
Option 1 An advert for Max Factor from the set edition of *Woman*.	The advert **denotes** a woman applying makeup as a man moves towards her and tries to gain her attention.	The woman's dress code and physical appearance have **connotations** of _____. The man's facial expression and body language **connote** _____.	The advert reinforces the **myth** that _____.
Option 2 An advert for Australian Sultanas from the set edition of *Woman's Realm*.	The advert **denotes** a woman on a surfboard riding a wave while balancing a silver platter of baked goods on one hand.	The image of the woman on the surfboard riding the wave **connotes** _____. The silver platter of baked goods has **connotations** of _____.	The advert reinforces the **myth** that _____.

(continued)

Magazine advert	Denotative meaning	Connotative meaning	Myth
Option 3 An advert for Imperial Leather from the set edition of *Vogue*.	The advert **denotes** a young child sitting on a woman's lap. The woman is leaning in towards the child. Both are smiling.	The image of the mother and child has **connotations** of _____. The woman's posture and gestural codes **connote** _____.	The advert reinforces the **myth** that _____

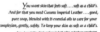

Representation

Revision Checklist for Representation

The following checklist outlines the key aspects of Representation that you need to know for the Magazine section of Component 2.

What it says in the spec	What you need to know
The way events, issues, individuals and social groups (including social identity) are represented through processes of selection and combination.	• How representations of social groups (e.g., men or women), social identity and, where relevant, individuals, issues or events in your set magazine product are constructed through the choices made by the magazine producers, and through the combination of different elements of media language.
The processes which lead media producers to make choices about how to represent events, issues, individuals and social groups.	• The factors that can be seen to shape and influence the representations in your set magazine product.
The effect of social and cultural context on representations.	• How the representations in your set magazine product are shaped by the social and cultural contexts in which they were produced (e.g., how they reflect particular social norms or cultural values).
How and why stereotypes can be used positively and negatively.	• The purpose and effect of any stereotypical representations that feature in your set magazine product.
How and why particular social groups, in a national and global context, may be under-represented or misrepresented.	• The extent to which particular social groups (such as black, Asian and minority ethnic groups) are under-represented or misrepresented in your set magazine (and in the media more broadly), and the reasons for this.

Top Revision Tip

When you are discussing your set magazine product, try to use appropriate semiotic terminology. Here are some semiotic terms that you may find useful:

- signifies
- denotes
- connotes
- paradigm
- syntagm
- polysemic.

If you need a reminder of what any of these terms mean, refer to the Year 1/AS student book.

Take it Further

5.7 Practise applying semiotic theory to other aspects of the set magazine product you have studied.

(continued)

What it says in the spec	What you need to know
How media representations convey values, attitudes and beliefs about the world and how these may be systematically reinforced across a wide range of media representations.	• How the representations in your set magazine product can be seen to express particular ideas or values, and how these representations relate to broader patterns within the media.
How audiences respond to and interpret media representations.	• The different ways in which audiences may read and respond to the representations in your set magazine product.

Revising Representations of Gender

A useful starting point when revising the representations of gender in your set magazine is to think about the messages and meanings that those representations can be seen to convey. Try using a 'What? Where? How?' approach, asking yourself the following questions:

- **What** messages does your set magazine convey about gender?
- **Where** are those messages articulated? In which specific parts of the magazine?
- **How** are those messages conveyed?

Presenting the answers to these questions in the form of a table, similar to the one below, will give you a handy revision aid.

What?	Where?	How?

The Cutex advert from the set edition of *Vogue* (left) and the Breeze advert from the set edition of *Woman* (far left).

How to Revise Gauntlett's Theory of Identity

A useful theory for exploring representations of gender, and one which you need to learn and be able to apply to your set magazine, is David Gauntlett's theory of identity.

KEY THEORY: David Gauntlett's Theory of Identity

- The idea that the media provide us with 'tools' or resources that we use to construct our identities.
- The idea that while, in the past, the media tended to convey singular, straightforward messages about ideal types of male and female identities, the media today offer us a more diverse range of stars, icons and characters from whom we may pick and mix different ideas.

When you are revising your set magazine product, consider whether it supports or challenges Gauntlett's suggestion that media representations from earlier historical periods tended to offer singular and straightforward messages about gender identity.

Link

For an explanation of Gauntlett's theory of identity see page 167 of the Year 1/ AS student book.

Top Revision Tip

Remember that magazines often carry contradictory messages, so you may find that some of the representations in your set magazine combine progressive ideas about gender with more traditional values.

Apply it!

5.17 Here are some examples of features or adverts from the set magazines that you could try applying Gauntlett's theory to. In each case, consider whether the representation is singular, straightforward or traditional, or whether it appears to be more diverse, liberal or progressive. Provide a brief explanation to support your point.

Woman magazine

Feature or advert	Singular, straightforward or traditional	Diverse, liberal or progressive
'Extra Special on Men' feature		
'Are You an A-Level Beauty?' feature		
'A Present for Your Kitchen' feature		
Women's Royal Army Corps advert		

The Sunday Cook

For the nicest, most leisurely, day of the week, Susan King chooses dishes with a difference for breakfast, lunch and tea

SUNSATIONAL SULTANAS

You want skin that feels soft . . . . soft as a child's. And for that you need Cussons Imperial Leather . . . . good, pure soap, blended with 9 essential oils to care for your complexion, gently, safely. To keep your skin as soft as a child's.

Enjoy Imperial Leather's perfume in bath cubes and talcum powder too.

IMPERIAL LEATHER

Woman's Realm magazine

Feature or advert	Singular, straightforward or traditional	Diverse, liberal or progressive
Atrixo advert		
'Bottled Beauty' feature		
'The Sunday Cook' feature		
Australian Sultanas advert		

Vogue magazine

Feature or advert	Singular, straightforward or traditional	Diverse, liberal or progressive
'Money: Questions and Answers' feature		
Imperial Leather advert		
Revlon advert		
'Heatwave Holiday' feature		

Revising Representations of Ethnicity

When revising your set magazine's representations of social groups and social identity, you should think about its representations of ethnicity as well as gender. In order to reacquaint yourself with some of the most significant issues relating to representations of ethnicity, try answering the following questions:

- How ethnically diverse is your set magazine? Are the representations in the magazine predominately white? Are black, Asian and minority ethnic groups under-represented in the magazine?
- Is there any evidence of tokenism in the magazine?
- Does the magazine misrepresent any particular ethnic group? Does it reinforce any ethnic stereotypes?

The extracts from the set magazines shown below may provide a useful focal point for your revision. Look carefully at the extract that has been taken from the magazine you have studied and answer the accompanying questions.

Apply it!

5.10

The advertising copy reads 'Eastern idol dominates, but fails to overwhelm the cool sophistication of the girl in Drogheda, tailored skirt …'

Eastern idol dominates, but fails to overwhelm the cool sophistication of the girl in Drogheda, tailored skirt with double pleats giving 'built in' movement. In 'Terylene'/Worsted. Price from 85/-.

- What binary oppositions does this advertisement set up?
- What do you notice about the language used to describe the white Western woman in the **advertising copy**? What qualities are ascribed to her?

Gor-Ray skirt advert taken from the set edition of *Woman's Realm*.

Quickfire Revision

5.17 What does the term 'advertising copy' refer to?

Take it Further

5.9 As well as looking at the extract from your own set magazine, you could also try analysing the representations of ethnicity in the other two extracts. This will help develop your analytical skills as well as deepening your understanding of relevant representational issues.

Apply it!

5.19

A BORN ENGLISHMAN

ALFRED HITCHCOCK

IN AN INTERVIEW WITH MARGARET HINXMAN

UNRAVELS THE MYSTERY OF BRITISH WOMEN

"THEY'RE LIKE SNOW-CAPPED VOLCANOES"

Selected extract from the article: 'Grace [Kelly] represented ideally the cool, tantalizing, British – or Nordic – type of beauty I look for in my actresses. […] Personally, I find this far more intriguing than the Latin brand of sex appeal that puts everything in the shop window.'

Extract and photos from an interview with the British film director Alfred Hitchcock, taken from the set edition of *Woman*.

Quickfire Revision

5.18 What is the white beauty myth?

- In what ways could this article be seen to reinforce the **white beauty myth**?
- To what extent does the article reinforce ethnic stereotypes?

A double page fashion spread from the 'Picnics Probable and Improbable' feature in the set edition of *Vogue*.

The copy reads: 'Dreamy golden silk kaftan, brightest lapis blue and sunset red embroidery. Jewels by the thousand – golden, pearly, glass bead necklaces, earrings, bracelets, anklets. […] Dream sequence – real desert: Karnac near Luxor.'

Quickfire Revision

5.19 What does the term 'exotic other' mean?

- In what ways does the framing and composition of this shot set up particular hierarchies and power relations? For example, consider who occupies the most and the least amount of space in the shot, who is positioned towards the centre and who is marginalised, etc.
- In what ways could this image be seen to reinforce the stereotype of the **exotic other**?

Industry

Revision Checklist for Industry

The following checklist outlines the key aspects of Industry that you need to know for the Magazine section of Component 2.

What it says in the spec	What you need to know
Processes of production, distribution and circulation by organisations, groups and individuals in a global context	• How (and by whom) your set magazine product was published and distributed.
The specialised and institutionalised nature of media production, distribution and circulation.	• The industrial and institutional context in which your set magazine product was made and distributed.
The significance of patterns of ownership and control, including conglomerate ownership, vertical integration and diversification.	• Whether your set magazine product is published by a media conglomerate. • Whether the publisher of your set magazine product is vertically integrated (i.e. has the means to print and/or distribute its own products). • Whether the company that owns your set magazine product has diversified into other media industries.
The significance of economic factors, including commercial and not-for-profit public funding, to media industries and their products.	• How magazine publishers generate revenue/profit and the impact that this can be seen to have on your set magazine product.
The regulatory framework of contemporary media in the UK.	• How the UK magazine industry is regulated (e.g., through IPSO and, prior to that, the PCC and the Press Council).

Revising Production, Distribution and Circulation

When you are revising, you will need to make sure that you are familiar with the basic processes of production, distribution and circulation that operate within the magazine industry. Here is a reminder of some of the key roles and stages in the magazine supply chain.

Publisher	The publisher employs the design and editorial teams who are responsible for the look and content of the magazine, as well as the sales team who are responsible for selling advertising space.

Printer	The next step in the supply chain is to print the magazines. This requires access to industrial printing presses as well as raw materials such as paper.

Distributor	Distributors are responsible for persuading wholesalers or retailers to take their magazines and for delivering stock to them. The physical transportation of the magazines requires access to a large fleet of vehicles.

Wholesaler	Wholesalers buy magazines in bulk from the distributors and sell them on to retailers. Large depots are generally required for storage.

Retailers	Retailers take magazine stock either directly from the distributors or from the wholesalers before selling the product to consumers.

Vertical Integration

One of the concepts you should be familiar with from your study of media industries is vertical integration. Remember that a vertically integrated company is one that has control over different stages in the supply chain. Therefore, in the magazine industry, an example of a vertically integrated company would be a publisher that also owns a printing company or paper mill, or one that is responsible for distributing as well as publishing magazines. Significantly, the publishers of the set magazines were both vertically integrated companies:

- IPC owned several printing companies, including Odhams (Watford) Ltd, which was the largest printing plant in the UK. This is where both *Woman* and *Woman's Realm* were printed.
- Condé Nast's acquisition of Arbor Press (later renamed the Condé Nast Press) in 1921 gave it one of the most efficient, high-quality printing plants in the world. The US edition of *Vogue*, along with many other American publications, was printed there. The printing of the British edition of *Vogue* was contracted out to a separate company though.

Revising Patterns of Ownership and Control

As part of your revision, you will also need to look at patterns of ownership and control in the magazine industry at the time your set product was published.

The chart on the right shows the market share of the largest and most powerful companies operating in the women's magazine sector during the mid-1960s.

IPC was by far the most powerful of these companies as it held a much larger share of the market than all the other companies combined. As the pie chart illustrates, by 1965 IPC accounted for 81% of all women's magazines sold.

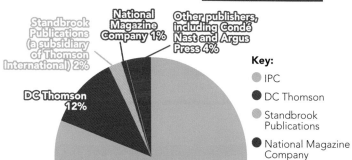

Market share of UK women's magazine publishers in 1965

Standbrook Publications (a subsidiary of Thomson International) 2%

National Magazine Company 1%

Other publishers, including Condé Nast and Argus Press 4%

DC Thomson 12%

IPC 81%

Key:
- IPC
- DC Thomson
- Standbrook Publications
- National Magazine Company
- Other (including Condé Nast and Argus)

How to Revise Curran and Seaton's Theory of Power and Media Industries

An important industry theory that you will have looked at when exploring patterns of ownership and control in the magazine industry is Curran and Seaton's theory of power and media industries.

KEY THEORY: James Curran and Jean Seaton's Theory of Power and Media Industries

- The idea that the media is controlled by a small number of companies primarily driven by the logic of profit and power.
- The idea that **media concentration** generally limits or inhibits variety, creativity and quality.
- The idea that more socially diverse patterns of ownership help to create the conditions for more varied and adventurous media productions

Curran and Seaton's theory is particularly useful for exploring patterns of ownership and control in the magazine industry in the 1950s and 1960s, as this was a time when companies such as IPC and Advance Publications (the owners of Condé Nast) sought to increase their power and control of the market through **horizontal integration**. The following timelines provide some examples of this, highlighting the main acquisitions that the companies made during this period.

Link

For an explanation of Curran and Seaton's theory of power and media industries see pages 172–173 of the Year 1/AS student book.

Quickfire Revision

5.20 What does the term media concentration refer to?

5.21 What does horizontal integration mean?

Top Revision Tip

When you are revising the key theories, it is important to remember that these are *ideas* that you need to engage with rather than just facts to be learnt. Wherever possible, as well as considering how the key theories can be applied to your set products, try to consider whether there are any alternative perspectives that offer a different viewpoint to those of the named theorists.

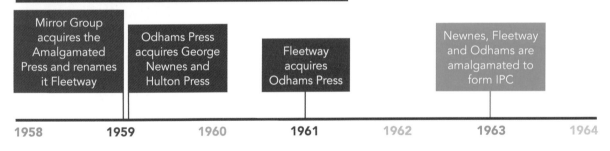

Timeline showing the series of acquisitions and mergers that culminated in the formation of IPC in 1963.

Mirror Group acquires the Amalgamated Press and renames it Fleetway

Odhams Press acquires George Newnes and Hulton Press

Fleetway acquires Odhams Press

Newnes, Fleetway and Odhams are amalgamated to form IPC

1958   1959   1960   1961   1962   1963   1964

Timeline showing some of the main acquisitions made by Advance Publications (parent company of Condé Nast) during the late 1950s/early 1960s.

Advance Publications acquires Condé Nast

Advance Publications acquires Street & Smith

Advance Publications acquires New Orleans Times-Picayune Group

1958   1959   1960   1961   1962   1963   1964

Apply it!

5.20 Read the following statements about the magazine industry. In each case, try to identify whether the statement supports or challenges Curran and Seaton's claim that media concentration generally limits or inhibits variety, creativity and quality. Then provide an explanation of *how* the statement can be seen to challenge or support this claim.

Statement	Conclusion Does the statement support or challenge Curran and Seaton's claim?	Explanation How does the statement support or challenge Curran and Seaton's claim?
When one large magazine company buys another, this has a negative impact on consumer choice as market competition is reduced and separate publications are often merged or closed down. For example, following its acquisition of Odhams Press in 1961, Fleetway merged its own leading weekly title, *Woman Illustrated*, with Odhams' leading title, *Woman*.		
'The large magazine [company] is better able than a [company] with only one periodical to cater for changing needs and tastes among readers by stopping one publication and launching another.' (Extract from *Royal Commission on the Press*, 1962, page 76)		

Revising Conglomerate Ownership and Diversification

Two other concepts you should be familiar with from your study of the magazine industry are conglomerate ownership and diversification. These concepts are relevant to the set magazine products as their publishers were owned by larger media conglomerates that operated across a range of different businesses and industries.

Top Revision Tip

Creating flashcards or glossaries is a useful way of learning key terms. Try writing a definition of the following industry terms:

- Conglomerate
- Subsidiary
- Diversification
- Vertical integration
- Oligopoly
- Monopoly

	Woman and Woman's Realm	*Vogue*
Publisher	Odhams	Condé Nast
Conglomerate owner of the publishing company	IPC	Advance Publications
Other notable magazines owned by the conglomerate	*Woman's Own* *Woman & Home* *Ideal Home* *Horse and Hound*	*Glamour* *Mademoiselle* *Brides* *House & Garden*

Through your study of the magazine industry, you will have seen that large conglomerates often extend their power and control by diversifying into other media industries or areas of business.

The graphics below show the different markets and industries that IPC and Advance Publications (the owners of Condé Nast) were operating in during the 1960s.

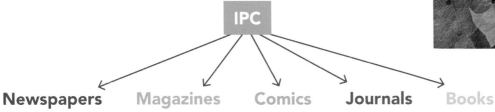

IPC

Newspapers   Magazines   Comics   Journals   Books

Advance Publications

Newspapers   Magazines   Television   Radio

Audiences

Revision Checklist for Audiences

The following checklist outlines the key aspects of Audiences that you need to know for the Magazine section of Component 2.

What it says in the spec	What you need to know
How audiences are grouped and categorised by media industries, including by age, gender and social class, as well as by lifestyle and taste.	• The way in which the magazine industry categorises readers according to demographic variables such as age, sex and socio-economic status, as well as their lifestyles, tastes and interests.
How media producers target, attract, reach, address and potentially construct audiences.	• What kind of readership the publishers of your set magazine product are trying to target, reach and attract. • The strategies used by the publishers of your set magazine product to target, reach and attract particular audiences. • The way in which the publishers of your set magazine product can be seen to construct their audience (e.g., cultivating particular attitudes, values and beliefs in their readers).
How media industries target audiences through the content and appeal of media products, and through the ways in which they are marketed, distributed and circulated.	• The way in which the genre, representations, subject matter and mode of address of your set magazine product create appeal for the target audience.
How audiences interpret the media, including how they may interpret the same media in different ways.	• The different readings that audiences might make of your set magazine product and the factors that might lead them to make different interpretations.

Revising Audience Targeting

By now you will know that one of the main ways of classifying audiences in the magazine industry is according to social grade. This is the system used by the Publishers Audience Measurement Company (PAMCo) and, prior to that, by the National Readership Survey (NRS).

Apply it!

5.21 In the following table, the social grades that were used by the NRS (now replaced by PAMCo) and the occupations they relate to have been jumbled up. Try to match the occupation to the relevant social grade.

Social grade	Occupation
A	Intermediate managerial, administrative and professional
B	Semi-skilled and unskilled manual workers
C1	State pensioners, casual and lowest grade workers, unemployed with state benefits only
C2	Supervisory, clerical and junior managerial, administrative and professional
D	Higher managerial, administrative and professional
E	Skilled manual workers

While *Woman* and *Woman's Realm* both had a broad cross-demographic appeal during the 1960s, as their readership was spread relatively evenly across all social grades, *Vogue* was targeted primarily at an ABC1 demographic. If you are studying *Woman* or *Woman's Realm*, you need to think about how your magazine was able to appeal to such a broad audience. If you are studying *Vogue*, you need to consider how it sought to attract a more affluent ABC1 audience.

Revising Audience Pleasures

Although Blumler and Katz's uses and gratifications theory is not one of the theories you are specifically required to study, it provides a useful model for exploring the appeal of magazines and how they are used by readers.

Apply it!

5.22 Complete the following table, identifying specific examples of how your set magazine addresses the needs outlined in Blumler and Katz's theory.

Audience need	Example of how the magazine addresses that need
The need for information	
The need for diversion, escapism or entertainment	
The need for personal identity	
The need for social interaction and integration	

Top Revision Tip

Make sure that you can explain some of the strategies the publishers of your set magazine used to attract and appeal to the target audience.

Take it Further

5.10 As well as defining the target audience of your set magazine in terms of demographics such as sex, age and social grade or social class, think about their values, attitudes and lifestyle. For example, the content of the magazine should give you a sense of the tastes and interests of the ideal reader.

Link

Check your answers by looking at the table on page 176 of the Year 1/AS student book.

Link

For an explanation of Gerbner's cultivation theory see page 177 of the Year 1/AS student book, and for an explanation of Hall's reception theory see pages 177–178 of the Year 1/AS student book.

How to Revise Gerbner's Cultivation Theory and Hall's Reception Theory

The two main audience theories that you will need to revise for Section B of Component 2 are George Gerbner's cultivation theory and Stuart Hall's reception theory.

KEY THEORY: George Gerbner's Cultivation Theory

- The idea that exposure to repeated patterns of representation over long periods of time can shape and influence the way in which people perceive the world around them (i.e. cultivating particular views and opinions).
- The idea that cultivation reinforces mainstream values (dominant ideologies).

KEY THEORY: Stuart Hall's Reception Theory

- The idea that communication is a process involving encoding by producers and decoding by audiences.
- The idea that there are three hypothetical positions from which messages and meanings may be decoded:
  - the dominant-hegemonic position: the encoder's intended meaning (the preferred reading) is fully understood and accepted
  - the negotiated position: the legitimacy of the encoder's message is acknowledged in general terms, although the message is adapted or negotiated to better fit the decoder's own individual experiences or context
  - the oppositional position: the encoder's message is understood, but the decoder disagrees with it, reading it in a contrary or oppositional way.

A BORN ENGLISHMAN

ALFRED HITCHCOCK
IN AN INTERVIEW WITH MARGARET HINXMAN

UNRAVELS THE MYSTERY OF BRITISH WOMEN

"THEY'RE LIKE SNOW-CAPPED VOLCANOES"

Look again at some of the articles, features or adverts from your set magazine and think about how Gerbner's cultivation theory and Hall's reception theory could be applied to each one, answering the following questions:

- What is the preferred reading of the article, feature or advert?
- What oppositional readings might a reader make?
- What views, opinions, attitudes or beliefs might the article, feature or advert help to cultivate?
- How might it help to cultivate those views, opinions, attitudes or beliefs?

You may find it useful to present your answers in the form of a table, as shown below. Alternatively, you could create a mind map or poster instead.

Title of article, feature or advert	Hall's reception theory		Gerbner's cultivation theory	
	Preferred reading of article, feature or advert	Oppositional reading of article, feature or advert	Views, opinions, attitudes or beliefs that might be cultivated	How views, opinions, attitudes or beliefs might be cultivated

The preferred reading is …

A possible oppositional reading would be …

Take it Further

The Sunday Cook

For the nicest, most leisurely, day of the week, Susan King chooses dishes with a difference for breakfast, lunch and tea

This helps to cultivate the view that …

This view or opinion is cultivated through the use of …

A mind map such as the one above, which is based around the 'Sunday Cook' feature in the set edition of *Woman's Realm*, may help you to revise Gerbner's and Hall's audience theories.

5.11 It is important to remember that Gerbner's cultivation theory is concerned with the way in which exposure to repeated patterns of representation cultivates particular ways of thinking; it doesn't suggest that single media products shape audience views and opinions immediately or in isolation from wider cultural trends. Therefore, in order to explore how your set magazine fits within broader patterns of representation, you may find it useful to look at covers or articles from similar types of magazine or from other editions of your set magazine. Thinking about what these magazines have in common with yours should help you identify the broader patterns of representation that helped to cultivate social and cultural attitudes during the 1950s and 1960s.

Top Revision Tip

When revising the influence of social, cultural and historical contexts on your set magazine, you should bear in mind that media products do not always respond to changes in the wider society or culture immediately. Social and cultural changes often take time to filter down into the media, resulting in a culture lag. Furthermore, some magazines may resist social and cultural change, clinging on to more traditional or established ideas and values, especially if they are integral to the magazine's brand identity or if the abandonment of those ideas and values risks alienating core elements of the magazine's readership.

Top Revision Tip

The problem pages in general interest women's magazines such as *Woman* and *Woman's Realm* often provide a useful insight into social and cultural attitudes and anxieties of the time. Don't overlook these pages.

Revising Social, Cultural and Historical Contexts

Apply it!

5.23 The following table shows some of the social and cultural changes that occurred during the 1960s. In order to support your revision of relevant contexts, consider which of these could be seen to have a particular influence on your set magazine.

Specific aspect of the social, cultural and historical context	Relevant part of the magazine and how it was influenced by the social, cultural and historical context
The growing independence of women in the 1960s (e.g., the Married Women's Property Act of 1964 gave women greater economic independence).	
Changing attitudes to marriage and the growing acceptance of divorce in the post-war period (eventually leading to the introduction of the Divorce Reform Act in 1969).	
The rise of the permissive society (e.g., with the advent of the sexual revolution and the introduction of the contraceptive pill in the 1960s).	
The rise of youth culture and the emergence of new countercultural movements such as the hippies in the 1960s.	
The growing interest in foreign travel during the 1960s.	
The advent of second-wave feminism in the 1960s (e.g., Betty Friedan's *The Feminine Mystique* was published in 1963).	
The continuing idealisation of the archetypal 'happy housewife' in the 1960s and the construction of the domestic sphere as a female space.	

Revising Economic Contexts

As well as revising social, cultural and historical contexts, you will also need to revise the economic context in which your set magazine was produced. The following table shows some of the economic issues that you may find useful to consider as part of your revision.

Economic issue	Influence on the magazine industry
The shift from post-war austerity to a new age of prosperity in the 1950s and 1960s.	A shift in ethos from 'make-do and mend' to 'shop and spend', as magazines embraced the new age of consumerism.
The end of paper rationing in the 1950s (paper rationing had been introduced during World War II).	More pages were available to carry advertising within magazines, enabling them to generate more revenue.
The high costs involved in producing and distributing magazines during the 1960s.	Large, vertically integrated companies such as IPC and Condé Nast tended to dominate the magazine industry because of their greater economic power.
The importance of market share within the magazine industry.	Large magazine companies often attempt to reduce competition through horizontal integration by acquiring or merging with rival publishers.
The importance of advertising revenue to the magazine industry and the need to sell or deliver audiences to advertisers.	Publishers may look to charge higher advertising rates either by delivering high circulation figures (e.g., *Woman*'s circulation in the mid-1960s was almost 3 million, while the circulation of *Woman's Realm* was 1.3 million), or by providing advertisers with access to a specific market (e.g., while *Vogue*'s circulation in 1965 was only 165,000, this consisted predominately of ABC1 readers with a specific interest in fashion and beauty).

⤈ Section C: Online Media

Set Product Options

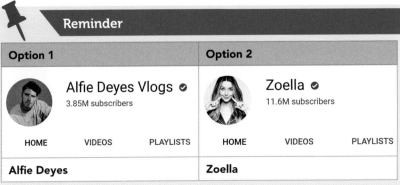

Reminder

Option 1	Option 2
Alfie Deyes Vlogs ✓ 3.85M subscribers HOME · VIDEOS · PLAYLISTS	**Zoella** ✓ 11.6M subscribers HOME · VIDEOS · PLAYLISTS
Alfie Deyes	**Zoella**

- For Section C of Component 2, you will have studied one of the two set online options shown above.
- You will have looked at the homepage of the product, linked blogs and/or YouTube channels, including relevant audio-visual material such as videos or vlogs, as well as links to social and participatory media such as Facebook, Twitter and Instagram.
- You will have looked at all four areas of the theoretical framework – Media Language, Representation, Media Industries and Audiences.
- You will have studied Barthes' theory of semiotics, Hall's theory of representation, Gauntlett's theory of identity, and Gerbner's cultivation theory, exploring how each of these theories can be applied to your set online product.
- You will also have considered the influence of relevant contexts on your set online product.

Top Revision Tip

In order to develop your understanding of the codes and conventions of online media, you could try creating your own revision blog. Some of the most popular blogging platforms, which are free to use, include:

- tumblr.com
- blogger.com
- wordpress.com.

Alternatively, you could set up a revision group on social media or share study tips on YouTube.

Revising Your Set Online Product

In this section, you will find revision checklists for each of the four areas of the theoretical framework, along with tips and suggestions about how to revise key topics.

Media Language

Revision Checklist for Media Language

The following checklist outlines the key aspects of Media Language that you need to know for the online media section of Component 2.

What it says in the spec	What you need to know
How the different modes and language associated with different media forms communicate multiple meanings.	• The multimodal nature of online media and the different ways in which images, sound, speech and/or writing convey meaning in the set online product.
How the combination of elements of media language influence meaning.	• How elements of media language, such as camerawork/photography, graphics, mise-en-scène, lexis and mode of address, work together in the set online product to convey meaning.
How developing technologies affect media language.	• The way in which digital technologies and the development of the internet in the Web 2.0 era have facilitated new forms of online communication, including blogs and vlogs.
The codes and conventions of media forms and products, including the processes through which media language develops as a genre.	• The codes and conventions of blogs and vlogs, and how they are used in the set online product. • The way in which blogs and vlogs can be classified into specific genres.
How audiences respond to and interpret the above aspects of media language.	• The different ways in which audiences may respond to the codes and conventions used in the set online product.

Reminder

The term blog is short for weblog. A blog is a regularly updated website or webpage that is typically comprised of a series of diary-like posts presented in reverse chronological order.

Revising the Codes and Conventions of Blogs and Vlogs

From studying your set online product, you will have seen that interactivity is a particularly important feature of these 'new' media forms.

Apply it!

5.24 The following table lists some of the interactive elements that are commonly used in blogs. Briefly explain how each element facilitates interaction and participation, thinking specifically about what it enables users of the blog to do.

Convention	Explanation
Menu or navigation bar	
Hyperlinks	
Social media icons	
Comments section	

Social media icons linking to Facebook pages, Twitter feeds, YouTube channels, Pinterest boards and Instagram accounts are a common feature of blogs.

Reminder

The term vlog is short for video blog. A vlog is essentially a blog in video form. As part of your revision of online media, you should make sure that you are familiar with the codes and conventions of blogs and vlogs.

Conventions of Vlogs and YouTube Videos

Vlogs and YouTube videos share some of the same conventions as blogs. For example, YouTubers' homepages often feature links to social media as well as a space in which users can post comments.

Alfie Deyes' main YouTube channel (see right) includes links to his Daily Vlogs channel as well as his Facebook, Tumblr and Instagram pages.

Apply it!

5.25 Some of the other conventions associated with vlogs and YouTube videos are shown in the following table. Find examples of each of these conventions from your set online product.

Conventions of vlogs and YouTube videos	Example from the set product (refer to specific vlogs or videos)
Metadata, including video titles, descriptions and tags	
A customary greeting at the start of the video	
A direct mode of address	
A call to action at the end of the video (e.g., a request to like, comment, follow, subscribe, etc.)	

Quickfire Revision

5.22 What term is used to describe the way in which vlogs, blogs and other forms of mass media create the illusion of face-to-face conversation through techniques such as a direct mode of address?

Revising Genre

When you are revising, you should make sure that you understand the way in which vlogs can be classified into genres.

Apply it!

5.26 The left-hand column below shows four of the most popular vlogging genres. In each case, match the genre to the relevant definition.

Genre	Definition
A. Personal vlogs	**1.** A broad genre that encompasses comedy sketches, pranks, challenges and competitions.
B. Fashion and beauty vlogs	**2.** A genre in which vloggers share their thoughts, experiences and feelings in the form of a video diary.
C. Entertainment vlogs	**3.** A genre that is commonly comprised of **walk-through** and **'let's play' videos**.
D. Gaming vlogs	**4.** A genre that encompasses demonstration or tutorial videos showing viewers how to achieve a particular style or look, as well as **haul videos** and reviews of products.

Link

If you need a reminder of how these different vlogging genres are defined, look at the information on pages 182–183 of the Year 1/AS student book.

Quickfire Revision

5.23 What are walk-through videos and 'let's play' videos?

5.24 What is a haul video?

YouTubers who work across more than one genre will often use separate channels for the different types of vlog they produce. A YouTuber may have one channel for their personal vlogs, for example, and another for their entertainment vlogs or their fashion and beauty vlogs.

Apply it!

5.27 Look again at the different YouTube channels linked to your set online product and make a note of the genre that each one belongs to.

Option 1: Alfie Deyes

YouTube channel	Alfie Deyes	Alfie Deyes Vlogs	PointlessBlogGames
Genre			

Option 2: Zoe Sugg

YouTube channel	Zoella	Zoe Sugg
Genre		

Link

For an explanation of Barthes' theory of semiotics in relation to blogs and vlogs see pages 183–184 of the Year 1/AS student book.

How to Revise Barthes' Theory of Semiotics

The key Media Language theory that you will need to look at when revising your set online product is Barthes' theory of semiotics.

KEY THEORY: Roland Barthes' Theory of Semiotics

- The idea that texts communicate their meanings through a process of signification.
- The idea that signs can function at the level of denotation, which involves the 'literal' or common-sense meaning of the sign, and at the level of connotation, which involves the meanings associated with or suggested by the sign.
- The idea that constructed meanings can come to seem self-evident, achieving the status of myth through a process of naturalisation.

Apply it!

5.28 As part of your revision, practise applying Barthes' theory to the following images, completing the statements about the connotations they convey.

A thumbnail image for the video 'EXPLORING THE MOST HAUNTED PRISONS/PART THREE' posted on the YouTube channel Alfie Deyes Vlogs.

Denotation	Connotation
The image **denotes** a Ouija board bearing the sign of a pentagram.	The Ouija board has **connotations** of _____ .
The image **denotes** a group of people huddled together; one has his head in his hands.	The body language and facial expressions of the people in the image **connote** _____ .
The main colours **denoted** in the image are green, black and red.	The colours used in the image have **connotations** of _____ .

A webpage from the 'Beauty' section of Zoella's website.

BEAUTY FOOD LIFE PLACES STYLE SHOP   SEARCH 🔍

Denotation	Connotation
The webpage **denotes** Zoella's name in a handwritten font.	The handwritten font has **connotations** of _____ .
The webpage **denotes** a series of lights.	The lights **connote** _____ .
The webpage **denotes** a number of makeup items.	The makeup has **connotations** of _____ .

 Take it Further

5.12 Now try applying Barthes' theory to another aspect of your set online product (another video or webpage you have studied, for example).

 Take it Further

5.13 As well as analysing how your set online product communicates at the level of denotation and connotation, consider the significance of the paradigmatic choices that have been made. For example, think about why one colour, image, font style or word has been chosen rather than another.

 Top Revision Tip

You may find it useful to consider the way in which your online product has changed or evolved over time. For example, Zoella's website was relaunched in November 2019, while Alfie Deyes dropped the *PointlessBlog* branding from much of his online content at the beginning of 2019, using his own name instead. Semiotic theory provides a useful framework for exploring the significance of these changes. For example, you could use Barthes' theory to compare the design and layout of Zoella's new website and logo with the previous version (shown on the left), or you could use it to analyse the connotative significance of branding in relation to Alfie Deyes and *PointlessBlog*.

Representation

Revision Checklist for Representation

The following checklist outlines the key aspects of Representation that you need to know for the online media section of Component 2.

What it says in the spec	What you need to know
The way events, issues, individuals (including self-representation) and social groups (including social identity) are represented through processes of selection and combination.	• How content creators construct representations by combining different elements of media language and through the choices they make regarding what to include in their blogs and vlogs and what to leave out.
The processes which lead media producers to make choices about how to represent events, issues, individuals and social groups.	• The factors that shape and influence the representations that content creators construct (e.g., the need to appeal to particular audiences, the need to generate revenue, the need to abide by regulatory guidelines, etc.).
The effect of social and cultural context on representations.	• How the representations in the set online product have been shaped by the social and cultural contexts in which they have been produced (e.g., how they reflect particular social norms and values).
How and why stereotypes can be used positively and negatively.	• The extent to which the set online product reinforces stereotypes and the purpose or function of any stereotypical representations that feature in the set product.
How and why particular social groups, in a national and global context, may be under-represented or misrepresented.	• The extent to which the set online product reflects the under-representation or misrepresentation of particular social groups.
How media representations convey values, attitudes and beliefs about the world and how these may be systematically reinforced across a wide range of media representations.	• How the representations in the set online product express social and cultural ideas or values, and how these representations relate to broader patterns within the media.
How audiences respond to and interpret media representations.	• The different ways in which audiences may read and respond to the representations in the set online product.

Revising Self-Representation

The way in which bloggers and vloggers represent themselves online is one of the topics you will need to consider when revising your set product. As part of your revision, try to refamiliarise yourself with two or three blogs or videos that the content creator you have studied has posted, thinking specifically about issues relating to self-representation. When you re-read or re-watch the blogs or videos, focus on the following:

- Mise-en-scène:
  - Where was the video shot or where were the photographs taken? How do these settings contribute to the content creator's self-representation?
  - What clothes is the content creator wearing and how do they help to convey a sense of the content creator's image or identity?
  - What props or objects appear in the blog or video? What do they signify or connote and how do they contribute to the content creator's self-representation?

- Lexis and mode of address:
  - What kind of language does the content creator use? How do they address the reader or viewer, and what impression of them does this help to convey?

- **Gatekeeping**:
  - What has the content creator chosen to include or disclose in the blog or video and how do their choices of what to include or disclose contribute to their self-representation?
  - Is there a focus on ordinary, everyday activities that the reader or viewer can identify with or relate to in the blog or video, or is the content more aspirational? (To what extent is the content creator constructed as the archetypal boy or girl next door?)

Quickfire Revision

5.25 What does the term gatekeeping refer to?

Revising Representations of Gender

As well as thinking about self-representation, you should also look at the representations of gender that feature in your set online product when you are revising.

Make a list of the following:

- Any blogs or vlogs you have studied that can be seen to reinforce gender stereotypes.
- Any blogs or vlogs you have studied that can be seen to challenge gender stereotypes.

In each case, make sure that you can explain *how* the blog or vlog either reinforces or challenges gender stereotypes. For example:

- Does the *content* or *subject matter* of the blog or vlog reinforce or challenge gender stereotypes?
- Does the content creator exhibit any stereotypically masculine or feminine traits in their blogs or vlogs?

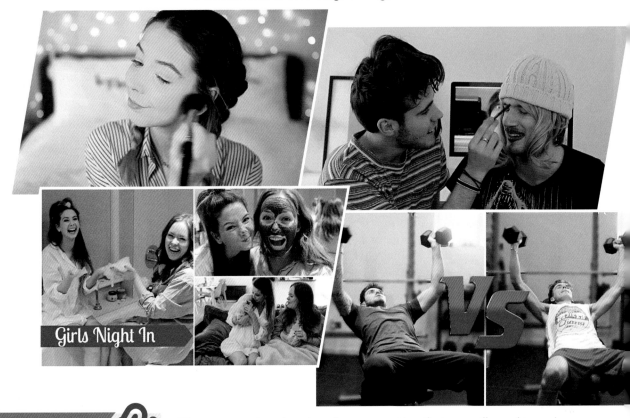

There are two key theories of representation that you will need to make sure you can apply to the online media product you have studied: Hall's theory of representation and Gauntlett's theory of identity.

Link

For an explanation of Hall's theory of representation in relation to online media see page 185 of the Year 1/AS student book.

KEY THEORY: Stuart Hall's Theory of Representation

- The idea that representation is the production of meaning through language, with language defined in its broadest sense as a system of signs.
- The idea that the relationship between concepts and signs is governed by codes.
- The idea that stereotyping, as a form of representation, reduces people to a few simple characteristics or traits.
- The idea that stereotyping tends to occur where there are inequalities of power, as subordinate or excluded groups are constructed as different or 'other' (e.g., through ethnocentrism).

How to Revise Hall's Theory of Representation

In order to revise Hall's theory of representation, look again at some of the blogs or vlogs you have studied and think about:

- how the representations are constructed through media language
- whether there are any examples of stereotyping in the set online product.

KEY THEORY: David Gauntlett's Theory of Identity

- The idea that the media provide us with 'tools' or resources that we use to construct our identities.
- The idea that while, in the past, the media tended to convey singular, straightforward messages about ideal types of male and female identities, the media today offer us a more diverse range of stars, icons and characters from whom we may pick and mix different ideas.

How to Revise Gauntlett's Theory of Identity

As part of your revision of Gauntlett's theory of identity, you should try to find examples showing how your set online product has been used as a tool or resource for identity construction. Comments posted by users in response to specific blogs or videos can be particularly revealing in this regard. See if you can find any examples of users discussing the way in which the content creator has influenced the user's own identity (e.g., in terms of their image, style or look, or their attitudes, values, beliefs or behaviours).

As well as considering identity construction, you should also think about the messages that your set online product conveys about ideal types of male and female identity.

- Does your set product define particular traits, values or interests as masculine or feminine, for example?
- Are the messages about gender diverse and complex, or are they more in keeping with the singular and straightforward messages that Gauntlett associates with media representations of the past?

Use the table below as a revision aid.

Key message regarding ideal types of male or female identity	Where the message is conveyed (i.e. specific blogs or videos)	How the message is conveyed

Top Revision Tip

The revision tasks on self-representation and representations of gender outlined on the previous pages should provide a useful starting point for your revision of Hall's theory as you will already have been thinking about aspects of media language such as mise-en-scène, language and mode of address, as well as stereotyping.

Link

For an explanation of how Gauntlett's theory of identity can be applied to online media see page 184 of the Year 1/AS student book.

☑ ☑ ☑
CHECKLIST

Industry

Revision Checklist for Industry

The following checklist outlines the key aspects of Industry that you need to know for the online media section of Component 2.

What it says in the spec	What you need to know
Processes of production, distribution and circulation by organisations, groups and individuals in a global context.	• How bloggers and vloggers produce and distribute content online.
The relationship of recent technological change and media production, distribution and circulation.	• The way in which digital technologies and the rise of the internet have changed the way in which media products are produced and distributed (e.g., enabling ordinary citizens to produce and distribute content online without the mediation of professional companies or organisations).
The significance of economic factors, including commercial and not-for-profit public funding, to media industries and their products.	• The different ways in which online content can be monetised.
The impact of 'new' digital technologies on media regulation, including the role of individual producers.	• The challenges that the internet and online media forms pose in terms of media regulation and the strategies that are being developed to deal with these challenges and issues. • The impact of media regulation on the producers of your set online product.

Revising Production, Distribution and Circulation

One of the things that you will need to consider when revising your set online product is the impact of recent technological change on media production, distribution and circulation. An important question to think about here is the extent to which 'new' digital technologies have democratised the media.

- What examples could you give to support the claim that new digital technologies have democratised the media? (E.g., how might these technologies be seen to challenge or disrupt the power and dominance of major companies and corporations?)

- What examples could you give to challenge the claim that new digital technologies have democratised the media? (E.g., how could you argue that major companies and corporations have used online platforms and technologies to consolidate or extend their control of the media?)

Another issue that you will need to consider when you are revising is the impact of economic factors on online media. This includes the way in which your set online product generates revenue.

Quickfire Revision

5.26 What is the difference between an advertisement and an advertorial?

5.27 What term is used for advertisements that appear beside or below an online video?

5.28 What is a pre-roll ad?

Link

If you need a reminder to answer these Quickfire Revision questions see pages 190 and 188 of the Year 1/AS student book.

Apply it!

5.29 Look again at your set online product and try to find at least one example of each of the sources of revenue shown in the following table.

Source of revenue	Example from the set product
Advertising	
Sponsorship and paid-for content (e.g., advertorials)	
Merchandising	

Take it Further

5.14 Do some further research into YouTube's 'Partner Programme' and the way in which it generates revenue by monetising content.

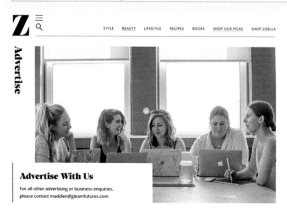

GRWM: Everyday Festive Glam Look | Zoella

1,627,078 views • 9 Dec 2017   71K   1.3K   SHARE   SAVE ...

Zoella ☺
11.6M subscribers   SUBSCRIBE

GRWM: Everyday Festive Glam
→ This video contains paid for advertorial for Benefit Cosmetics

#WorldNutellaDay

Big Nutella Celebrations In The Office!

285,220 views • 4 Feb 2019   11K   238   SHARE   SAVE ...

Alfie Deyes Vlogs ☺
3.8M subscribers   SUBSCRIBE

▶ Big Nutella Celebrations In The Office!
This Video contains a paid for advertorial
https://www.nutelladay.com/

In order to comply with the ASA's CAP Code and Consumer Protection Laws, paid-for content such as Zoella's advertorial for Benefit Cosmetics and Alfie Deyes' advertorial for Nutella has to be clearly signalled to viewers.

Revising Regulation

Through your study of online media, you should have developed an understanding of the impact that 'new' digital technologies have had on regulation and the challenges that online media forms pose for regulators. Recent debates regarding online media regulation have tended to focus on:

- concerns about online privacy and data collection
- concerns about online advertising and consumer protection (e.g., the need for paid-for content to be clearly declared)
- concerns about the amount of time young people spend online and the need for screen time limits
- concerns about younger audiences accessing unsuitable material online
- concerns about who should be held accountable for material posted online (e.g., the question of whether Twitter, Facebook and YouTube should be treated merely as platforms or as publishers).

Apply it!

5.30 The following table shows some of the bodies responsible for regulating online media in the UK. To support your revision of this topic, provide some specific examples of what their rules and guidelines say about online media. Where possible, try to indicate how these rules and guidelines relate to and impact on your set online product.

Regulator	Relevant rules, laws, codes or guidelines	What the rules state and how they apply to online media
YouTube	YouTube Community Guidelines	
Advertising Standards Authority (ASA)	The CAP Code (UK Code of Non-Broadcast Advertising and Direct and Promotional Guidelines)	
Competition and Markets Authority (CMA) (this role was previously performed by the Office of Fair Trading)	Consumer Protection Laws (e.g., those relating to online endorsements and advertising)	
The Information Commissioner's Office (ICO)	General Data Protection Regulation (GDPR) The Data Protection Act (2018)	

Audiences

Revision Checklist for Audiences

The following checklist outlines the key aspects of Audiences that you need to know for the online media section of Component 2.

What it says in the spec	What you need to know
How audiences are grouped and categorised by media industries, including by age, gender and social class, as well as by lifestyle and taste.	• The way in which online audiences can be placed in particular demographic or psychographic categories. • The way in which data gathered about the online habits and behaviour of users enables more accurate audience profiles to be constructed.
How media producers target, attract, reach, address and potentially construct audiences.	• The different strategies used by the producers of the set online product to target, attract, reach and address particular audiences. • The way in which the producers of the set online product cultivate particular attitudes, values and beliefs, thereby constructing their audience.
How media industries target audiences through the content and appeal of media products, and through the ways in which they are marketed, distributed and circulated.	• How the representations, subject matter and mode of address in your set online product create audience appeal and enable content creators to target audiences. • The different strategies used to market and promote the set online product.
The interrelationship between media technologies and patterns of consumption and response.	• The way in which digital technologies in the Web 2.0 era facilitate audience participation and interaction.
How audiences interact with the media and can be actively involved in media production.	• The way in which content creators solicit feedback from audiences and use this to shape and inform future media content. • The way in which digital technologies can be seen to have democratised the internet, enabling media users to become **prosumers**.

Quickfire Revision

5.29 What is a prosumer?

You should also be prepared to discuss the way in which the content and appeal of your set online product is used to target audiences. Consider, for example, the topics that the blogger or vlogger explores, the mode of address that they use and the way in which this facilitates para-social interaction.

Revising Audience Targeting and Audience Appeal

As part of your revision, you should look again at how your set online product has been promoted and marketed, and the different strategies it uses to target audiences.

Apply it!

5.31 Some examples of techniques commonly used by the producers of online products to target audiences are shown in the following table. Identify those that are relevant to the set online product you have studied and explain how they have been used to target particular audiences.

Strategy used	How the strategy is used to target particular audiences
Collaboration videos	
Appearances at festivals, conferences or conventions	
Appearances at red carpet events (film premieres, awards ceremonies, etc.)	
Other media appearances (e.g., television or radio programmes, music videos, newspaper or magazine features, etc.)	

Collaboration videos such as the 'The Mad Lib Story Challenge' (left) and 'Tanya Burr and Zoella 5 Minute Makeup Challenge' (right) are useful ways of broadening a YouTuber's audience reach.

Revising Patterns of Audience Consumption and Response

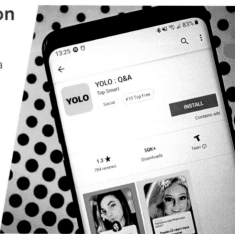

Another topic you will need to revise is the relationship between media technologies and patterns of consumption and response. In particular, you will need to think about the way in which the internet and digitally convergent technologies have not only changed the way in which audiences consume media products but also have enabled audiences to 'speak back' to the media in various ways.

Linked to this, you should consider the different ways in which audiences in the online age are able to interact with media products and the way in which digital technologies have enabled them to become more actively involved in media production.

Apply it!

5.32 With this in mind, try to find an example of each of the following from your set online product:

- An online Q&A session involving interaction between the content creator and audience members.
- Comments posted by an individual audience member in response to a particular blog or vlog, or an online conversation about a particular blog or vlog.
- A video created by an audience member in response to a blog or vlog.
- Fan art or fan fiction inspired by the content creator that an audience member has posted online.
- A blog or vlog that the content creator has produced in response to audience feedback.

An example of a Q&A session that Alfie Deyes held on Instagram in December 2018.

The 'Get in touch' page that appears on Zoella's website, inviting audience interaction.

Link

For an explanation of how Gerbner's cultivation theory can be applied to online media products such as blogs and vlogs see page 194 of the Year 1/AS student book.

Take it Further

5.15 Try to identify patterns of representation that run across the set online product you have studied. (Is there a certain consistency in terms of how gender is represented, for example?) Then consider how these patterns of representation might cultivate particular views and opinions among regular users of the online product.

How to Revise Gerbner's Cultivation Theory

A key audience theory that you need to make sure you can apply to your set online product is Gerbner's cultivation theory.

KEY THEORY: George Gerbner's Cultivation Theory

- The idea that exposure to repeated patterns of representation over long periods of time can shape and influence the way in which people perceive the world around them (i.e. cultivating particular views and opinions).
- The idea that cultivation reinforces mainstream values (dominant ideologies).

As Gerbner's theory suggests that cultivation reinforces mainstream values, a useful starting point for your revision of this theory would be to identify some examples of mainstream values and dominant ideologies that your set online product could be seen to reinforce.

These mainstream values or dominant ideologies might include prevailing cultural attitudes towards capitalism, consumerism, materialism or gender roles within Western culture.

Use the following table to structure your revision.

Mainstream value or dominant ideology	Where the value or ideology is reinforced (i.e. specific blogs or videos)	How the value or ideology is reinforced

Revising Relevant Contexts

Relevant context	Points to consider
Social and cultural context	• The effect of social and cultural context on the representations of gender in the set online product.
	• The extent to which the values, attitudes and beliefs expressed in the set online product have been influenced by the wider social and cultural context in which the product was produced.
	• The way in which audience responses to the set online product may be influenced by social and cultural context.
Economic context	• The various ways in which online content can be monetised.
	• The importance of advertising, sponsorship and merchandising to the online industry.
	• The extent to which the online media landscape is controlled by large organisations and companies whose primary purpose is to make profit.

STYLE   BEAUTY   LIFESTYLE   RECIPES   BOOKS   SHOP OUR PICKS   SHOP ZOELLA

FIND FILMM ON THE APP STORE

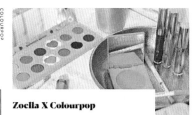

Zoella X Colourpop

The limited edition Zoella X Colourpop Brunch Date collection is nearly sold out so won't be sticking around for long, so be sure to grab it while you still can!

SHOP ZOELLA X COLOURPOP BRUNCH DATE

Cordially Invited

Published in October 2018, Cordially Invited is a blueprint for making an event and a memory out of each day. Packed full of ideas, inspiration and DIYs for making any day a celebration, the book is split into seasons, so you can open it up every month and find something amazing to make.

SHOP CORDIALLY INVITED

6

Component 2: Investigating Media Forms and Products: Assessment

Top Revision Tip

For the AS Level Component 2 examination, you are only required to study one set product for each of the three media forms. If you are taking the A Level course, you are required to study an additional set product for each media form. Details of the additional set products for the A Level Component 2 examination can be found in the Year 2/A Level student book and the Year 2/A Level revision guide.

How Will I Be Assessed?

The Component 2 examination assesses your understanding of the theoretical framework in relation to three media forms: television, magazines and online media. It consists of three sections – one on each of the media forms you have studied.

There will be two extended response questions and one two-part question. Each question will be worth a total of 20 marks.

Section	Media form	Set product	Question
Section A	Television	*Life on Mars* or *Humans* or *The Jinx*	Either one extended response question or one two-part question
Section B	Magazines	*Woman* or *Woman's Realm* or *Vogue*	Either one extended response question or one two-part question
Section C	Online media	Alfie Deyes or Zoella	Either one extended response question or one two-part question

What Theories and Contexts Do I Need to Revise?

	Media Language theories	Representation theories	Industry theories	Audience theories	Contexts
Section A: Television	Narratology (including Todorov) Genre theory (including Neale)	Theories of representation (including Hall)	N/A	Reception theory (including Hall)	Historical Social and cultural Economic
Section B: Magazines	Semiotics (including Barthes)	Theories of identity (including Gauntlett)	Power and media industries (including Curran and Seaton)	Cultivation theory (including Gerbner) Reception theory (including Hall)	Historical Social and cultural Economic
Section C: Online media	Semiotics (including Barthes)	Theories of representation (Hall) Theories of identity (including Gauntlett)	N/A	Cultivation theory (including Gerbner)	Social and cultural Economic

 Top Revision Tip

The table above only shows those theories that are required for the AS Level Component 2 examination. If you are taking the A Level course, there are additional theories that you are required to study. You can find details of these in the Year 2/A Level student book and Year 2 A Level revision guide.

 Top Revision Tip

As with Component 1, you can refer to other theories besides the required ones outlined here if you wish, provided they are relevant to the question. Try not to just include theories for the sake of it though; the theories that you refer to should always make a meaningful contribution to your response.

Component 3: Media Production

Quickfire Revision

7.1 What elements of the theoretical framework will you be required to demonstrate in your production?

Top Revision Tip

Whatever form you choose or are directed to work in, what you produce needs to be your own work. All the images should be taken by you and not downloaded from the internet, for example. There are a few exceptions, including industry and social media logos and magazine barcodes.

Reminder

- Component 3 is the non-exam assessment unit of the AS/Year 1 course that you will complete in your centre and it is then assessed by your teachers.

- Component 3 is designed to allow you to demonstrate your knowledge and understanding of media products and the theoretical framework, and illustrate your skills in research, planning and production.

- It brings together elements you have learned during the course and allows you to show your knowledge and understanding in a practical way.

- The briefs will be released each year by Eduqas and you need to follow these briefs closely. Your teacher or centre may decide to offer all these briefs, or they may select a menu of briefs for you to choose from.

- You should create an individual production piece. However, you may use unassessed students and others, for example members of your family, in your work.

- You should create original material for your production. You will need to consider this when you make decisions about what you want to create.

- For the music video brief, you can use an existing song by a band or artist, but this should not have an existing music video.

- For the television brief an existing music soundtrack can be used but this must be copyright free.

- All non-original music used must be acknowledged on the cover sheet.

- It is acceptable to use a template or web design software for the web pages, but it must not contain pre-populated content. All content, for example images, graphics and audio-visual material, needs to be original and learners must be responsible for the design of the website.

- You will be monitored throughout the production process in order to ensure that your work is authentic and has been created by you. This is also an opportunity for your teacher to give you advice and guidance.

The choice of briefs offered may depend on the equipment available at your centre.

Checklist of key points

Elements of the briefs will change each year, for example the intended target audience and the **industry context**, but for AS you will always have the following choices:

- ⊘ A sequence from a new television programme or a website to promote a new television programme.
- ⊘ A print marketing campaign or a website to promote a new film. For this brief the campaign or website must not include a complete short film, film sequence or trailer.
- ⊘ A music video or a website to promote a new artist or band.
- ⊘ A new print or online magazine.

 Apply it!

7.1 How many marks are available for each element of this component? Write your answers in the third column of the following table.

What it says in the spec	What you need to know	How many marks?
Produce a Statement of Aims and Intentions to create a media product for an intended audience.	• The Statement of Aims and Intentions needs to be completed after the research and planning and before you start the production. It is not an evaluation. • It should demonstrate how you will use your research to apply the codes and conventions of the chosen genre and construct purposeful representations. • You should use appropriate subject-specific terminology and demonstrate how you will apply your knowledge and understanding of the theoretical framework.	
Create a media production that meets the requirements of the set brief, including suitability for the chosen form, genre, industry context and target audience.	• You need to adhere to all elements of the brief and complete them fully. Use the requirements set out in the brief as a checklist as you work through your production. • Your research into existing products will help you to employ the relevant codes and conventions and demonstrate understanding of the industry context. • You should consider how your production will target the audience set out in the brief. This needs to be the full range, not a selected audience.	

(continued)

 Quickfire Revision

7.2 What is meant by the industry context?

7.3 What elements do you need to submit for Component 3?

 Top Revision Tip

It is essential that you complete all the requirements of the brief, as they are an important part of the assessment for this component.

 Top Revision Tip

Consider your choice of brief carefully, bearing in mind your interests, skills and the equipment at your disposal.

 Quickfire Revision

7.4 How long are you expected to spend on this component?

7.5 Why is it important that you complete all the requirements of the brief fully?

Top Revision Tip

Consider how you can use what you have learned during the course to help with your production:

You have studied all the production forms:

- C1
  - Music videos.
- C2
  - Magazines in print and online
  - Television.

You can apply what you have learned to any product, form or genre:

- The codes and conventions of the form and how media language is used to convey meanings.
- How representations appropriate to the form are constructed.
- How media products target, reach, address and construct audiences.
- Industry issues related to the form and products.

What it says in the spec	What you need to know	How many marks?
Create a media production that uses media language to communicate meaning and construct representations.	• Here you can apply the knowledge and understanding of the theoretical framework that you have gained through the study of the set products during the course. • Media language, including visual, technical and language codes, should be used to create meanings and construct representations appropriate to your product. • The design (print briefs) or narrative (audio-visual briefs) should be well constructed and appropriate to the form.	

Deconstructing the Briefs

Sample briefs

This film marketing brief is taken from the AS Sample Assessment Materials and is annotated to illustrate some of the common requirements for all briefs offered.

The brief will tell you exactly what you need to produce. You need to study this carefully for specific requirements. Here you need to understand the difference between a 'teaser' and a 'theatrical' poster.

You will need to choose a film **genre** and engage in relevant research. This will enable you to employ appropriate codes and conventions to demonstrate your knowledge and understanding of the theoretical framework.

Create a DVD front and back cover, a 'teaser' poster and a main theatrical poster for a new film in a genre of your choice.

You may choose to produce marketing materials for a hybrid or sub-genre of the film.

You should create a product for **an independent UK film company** (such as WARP or DNA), targeting an audience of **16–34 year old fans of your chosen film genre.**

Length: 4 pages

The media production should not include a complete short film, film sequence or trailer.

The brief will detail the **industry context**, this will change from year to year. The examples given will help you to focus your research and allow you to apply the relevant codes and conventions to your marketing campaign.

The brief will clearly identify the **audience** and this must be adhered to. It will always give an age range but may also contain other information, for example a psychographic group.

The brief will specify the **length** or quantity you should produce. Ensure that you adhere to this. If you produce too much, only the specified amount will be assessed. If you produce too little you are unlikely to meet all the requirements.

The brief will also include more detailed information about the minimum requirements you should complete, for example the amount of images, locations and characters.

Apply it!

7.2 Use this method to deconstruct your chosen brief.

Apply the knowledge and understanding gained in Components 1 and 2 to your own production.

Quickfire Revision

7.6 What is the difference between primary and secondary research?

Top Revision Tip

Make sure you have a way of recording your research findings so that you can refer to them when you start creating your product.

Research

Reminder

- Research and planning are not assessed but it is essential that they are undertaken. You cannot produce a professional and valid piece of production work without first researching the form and sub-genre in which you are working.
- It is also essential that you research the audience who may consume your particular product, in order to discover their opinions.
- Thorough and useful research will help you to create a better media production. You need to employ the most appropriate research for the product you intend to create.
- It is also important that you are clear about what specifically you want to find out and how it will help you to create your product. Both primary and secondary research will be useful.

Checklist of Key Points: What Research is Appropriate?

Product analysis: Analyse the way media language is used to construct meanings and how representations are constructed in media products similar to the one you want to produce. This may focus on layout and design, mode of address and the use of technical and audio codes. You will also need to research specific genre conventions and characters, narrative and settings, depending on the brief you have chosen.

Industry context: Will involve research into the organisations that produce the type of product you want to create, including how the product may be produced, distributed and marketed, and how your chosen industry is regulated. You should consider how the results of this research impact upon a product. Your research should be guided by the industry context detailed in the brief, for example Hearst or Time Inc. UK for a mainstream magazine.

Secondary audience research: For example, media packs and details of marketing strategies. Relevant academic theories may help to develop your understanding and support your analysis.

Audience research: Will focus on how particular industries and organisations appeal to, engage and position audiences, the different and complex ways in which audiences interact with media products and how audiences may respond to media products.

Primary audience research: May be appropriate. In industry, a media product would not be created without first conducting research into the audience who will consume it. Conducting research with a focus group allows you to gather more detailed information and have more control over the situation, and to direct the questions and feedback.

Planning

Link

More detailed research and planning tasks appropriate to each form can be found on pages 204–238 of the Year 1/AS student book.

Reminder

- Your research should inform your planning. Planning is another essential element of the production process and good planning will help to ensure that your final product is successful.
- Ensure that your planning includes the required elements of the brief.
- If you have done your research well you will have developed your knowledge and understanding of the product you are about to create, this will then inform your planning.
- Use all elements of the theoretical framework in your planning.

Checklist of Key Points: What Planning Tasks are Appropriate?

A treatment: A brief synopsis of ideas for a media project. It serves two purposes: to summarise elements of the idea, for example the plot and main characters, as well as to sell your idea to a producer. A treatment should communicate your idea in a concise but compelling manner.

A pitch: Present the ideas for your new product to a selected audience, with the aim of persuading them of the viability of the project. You can then adapt these in response to the feedback.

Top Revision Tip

Although research and planning are not formally assessed, they are vital to the production process. You need to engage in careful planning to ensure you are meeting the requirements of the brief and applying your knowledge and understanding of the theoretical framework.

Apply it!

7.3 Present your treatment to a group of your peers. Ask them for feedback and review your planning in the light of this.

A storyboard: Plan the shots and narrative before you start filming. This can be informed by a **recce** of the locations you intend to use. Taking photographs of these is a useful planning task and can be used for later reference.

A project plan: Includes a timeline or Gantt chart and planned use of, for example, resources. This will be particularly important if you will have to share equipment with other students.

Mock-ups of magazine pages or DVD covers: This will help to ensure that you have incorporated all the elements of the brief before you start creating your product.

A script: May be appropriate for the television brief and for elements of the online briefs. This task also allows you to consider how you will use an appropriate mode of address to target the intended audience.

Top Revision Tip

When you are researching existing products, you should be clear what you want to find out. Your research should be focused on the requirements of the brief and how your findings will influence your production decisions.

Top Revision Tip

The table on the right will be useful in the monitoring discussion you will have with your teacher. It will allow them to see how your thought processes and ideas for your own production are influenced by your research.

Being organised is key to a successful production.

Apply it!

7.4 Research and planning checklist

Use the table below to help plan your production.

Chosen brief and genre/sub-genre:		
Interpreting the brief	**Application to your production**	**Date completed**
What are the specific requirements of this set brief? • Key elements • Target audience • Industry context		
What existing products will I research? How are they relevant to the brief? What specifically am I looking for?		
What primary audience research will I undertake? How will this be helpful to my production?		
What secondary audience research will I undertake?		
What did my research illustrate about how media language communicates meaning?		
How did my research into existing similar products show the way that representations are constructed?		
Summary of production ideas.		
What planning tasks will be relevant to my production?		
How will I organise my time to ensure I complete my production by the deadline?		
What resources will I need?		
How will my research and planning influence my Statement of Aims and Intentions?		

Television and Online Options

Reminder

You need to fulfil the minimum requirements for the brief. These are likely to include:

- a specific number of locations
- the number of characters to be included and construct representations of social groups
- specific pages to be included in the website, for example an 'Episodes' page
- guidance in relation to the narrative structure, for example the inclusion of an equilibrium and a conflict
- audio which may give specific detail of diegetic and non-diegetic sound
- editing – this may include specific requirements, for example montage or continuity
- graphics, if appropriate to the set brief, for example the title of the programme.

You should also ensure that you use media language to communicate meaning and construct representations.

Checklist of key points

☑ Use your research findings and planning to influence the decisions you make about your production.

☑ Make sure that your planning includes all the requirements of the brief and use this as a checklist while you work.

☑ Check the equipment available to you and practise using it in advance so that you are sure about how it works.

☑ Pay attention to the audio you want to use; poor audio will reduce the effectiveness of your sequence. If you are filming outside you will need a suitable microphone.

☑ Be organised – plan a schedule and stick to it! Give clear instructions to your actors and people who are part of your crew. This is your project, not theirs.

☑ Use your storyboard – it will give a structure to your filming. However, it is also a working document and can be tweaked and amended should you have new ideas.

☑ Always film more footage/take more photographs than you need – this gives you flexibility when editing. Avoid zooming in and out or panning quickly unless you want to create that effect. Be clear about what you want your actors to do and they should know exactly when filming starts and stops.

Link

More detail about the television and online production brief is available on pages 213–225 of the Year 1/AS student book.

Top Revision Tip

If you are producing online pages for your television programme, the planning tasks will be similar to those for the television extract as your website pages will also include original audio-visual footage.

Top Revision Tip

If you are adding post-production sound, make sure the sound quality matches the location. For example, if your sequence is filmed outside and you record the dialogue separately inside, it will not sound realistic.

Top Revision Tip

Don't forget about continuity! If you take a break in filming a scene and return to film the next day, make sure your actors are wearing the same clothing, that the weather hasn't changed dramatically and the locations are similar.

Quickfire Revision

7.7 Are you allowed to use existing music in your production?

Magazines and Online Options

Link

More detail about the magazines and online production brief is available on pages 205–212 of the Year 1/AS student book.

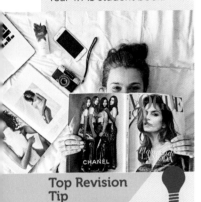

Top Revision Tip

The brief will specify the target audience and the industry context. Examples of the publisher may be given; this will guide your research and production.

Top Revision Tip

Your study of magazine conventions in Component 2 will help in creating your production.

Top Revision Tip

Use the key points for the Television/Online option to help with the audio-visual element of the website.

Quickfire Revision

7.8 Must all the images on your magazine pages be original, i.e. taken by you?

7.9 What elements of media language will help you to construct representations in your print or online magazine?

Reminder

You need to fulfil the minimum requirements for the brief. These are likely to include:

- the number and type of pages you need to include, for example a front cover, contents page and a double-page spread, or a homepage and other linked pages for a website
- the number of images and where these should be
- the specific features of a magazine or website, for example a standfirst and subheadings or an audio-visual interview
- the word length for particular features or articles
- the representations of social groups you need to construct.

Checklist of key points

- ☑ Ensure that you adhere to the codes and conventions of your chosen genre/sub-genre. Bear in mind what you found out in your research into similar print and online products.
- ☑ Consider what you want your photographs/images to look like before you take them. Do a recce of possible locations, select appropriate subjects and consider the framing of your photograph.
- ☑ Direct your models, bearing in mind the focus of the assessment – use media language to communicate meaning and construct representations.
- ☑ Use your own images. You do not need to have a high-specification camera – many mobile phones can take adequate photographs for the purpose. You cannot be given credit for photographs you have not taken, even if you have manipulated them digitally.
- ☑ Take more photographs and audio-visual footage than you need. Be creative! Experiment with taking the same model from different angles. However, remember not to replicate images in your production work.
- ☑ Consider how you will create a house style for your magazine. Each page should link together stylistically in some way so that it is evident they are from the same magazine.
- ☑ Use an appropriate typography that is suitable for the magazine sub-genre and a mode of address that effectively targets the set audience.
- ☑ Use the coverlines on a front cover to help construct representations and to reflect the magazine's genre and industry context. For example, the themes and topics included in a mainstream magazine may be very different from those featured in a more niche, independent magazine.
- ☑ Use an editing package that allows you to produce work of a high standard.

Consider how clothing and expression can construct representations.

Film Marketing Option

Reminder

You need to fulfil the minimum requirements for the brief. These are likely to include:

- Specific detail regarding images, locations and characters. The total amount of images will usually be given as well as details of where these should be divided between the elements of the campaign.
- Details about aspect ratios for posters, for example a portrait 'teaser' poster.
- Formulaic elements to be included, for example taglines, release date, billing block, and the names of the director and actors.
- Word length for elements, including the blurb. There may also be specific requirements about the blurb's content, for example narrative conflict or an enigma.

Checklist of key points

- ⊘ Consider how you can employ the research you have undertaken into media language, including the conventions of the specific film sub-genre. This can be reflected in the layout and composition, the choice and use of original images and the selection of iconography.
- ⊘ Carefully construct the blurb or promotional text on your DVD cover and website page. The mode of address and use of appropriate language will allow you to communicate meaning about the sub-genre and narrative of your film.
- ⊘ Pay careful attention to the construction of the representation of the film sub- genre and the characters within this genre. This can be achieved through attention to visual codes, including clothing and expression. The choice and construction of the central image can also create a narrative, for example an enigma.
- ⊘ The choice of images in the thumbnails and on the website pages can demonstrate elements of the narrative and generic conventions.
- ⊘ The images need to be original and demonstrate evidence that instruction has been given to the models about gesture, expression and clothing in order to establish purposeful representations.
- ⊘ Ensure that the conventions reflect the industry context specified in the brief. For example, an independent film is less likely to feature names of star actors, whereas a mainstream film will use these as part of the film's appeal.

Consider how you will use media language to communicate meanings and construct representations.

As part of your research explore the conventions of the front and back of DVD covers.

Link

More detail about the film marketing production brief is available on pages 225–233 of the Year 1/AS student book.

Top Revision Tip

Ensure that your research covers all elements of the brief so that you are aware of the specific codes and conventions.

Top Revision Tip

Your study of the conventions of film posters in Component 1 will help in planning and creating your production. However, you should ensure that you also research other elements of the brief required, for example the back of DVD covers.

Top Revision Tip

Consider how the choice of film title, font style and colour palette can help to construct the sub-genre.

Apply it!

7.5 Practise combining different titles and fonts until you find a design that is successful.

Music Marketing Option

Link

More detail about the music marketing production brief is available on pages 233–241 of the Year 1/AS student book.

Top Revision Tip

Remember that you can use an existing song, but you need to choose a track that does not have an existing official music video. This will allow you to be more creative and original. Making the right choice about the song you choose is important and must suit the sub-genre of music and the representation of your band/artist.

Top Revision Tip

Always have a back-up copy of your footage and your edit, just in case!

Apply it!

7.6 Set up a practice shoot with your performer to ensure your audio is unproblematic.

Quickfire Revision

7.10 Are you allowed to use an existing song for your music video?

Consider how you can use costume, gesture and setting to construct a representation of your artist.

Reminder

You need to fulfil the minimum requirements for the brief. These are likely to include:

- details of specific locations
- range of shots, angles and movement
- types of footage, for example performance
- elements of narrative, for example conflict
- representations of a social group
- editing of footage to track
- graphics, for example name of band/track title.

Checklist of key points

- Consider what equipment you need to produce your music video. You may need to film with more than one camera in order to construct interesting representations of your artist/band.
- In your music video or website you may want to vary your filming/taking of photographs between the external and internal settings by experimenting with the lighting.
- Lip-synching is very important and very obvious if it is not executed correctly. It needs careful consideration. If you are going to dub the sound on post-production then it is important that your artist sings along to the track playing while you are filming and does not try to mime, this will make the post-production process much easier.
- Film more than you need and experiment by filming with two video cameras or using different camera angles to construct representations.
- Consider what iconography you intend to include in your music video or website to reflect the style of the music video and reinforce the representation of the artist/band.
- Consider how you can establish a house style for your website pages that reflect the genre of music and the representation of your artist/band.
- It is your role to direct your actors and crew in order to demonstrate your understanding of the theoretical framework and your production aims. Consider how you want your artist/band to dress, their gestures and expressions in order to construct a representation appropriate to the sub-genre.
- Make sure that you film in enough time – editing always takes longer than you think. Build in 'disaster time' in case you lose footage and have to re-shoot a scene.

Factor in plenty of time to edit your music video.

Production Tips

Do	Don't
Make sure you complete all tasks and minimum required elements in the brief.	Don't use 'found' images, footage or written text other than that allowed in the specification, for example magazine barcodes.
Consistently use the conventions of your chosen form and sub-genre.	Don't use pre-populated templates, for example for websites. Web design software or templates are acceptable for the online options; however, you should be responsible for the design of the website and all content needs to be original.
Apply knowledge and understanding of the theoretical framework: Media Language, Representations, Media Industries, Audiences.	
Engage and position the target audience through mode of address.	
Create and design all elements of the production, including images, footage and text.	Don't submit incomplete work or a production that is under the required time/length.
Use original images, with the exception of those that are allowed, for example industry logos.	Don't exceed the word limit for elements of the production or the Statement of Aims and Intentions.
Act on the advice given by your teacher at the key monitoring stages.	Don't leave filming until the very end of the schedule; you need to build in time for the editing process or to re-shoot scenes/take additional photographs.
Be organised! Make a time plan and stick to it.	

Apply it!

7.7 Film more footage than you need, which will enable you to have options when editing. Do not forget about continuity.

7.8 Take more photographs than you need in one shoot and consider how you will use media language to communicate meaning through clothing, expression and gesture.

Take a range of photographs to give you options during editing.

Listen to advice given by your teacher during the monitoring process and act upon it.

Component 3: Statement of Aims and Intentions

Apply it!

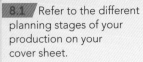

8.1 Refer to the different planning stages of your production on your cover sheet.

Completing the Cover Sheet

The cover sheet is an important working document that should be used throughout the Component 3 process. It is a record of your work and fulfils official authentication requirements. It is also the way in which you submit your Statement of Aims and Intentions and how your teacher records and justifies their assessment of your work.

In addition to completing your production you must submit:

* a cover sheet
* a Statement of Aims and Intentions.

Section A

✓ Checklist of key points

Fill in the appropriate personal details and those of your production.

Give details of the specific planning tasks you have undertaken and how these have been influenced by your research into existing products. Avoid generalisations, refer specifically to your production. You should aim to write approximately 100 to 150 words here.

Give brief details of how you approached your production in order to realise the set brief you chose, including the drafting process.

Here, give specific details of what you intend to submit for assessment. Include the URL if you have produced a website.

You must acknowledge your use of any non-original material used in the production, for example copyright-free music and software packages you have used, and how they have been employed.

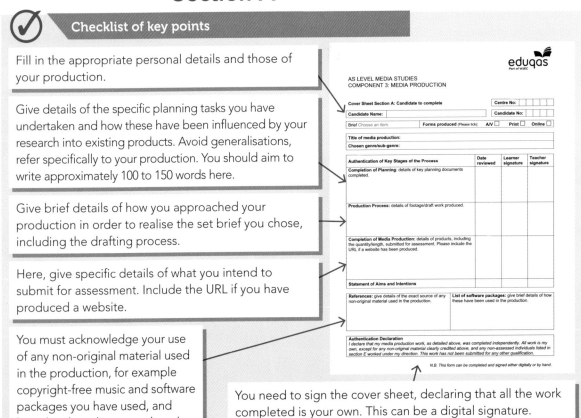

You need to sign the cover sheet, declaring that all the work completed is your own. This can be a digital signature.

There is space on the final page of the cover sheet where you should acknowledge any non-assessed people who have taken part in your production.

Completing the Statement of Aims and Intentions

Reminder

- The Statement of Aims and Intentions should be completed after the research and planning and before the production is started.
- It is not an evaluation; it sets out your aims and how you intend to fulfil the requirements of the brief and demonstrate your knowledge and understanding of the theoretical framework.
- Ensure that you refer to the requirements of the brief and how you intend to fulfil them.
- Use relevant subject-specific terminology.
- Incorporate theories and theoretical perspectives where appropriate, for example feminist perspectives may be relevant in relation to how you intend to construct representations.
- It is relatively brief and cannot exceed 350 words, but is a compulsory component.
- You can use bullet points or write in continuous prose.

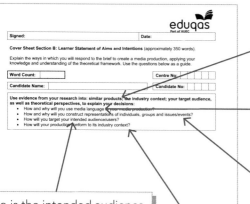

The Statement of Aims and Intentions should refer specifically to the research you have undertaken into all elements of the theoretical framework.

Explain how you intend to use media language in your production, for example visual codes, technical codes, narrative and design.

You should include people in your production to allow you to construct appropriate representations. Outline how you intend to do this, for example clothing, expression, gesture and setting. Are the representations appropriate to your chosen genre/sub-genre?

Who is the intended audience for your production? How do you intend to realise the set brief in order to target this audience? How do you intend to use mode of address to target the audience?

How do you intend to use the conventions of the genre to illustrate the industry context? How does the chosen industry context relate to the requirements of the brief?

9 Examination Preparation

Link

Further information on approaching Section A of the examination and example questions is available on pages 244–251 of the Year 1/AS student book.

Top Revision Tip

There will always be a print and audio-visual unseen resource in Section A of the examination.

Top Revision Tip

In Question 2, the unseen resource may be in the same or a different form as that of the set product.

Top Revision Tip

Familiarise yourself with the Assessment Objectives, what they mean and where they will be assessed.

Top Revision Tip

You can see that AO1 is assessed in Section B and AO2 in Section A, this will help to focus your revision.

≫ Component 1: Investigating the Media

Reminder

In this assessment you will be required to:

- analyse critically and compare how media products construct and communicate meanings
- use key theories and theoretical perspectives
- employ relevant subject-specific terminology
- debate key questions relating to the social, cultural, political and economic role of the media
- construct and develop a sustained line of reasoning that is coherent, in an extended response.

Addressing the Assessment Objectives

It is important that you understand which Assessment Objectives you need to address in which question.

AO1a: Demonstrate knowledge of the theoretical framework of the media.	Assessed in questions: 3 4
AO1b: Demonstrate understanding of the theoretical framework of the media.	
AO1 2a: Demonstrate knowledge of contexts of media and their influence on media products and processes.	
AO1 2b: Demonstrate understanding of contexts of media and their influence on media products and processes.	
AO2 1: Apply knowledge and understanding of the theoretical framework of media to analyse media products, including in relation to their contexts and through the use of academic theories.	Assessed in questions: 1 2
AO2 2: Apply knowledge and understanding of the theoretical framework of media to make judgements and draw conclusions.	Assessed in questions: 1 2

Section A: Investigating Media Language and Representation

Reminder

- This section is worth 35 marks.
- The focus is Media Language and Representation assessed in relation to two of the forms studied for this section: advertising, marketing, music videos or newspapers.
- There will be two questions in Section A.
- **One question** will assess Media Language and will require you to analyse an unseen print or audio-visual media resource from one of the forms you have studied for this section.
- **One question** will assess Representation. This will require you to compare one set product with an unseen print or audio-visual product from any of the forms studied for this section. This is an extended response question. You will need to refer to relevant contexts.
- The question referring to the audio-visual unseen resource will always come first on the paper.

Checklist of key points

- ⊘ You will be given time at the start of the examination to read the questions, this will help you to prepare.
- ⊘ Use the mark-a-minute rule to guide you as to the time you need to spend on your response. You should also factor in time to make notes on the unseen resources.
- ⊘ For the unseen products you will need to take notes.
- ⊘ The Representation question is a comparison question with a higher mark tariff. The question will include bullet points, use these to guide your note-taking.
- ⊘ Ensure that you prepare the print unseen as well as the audio-visual resource before embarking upon your response.
- ⊘ Designing a grid or format to ensure that you make useful notes is helpful. This will help you to focus on the most relevant aspects of the unseen products.
- ⊘ Ensure that you avoid merely describing what you can see; consider how meanings are communicated through media language and how representations are constructed according to the question.
- ⊘ Use subject-specific terminology related to the form in your response.
- ⊘ For the representation question, consider carefully how you will structure your response in comparing the two products. Use terminology related to comparison in your answer to signal that you are highlighting the similarities and differences.

Top Revision Tip

Structuring your response to the longer questions and including relevant terminology can enhance your answer.

Quickfire Revision

9.1 What mark tariff would you expect to see for a question that purely assesses knowledge, for example AO1a?

You need to manage your time carefully in the examination, using the question tariffs to help you

A revision checklist helps to ensure that you have covered all elements of the examination paper.

Top Revision Tip

Use the Specimen Assessment Materials (SAMs) and past papers to help guide your revision.

Top Revision Tip

Remember that from 2021 you will be required to study a different front page and article from the *Daily Mirror*.

Top Revision Tip

You will see the audio-visual unseen three times regardless of whether it is a Media Language or a Representation question. For the first viewing you will just watch. Consider how you will plan your note-taking for viewings two and three.

Top Revision Tip

The unseen resources will always be taken from a form you have studied for Section A.

Apply it!

9.1 Using the appropriate terminology related to making comparisons in the Representation question will help you to structure your response more effectively. These terms can be used as connectives or as sentence/paragraph starters.

In the following table decide which words or phrases would be used for similarities, which for differences and which are more general.

Key terminology	Similarity/difference? Connective/starter?	Key terminology
Just as		In the same way
On the contrary		Conversely
Similarly		On the other hand
Alternatively		In a similar fashion
Equally		Furthermore
Just as … so too		Likewise
Whereas		In contrast to

Component 1 Revision Checklist Section A

Apply it!

9.2 Tick the 'Done' box once you have revised each of the topics and are happy that you understand it.

Topic	Areas to revise	Done
General	• Codes and conventions of the form and genre/sub-genre • Subject-specific terminology appropriate to the form • Analytical terminology • Terminology related to making comparisons	
Advertising and marketing	• Media Language, Representations and Media contexts in *Tide* • Media Language, Representations and Media contexts in *WaterAid* • Media Language, Representations and Media contexts in *The Kiss of the Vampire* • Analysing unseen products from the set form (SAMs: Barnardo's *Believe in Me* advert) • Practise planning the extended response comparison question using an unseen and a set product (2018: *Tide* and *Wonder Woman*)	
Music video	• Media Language, Representations and Media contexts in *Formation* or *Dream* • Analysing unseen products from the set form (2018 paper Ed Sheeran, *Shape of You*) • Practise planning the extended response comparison question using an unseen and a set product (SAMs: *Dream/Formation* and *Hidden Figures* film poster)	
Newspapers	• Media Language, Representations and Media contexts in the *Daily Mirror* (10 November 2016) • Analysing unseen products from the set form • Practise planning the extended response comparison question using an unseen and the set newspaper product	
Theoretical perspectives	• Media Language: Semiotics (including Barthes) • Representation: Theories of Representation (including Hall) • Theories of identity (including Gauntlett): Advertising and marketing and Music video	

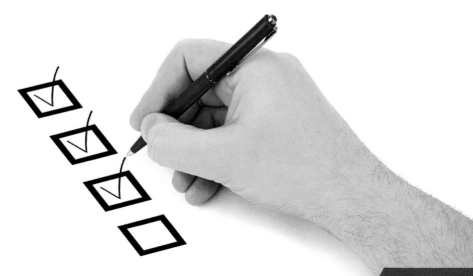

Deconstructing the Questions: AS Examination 2018, Section A

Question 1

The unseen resource for this question in 2018 was an extract from the music video *Shape of You* (Ed Sheeran, 2017).

Assesses AO2 1: Apply knowledge and understanding of the theoretical framework of media to analyse media products.

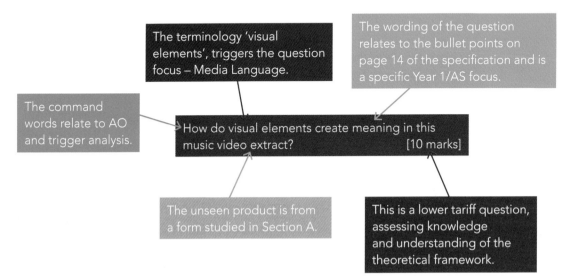

The terminology 'visual elements', triggers the question focus – Media Language.

The wording of the question relates to the bullet points on page 14 of the specification and is a specific Year 1/AS focus.

The command words relate to AO and trigger analysis.

How do visual elements create meaning in this music video extract?   [10 marks]

The unseen product is from a form studied in Section A.

This is a lower tariff question, assessing knowledge and understanding of the theoretical framework.

Top Revision Tip

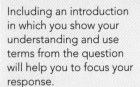

Including an introduction in which you show your understanding and use terms from the question will help you to focus your response.

Top Revision Tip

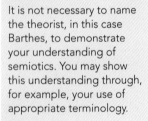

It is not necessary to name the theorist, in this case Barthes, to demonstrate your understanding of semiotics. You may show this understanding through, for example, your use of appropriate terminology.

Question 1 Responses

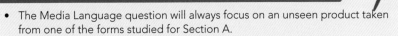

Reminder

- The Media Language question will always focus on an unseen product taken from one of the forms studied for Section A.
- Any of the areas of media language listed in the specification can be assessed.
- The focus of the question will be taken from the bullet points on page 14 of the Year 1/AS specification.

On the next page is an extract from a candidate's response to Question 1 (2018). The complete answer was placed in Band 5 because it fulfils the criteria from the marking scheme:

- Excellent, consistent and accurate application of knowledge and understanding of the theoretical framework to analyse the unseen music video extract.
- Analysis of the music video is perceptive, detailed and may be informed by relevant theories.

There are a multitude of methods used to create meaning through denotation and connotation throughout the extract. Meaning is achieved through the encoding by the producers of a combination of elements including technical, visual and gesture codes.

One way in which the visual elements construct meaning is through the technical code of lighting. During the introduction, the mise-en-scène is primarily dark, connoting mystery. This works in combination with a close-up camera shot of the faces close together as they work, foreshadowing the narrative later in the extract. This sets up an effective juxtaposition when later in the video the code changes to bright lighting. This symbolises the growth of their relationship, from dark to light.

Another way in which visual elements create meaning is through gesture codes. In the beginning there are fast-paced, aggressive movements from both characters effectively intertwined with moody lighting. This, combined with the semantic field of boxing including the iconography of gloves and the punchbag, symbolises aspects of the characters' lives.

Take it Further

9.1 Watch the first 2 minutes of the Ed Sheeran music video 'Shape of You': www.youtube.com/watch?v=JGwWNGJdvx8, and write two more paragraphs in response to the question, trying to target the Band 5 criteria.

Remember to support your points with specific examples from the product.

Top Revision Tip

In Question 2 you will be required to refer to contexts.

9.3 Annotate the following extract from a response in different colours, highlighting where it:

- uses terminology related to the theory of semiotics
- demonstrates knowledge and understanding of the theoretical framework through their use of specific examples from the music video
- engages in perceptive analysis
- uses subject-specific terminology
- suggests intended meanings.

The extract was awarded a mark in Band 3 as it fulfils the following criteria:

- Satisfactory, generally accurate application of knowledge and understanding of the theoretical framework to analyse the unseen music video extract.
- Analysis of the music video is reasonable and straightforward.

> *In the beginning of the music video there is very low lighting and a low-angle mid-shot of the singer Ed Sheeran sitting on a chair. This creates the meaning of loneliness setting a sad atmosphere for the audience.*
>
> *A mid close-up of the female main character, centrally framed and hanging from the punch bag directs the audience's attention to her.*
>
> *In the beginning of the music video both main characters are alone in the frames. However, a shot reverse shot showing that they are looking at one another through the boxing ring ropes creates the idea that they are attracted to one another. Montage editing also creates this effect.*

1. What satisfactory points does this candidate make?
2. What advice would you give to improve the response?
3. Re-write the three paragraphs incorporating your suggestions for improvement.

Deconstructing the Representation Extended Response Question

Reminder

- In this question you are required to compare an unseen product with one of the set products studied for Section A.
- To achieve higher marks, you should write a response that constructs and develops a sustained line of reasoning, and which is coherent, relevant, substantiated and logically structured.
- You need to address all the bullet points in the question, but there is no expectation that these will be treated equally.

Assesses AO2 1 and 2: Apply knowledge and understanding of the theoretical framework of media to analyse media products including in relation to their contexts and through the use of academic theories.

This command word relates to the AO and indicates that it is an analysis question.

The focus of the question is representation with specific focus on the use of stereotypes.

The higher mark tariff indicates that this is the extended response question assessing your ability to construct and develop a sustained line of reasoning.

You are required to compare a set product (film poster) with one from a form studied for Section A (advertisement).

Compare how stereotypes are used in the film poster for *Wonder Woman* and the advertisement for *Tide*. **[25 marks]**

In your answer you should consider:
- the similarities and differences in how stereotypes are used in the products
- how the representations convey values and attitudes
- how far the representations reflect historical and cultural contexts.

The command words 'how far' triggers that you need to make judgements and draw conclusions.

The bullet points are related to elements of the specification found on page 15 of the Year 1/AS specification, so are included to help you structure your response. You need to address all of them.

Planning an Extended Question

It is important to spend about 10 minutes planning your response to this question. As practice, use the table below to plan a response to the question on the previous page. Some points have been made for you.

Consideration	Tide	Wonder Woman
• The similarities and differences in how stereotypes are used in the products.		• Appeals to an audience to sell a product through the construction of recognisable social stereotypes.
• How the representations convey values and attitudes.	• The stereotype is narrow and patriarchal. • The role model for the time is questionable. • The advert constructs an image of unattainable domestic perfection.	
• How the representations convey attitudes and values.		• Women are as powerful as men. • The film genre has changed and adapted to reflect social change. • The protagonist suggests a change in audience perceptions of this genre.
• How far the representations reflect historical and cultural contexts.	• Reflects the 1950s post-war role of women. • Stereotypical construction of the female through visual codes and language reflects context.	

Section A Summary

Assessment Objective assessed	Concepts to be assessed	Products assessed	Typical command words
AO2 1 and 2 Apply knowledge and understanding of the theoretical framework of media to: • Analyse media products, including in relation to their contexts and through the use of academic theories. • Make judgements and draw conclusions.	Representation	Comparison of one set product and an unseen audio-visual or print product from any of the forms studied for this section.	Compare Compare how
AO2 1 Apply knowledge and understanding of the theoretical framework of media to analyse media products, including in relation to their contexts and through the use of academic theories.	Media Language	An unseen audio-visual or print resource from any of the forms studied for this section.	Explore how How does

Notes:

• Questions 1 and 2 will assess Representation and Media Language and can appear in either order on the paper according to the unseen form.

• The Media Language question will always assess AO2 1.

• The Representation question will always assess AO2 1 and 2.

• Question 1 will always relate to an unseen audio-visual resource.

• Question 2 will always relate to an unseen print resource.

• Comparison of set products from the same form or from different forms may be required.

• Reference to relevant contexts will be required for the representation question.

Top Revision Tip

Structuring a response

• Use subject-specific terminology including vocabulary related to the media form as well as that related to concepts.

• Structure paragraphs to create a sustained line of argument, this is particularly important for the higher tariff questions. The final sentence of one paragraph should link to the starting sentence of the next paragraph.

• Use connectives to construct more complex sentences.

• Support your points with specific examples.

• Avoid generalisations and description.

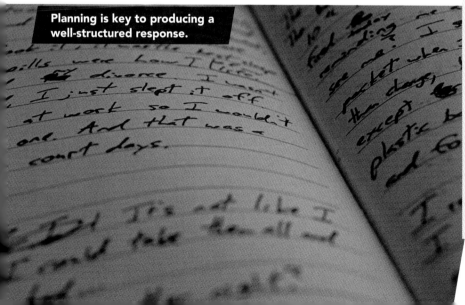

Planning is key to producing a well-structured response.

Link

Further information on approaching Section B of the examination and example questions is available on pages 251–254 of the Year 1/AS student book.

Section B: Investigating Media Industries and Audiences

Reminder

- This section is worth 25 marks.
- It assesses only AO1.
- The focus is Media Industries and Audiences, assessed in relation to two of the forms studied for this section: advertising, film, newspapers, radio and video games.
- There will be two questions in Section B.
- **Question 3** will assess Media Industries. It will be a stepped question assessing knowledge and understanding of media industries in relation to one of the forms you have studied.
- **Question 4** will assess Audiences. It will be a stepped question assessing knowledge and understanding of audiences in relation to one of the forms you have studied. This will be different from the form used in Question 3.

Checklist of key points

- ⊘ There are no unseen products in this section of the examination paper.
- ⊘ In this section you are not required to textually analyse the set products; the focus is on the products as examples of the related media industries and audiences.
- ⊘ Advertising in only studied in relation to Audiences.
- ⊘ Film is only studied in relation to Media Industries.
- ⊘ Contemporary and emerging media in relation to the set product should also be considered to enhance understanding.
- ⊘ Some of the questions will be low tariff, specifically assessing knowledge or knowledge and understanding. You should not spend too long on these questions.
- ⊘ In one of the questions in Section B you will be rewarded for drawing together your knowledge and understanding from across the full course of study, including different areas of the theoretical framework and media contexts. You will be informed of this on the examination paper.

Film is only studied in relation to Media Industries.

In Section B you are required to demonstrate your understanding of the radio industry and audiences.

Component 1 Revision Checklist Section B

Apply it!

9.5 Tick the 'Done' box once you have revised each of the topics and are happy that you understand it.

Topic	Areas to revise	Done
General	• Subject-specific terminology appropriate to the form, for example video games, and the concept, for example Media Industries. • Analytical terminology. • Relevant contexts appropriate to the form.	
Advertising	• Audience issues in relation to *Tide*. • Audience issues in relation to *WaterAid*. • Planning and writing answers to advertising audience questions.	
Film	• Media Industry issues in relation to *Straight Outta Compton*. • Planning and writing answers to film industry questions.	
Newspapers	• Media Industry issues in relation to the *Daily Mirror*. • Audience issues in relation to the *Daily Mirror*. • Planning and writing answers to newspaper industry questions (2018 examination). • Planning and writing answers to newspaper audience questions.	
Radio	• Media Industry issues in relation to *Late Night Woman's Hour*. • Audience issues in relation to *Late Night Woman's Hour*. • Planning and writing answers to radio industry questions (SAMS). • Planning and writing answers to radio audience questions.	
Video games	• Media Industry issues in relation to *Assassin's Creed III: Liberation*. • Audience issues in relation to *Assassin's Creed III: Liberation*. • Planning and writing answers to video games industry questions. • Planning and writing answers to video games audience questions (SAMS and 2018 examination).	
Theoretical perspectives	• Media Industries: Power and media industries (including Curran and Seaton). • Audiences: Media effects (including Bandura): Video games, Advertising. • Cultivation theory (including Gerbner): Advertising, Newspapers. • Reception theory (including Hall): all forms.	

Top Revision Tip

For assessment from 2021 the Year 1/AS film product will be *Black Panther*.

As part of your revision programme, practise writing examination questions under timed conditions.

Deconstructing the Questions: AS Examination 2018, Section B

Question 3 is a stepped question, but the number of steps may differ.

(a) Name the organisation that owns the *Daily Mirror*.

(b) Identify two ways in which newspapers are distributed.

(c) Briefly explain an advantage of **one** of these ways.

(d) Explain how political contexts affect the newspaper industry. Refer to the *Daily Mirror* to support your points.

Question 3(d) responses

Following is an extract from a candidate's response to Question 3 (d) (2018). The complete answer was placed in Band 5 because it fulfils the criteria from the marking scheme:

- Excellent, detailed and accurate knowledge and understanding of political contexts and their effect on the newspaper industry.
- Detailed reference to the set newspaper to support points.

A newspaper's primary purpose is to deliver information, although this can be influenced by the political standing of the newspaper which is more evident in the editorial and opinion pieces. Newspapers report the news of the day but also operate political bias and the newspaper's readers will have expectations of how stories will be treated.

The ownership of the newspaper is also important in terms of how news stories are represented as the views and ideology of the owner may be apparent in the newspaper.

Tabloid newspapers tend to make their political allegiance more explicit than broadsheet newspapers. The Daily Mirror, for example is a left-wing popular newspaper so the stories will appeal to a left-wing readership.

For example, the issue of the Daily Mirror published before the EU referendum in 2016 clearly states a political view, 'vote remain tomorrow'. It also uses lexis to overtly criticise the right-wing government 'the most divisive, vile and unpleasant political campaign in living memory', clearly suggesting its opposition to this party. The inner pages and the editorial further reinforce this view. The front page image conforms to Barthes' semiotic theory employing the iconography of blue skies and hands holding up a 'Future' sign symbolising the result of a positive outcome in order to persuade the reader to vote to remain.

Apply it!

9.7 Annotate the Band 5 response on the previous page in different colours, highlighting where this response:

- demonstrates understanding of the newspaper industry
- demonstrates understanding of political contexts and their effect on the newspaper product
- uses subject-specific terminology
- draws together knowledge from across the full course of study.

Apply it!

9.8 Using this question and the specific edition of the *Daily Mirror* you have studied in class, write a 3(d) response aiming to target all aspects of the Band 5 criteria.

Apply it!

9.9 Using what you understand of the requirements for this question, read the extract below from the Band 3 response and suggest:

1. What the candidate does successfully.

2. What they could have done to improve the response.

The following extract from a response was awarded a mark in Band 3 as it fulfils the following criteria:

- Satisfactory, generally accurate knowledge and understanding political contexts and their effect on the newspaper industry, although this may lack development.
- Appropriate reference to the set newspaper to support points.

Newspapers like the Daily Mirror consistently maintain showing their political views through their articles. This could help to increase the sales as the dominant ideology would relate to the views the newspaper is portraying and their readers.

For example, the Daily Mirror front page with the headline 'You Are Not Welcome Here, Mr President' suggests that the paper is anti-Trump and does not support the Republican party views in America.
A binary opposite between the UK and Trump is created and the image used is unflattering.

This particular article had a large amount of interest as it mirrored the thoughts of many of the readers of the newspaper meaning it was their preferred reading in Hall's reception theory.

Question 4

Assesses AO1a and 1b: Demonstrate knowledge and understanding of the theoretical framework of media.

Question 4(b)

The command word relates to the AO indicating a knowledge and understanding focus.

The question has two stems: one with the audience focus and one indicating the product to be referred to in support of points made about audiences.

The word 'interact' refines the focus of the question and is relevant to the video game form.

The concept focus is audience.

Explain how audiences interact with video games. Refer to *Assassin's Creed III: Liberation* to support your points. **[8 marks]**

This is a question with a lower tariff, indicating that you should spend approximately 8 minutes answering it, making a range of points demonstrating specific knowledge and understanding.

Apply it!

9.10 Using the above Question 4(b), write a response, spending approximately 8 minutes on it.

Section B Summary

Section B: Understanding Media Industries and Audiences (45 marks)				
Question	Assessment Objective assessed	Concepts to be assessed	Products assessed	Typical command words
3: stepped question	**AO1 1 and 2:** Demonstrate knowledge and understanding of: the theoretical framework of media contexts of media and their influence on media products and processes	Media Industries	Set products for: • Film • Newspapers • Radio • Video games, excluding advertising product	Briefly explain How have/Explain how What is/Identify Explain how/ Explain why
4: stepped question	**AO1 1 and 2:** Demonstrate knowledge and understanding of: the theoretical framework of media contexts of media and their influence on media products and processes	Audiences	Set products for: • Newspapers • Radio • Video games, excluding film product	Explain how/ Explain why How do/Explain how

Notes:

• Two different forms will be assessed in Section B.

• The questions will always assess AO1 – demonstration of knowledge/knowledge and understanding/ understanding of contexts.

• The command words will change according to the focus and mark tariff of the question.

• The questions will always be stepped, but the number of steps and mark allocation may differ.

• Section B will always include an opportunity for learners to draw together their knowledge and understanding from across the full course of study.

Designing Your Own Questions

Apply it!

9.11 Using what you have learned in this chapter, design a question for Section A or B, using the following format to help you.

2. **Label** your question with:
- command word
- Assessment Objective assessed
- concept being assessed
- product(s) being discussed
- tariff – what does this indicate that the learner is being asked to do?

1. **Write** your question here.

3. **Indicative content**

What key points would you be looking for in a response to this question?

4. **Evaluation**

Show your question to someone else and ask them to comment on:
- strengths
- weaknesses
- elements that could be improved.

Apply it!

9.12 Use the above grid to design a range of possible questions that could be asked in Section A or B of Component 1. Consider:
- the appropriate wording of the question to target what is being assessed
- if it can be answered – writing the indicative content will help here
- using the correct command words
- addressing the appropriate Assessment Objectives.

⌄ Component 2: Investigating Media Forms and Products

Link

Further information on approaching the Component 2 examination and example questions can be found on pages 255–261 of the Year 1/AS student book.

Reminder

- This examination assesses your knowledge and understanding of Media Language, Representation, Media Industries, Audiences and Media contexts.
- You will be assessed on your use of relevant theories or theoretical approaches and relevant subject-specific terminology.
- The paper is comprised of **three sections** – Section A: Television, Section B: Magazines, Section C: Online media.
- Each section is worth **20 marks**.
- Each section will feature either one **two-part** question or one **extended response** question.

Top Revision Tip

As with Component 1, use the SAMs and past papers to help guide your revision.

Interpreting the Question and Understanding Assessment Objectives

It is important to take some time in the exam to make sure that you understand what the question is asking and what you are required to do. A basic understanding of the two main AOs that the exam addresses can be useful in this regard:

- **AO1** requires you to *demonstrate* knowledge and understanding.
- **AO2** requires you to *apply* knowledge and understanding.

These two assessment objectives are further subdivided into the following strands:

AO1 1	Demonstrate knowledge and understanding of the theoretical framework of the media.
AO1 2	Demonstrate knowledge and understanding of contexts of media and their influence on media products and processes.
AO2 1	Apply knowledge and understanding of the theoretical framework of media to analyse media products, including in relation to their contexts and through the use of academic theories.
AO2 2	Apply knowledge and understanding of the theoretical framework of media to make judgements and draw conclusions.

The following table shows some of the command words and question stems that are commonly used to target the different Assessment Objectives.

Assessment Objectives		Command words and question stems
AO1 1 and 2	Demonstrate knowledge and understanding.	Define Explain
AO2 1	Apply knowledge and understanding to analyse media products.	Analyse Explore
AO2 2	Apply knowledge and understanding to make judgements and draw conclusions.	To what extent …? How far …? How important …?

Some questions may address more than one Assessment Objective. For example, questions that require you to make judgements and draw conclusions (AO2 2) will generally address another AO in addition to this. They may require you to analyse a media product, for instance, (AO2 1) or to demonstrate your knowledge and understanding of either the theoretical framework (AO1 1) or the influence of media contexts (AO1 2).

Look at the following questions from the SAMs provided by the awarding body. In each case, make a note of the command word that has been used and try to identify the Assessment Objective(s) that the question is targeting.

Specimen question	Command word/question stem	Assessment Objective
To what extent does the set episode of *Life on Mars/Humans/The Jinx* conform to Todorov's theory of narrative equilibrium?		
With reference to the front cover of the set edition of *Woman/Woman's Realm/Vogue*, explain the difference between denotation and connotation.		
How far do the representations in the set edition of *Woman* (1964)/*Woman's Realm* (1965)/*Vogue* (1965) reflect social and cultural contexts?		
Explain the strategies that the producers of blogs and vlogs use to attract their audiences. Refer to *PointlessBlog/Zoella* in your response.		

Exploring Past Papers

Looking at past papers, SAMs and marking schemes is a useful way of developing your understanding of the requirements of the exam.

Using the AS Level Component 2 paper from Summer 2018 as an example, the following pages show you how to deconstruct different types of exam question. This will give you a greater understanding of how to approach the tasks that you will be required to undertake in the exam.

Section A: Television

The following questions are taken from Section A of the Summer 2018 Component 2 exam.

Top Revision Tip

Past papers and SAMs can be found in the Media Studies section of the Eduqas website.

Top Revision Tip

Highlighting or underlining the keywords in the question will help you to identify the most important aspects of the task.

Option 1: *Life on Mars*

0 1 (a) Explain what you understand by intertextuality. Refer to the set episode of *Life on Mars* to support your response. **[5]**

(b) To what extent does the set episode of *Life on Mars* support Steve Neale's suggestion that genres change over time? **[15]**

Or,

Option 2: *Humans*

0 2 (a) Explain what you understand by intertextuality. Refer to the set episode of *Humans* to support your response. **[5]**

(b) To what extent does the set episode of *Humans* support Steve Neale's suggestion that genres change over time? **[15]**

Or,

Option 3: *The Jinx*

0 3 (a) Explain what you understand by intertextuality. Refer to the set episode of *The Jinx* to support your response. **[5]**

(b) To what extent does the set episode of *The Jinx* support Steve Neale's suggestion that genres change over time? **[15]**

Section A (Part a) (2018): Deconstructing the Question

Section A of the 2018 Component 2 exam features a two-part question comprised of one short answer question, which is worth 5 marks, as well as a 15-mark question. We will now look at each part of the question. The key elements of the question have been highlighted and annotated to give you a clearer understanding of the requirements of the task.

The command word tells you what you need to do in order to answer the question. In this case, you are required to **explain** a key concept. This requires you to demonstrate knowledge and understanding of the theoretical framework (**AO1 1**).

The question is assessing your knowledge and understanding of **intertextuality**. This is a specific aspect of media language that the specification requires you to study in relation to television (see the revision checklist on page 169 of Chapter 5).

Explain what you understand by intertextuality. Refer to the set episode of *Life on Mars/Humans/The Jinx* to support your response. [5]

This question asks you to **support your response** by *referring* to the set product you have studied. There is a slightly different emphasis in questions such as this, which assess knowledge and understanding (AO1) rather than analysis (AO2), as the set product is simply a vehicle for you to demonstrate your knowledge and understanding.

The number in brackets at the end of the question tells you how many marks the question carries. This should dictate the length of your response and how long you should spend on each part of the question. In this case, there are 5 marks available so you should spend significantly less time on this part of the question.

Section A (Part a) (2018): Assessment Criteria and Sample Responses

Here is the assessment grid for the sample question shown on page 266:

Band	AO1 1a and 1b Demonstrate knowledge and understanding of the theoretical framework of media.
5	**5 marks** • Excellent, detailed and accurate knowledge and understanding of intertextuality • The concept of intertextuality is precisely explained and clearly exemplified with detailed reference to the set episode
4	**4 marks** • Good, accurate knowledge and understanding of intertextuality • The concept of intertextuality is generally well-explained and exemplified in a secure manner with appropriate reference to the set episode
3	**3 marks** • Satisfactory knowledge and understanding of intertextuality • The concept of intertextuality is fairly well-explained and reasonably well-exemplified with some reference to the set episode, although there may be some minor inaccuracies or inconsistencies
2	**2 marks** • Basic knowledge and understanding of intertextuality • Explanation of intertextuality lacks clarity, demonstrating only a basic or partial understanding. Exemplification through reference to the set episode is likely to be basic or partially flawed
1	**1 mark** • Minimal knowledge and understanding of intertextuality • There is a significant degree of inaccuracy, demonstrating a very limited understanding of intertextuality. Exemplification is likely to be limited or significantly flawed
	0 marks • Response not worthy of credit

As well as the assessment grid, the marking scheme also includes the following guidance:

> *Responses in the higher bands are likely to demonstrate knowledge and understanding of the function of intertextuality (e.g., the way that it is used to convey meanings).*
>
> *Responses in Band 3 are likely to offer a straightforward definition of the term without explaining its use or function.*
>
> *In the lower bands, understanding of intertextuality is likely to be less secure.*

Top Revision Tip

While the assessment grids included in the marking scheme are tailored according to the particular requirements, AOs and topic areas of each individual question, the descriptors used for each of the five bands tend to be fairly consistent. You may find it useful to highlight the keywords associated with responses in the top bands, as this will help you to understand the qualities that the examiners are looking for.

Sample Response 1

The following is an example of a Band 3 response to Question 1(a) on page 265.

This meets the criteria for a Band 3 response as the candidate demonstrates a 'satisfactory knowledge and understanding of intertextuality'. In order to access the higher bands, the candidate would need to offer more than a straightforward definition of the term, explaining its use or function instead.

Intertextuality is when one text refers to another.

For example, in one scene in 'Life on Mars' we see a film poster of 'High Noon' on the wall of Gene Hunt's office.

The candidate demonstrates their knowledge and understanding of intertextuality by identifying a relevant example from the set episode. However, they could have developed this further by briefly explaining how or why the intertextual reference is used in the programme.

Sample Response 2

The following is an example of a Band 5 response to the same question. Notice the differences compared with the previous response. Look at the annotations and think about what enables this response to take it into the higher band.

The key concept of intertextuality is neatly and precisely defined in the first two sentences. What really differentiates this response from the previous one is the way in which the candidate goes on to explain the purpose or function of intertextual references in the second paragraph. It is this that enables the response to access the higher bands.

The reference to the set episode is more detailed compared with the first response. Crucially, the candidate again demonstrates knowledge and understanding of the function and purpose of the intertextual reference that is used.

Intertextuality refers to the relationship between different texts. It occurs when one text refers or makes allusion to another.

Intertextual references can have a variety of different functions, but they generally add to the meaning of the text in which the reference appears. For instance, an intertextual reference may encourage the audience to make a preferred reading of a particular character or scene.

For example, the poster of the western movie 'High Noon' that can be seen on the wall of Gene Hunt's office in the set episode of 'Life on Mars' has an important intertextual function; this aspect of the mise-en-scène suggests that Hunt sees himself as a sheriff-like figure, imposing law and order and administering justice in the 'Wild West' of 1970s Britain.

The candidate also demonstrates their understanding of the theoretical framework by making appropriate reference to relevant critical terminology. The reference to the preferred reading, for example, shows knowledge and understanding of Hall's reception theory, while the reference to mise-en-scène shows knowledge and understanding of another aspect of media language. Importantly, though, these terms are not just included randomly; they are entirely relevant as they help the candidate to answer the question.

Section A (Part b) (2018): Deconstructing the Question

Shown below is the second part of the Television question from the Summer 2018 Component 2 exam. Again, the key elements of the question have been highlighted and annotated to give you a clearer understanding of the requirements of the task.

The question stem, which uses the phrase '**To what extent ...?**', tells you that you will need to make judgements and draw conclusions (**AO2 2**) in your response.

This question requires you to analyse **the set episode** of the television product you have studied in relation to Neale's theory of genre. Therefore, you will need to find specific aspects of the set episode that either support or challenge Neale's suggestion that genres change over time.

To what extent does the set episode of *Life on Mars/Humans/The Jinx* support Steve Neale's suggestion that genres change over time? [15]

The focus of this question is on a specific aspect of **Steve Neale's theory of genre**. It is assessing your ability to use academic theory to analyse your set television product (**AO2 1**).

As this is a 15-mark question, you should spend approximately three times as long on this as you would on a 5-marker. Including planning and proofreading time, you should spend about 30 minutes on this question.

Quickfire Revision

9.5 Look carefully at the extract from the assessment grid. What particular skills and abilities does it suggest you will need to demonstrate in your response?

The following extract is taken from the assessment grid for this question showing the criteria for a Band 5 response.

Band	AO2 1 and 2
	Apply knowledge and understanding of the theoretical framework of media to:
	• **analyse media products, including in relation to their contexts and through the use of academic theories**
	• **make judgements and draw conclusions.**
5	**13–15 marks**
	• Excellent, detailed and accurate application of knowledge and understanding of the theoretical framework to analyse the set product
	• Analysis of the set episode is perceptive and insightful
	• Judgements and conclusions regarding the extent to which the television product supports Neale's suggestion that genres change over time are perceptive and fully supported with detailed reference to specific aspects of the set episode

Apply it!

9.13 Using this structure as a guide, write a detailed plan showing how you would answer this question. Make a note of the key points you would make in each paragraph and the specific evidence from the set episode you would use to support your argument.

Section A (Part b) (2018): Planning and Structuring a Response

While there is no set formula that you have to follow when writing an exam response, you may find the following model provides a useful structure that can easily be adapted to suit the requirements of different types of question.

Paragraph	What to do and what to include
Introductory paragraph	There are various ways of writing an effective introduction. The most important thing you need to do is engage with the question and show that you understand what it is asking. Consider doing one or more of the following: • Briefly summarise relevant aspects of Neale's theory and introduce the genre of your set product. • Provide a quick overview of the ground your response will cover. • Briefly outline the basic premise or angle of your argument.
Paragraph 2	Make your first key **point** (e.g., outline one of the ways in which your set product either supports or challenges Neale's suggestion that genres change over time). Use **evidence** from the set episode to support and illustrate this point. **Explain** how this aspect of the set episode supports or challenges Neale's theory (provide analysis).
Paragraph 3	Make your next key **point** (e.g., outline another way in which your set product either supports or challenges Neale's suggestion that genres change over time). As before, use **evidence** from the set episode to support and illustrate your point. Again, **explain** how this aspect of the set episode supports or challenges Neale's theory (provide analysis).
Paragraph 4	Here, if you have enough time, you could either make another point, following the same structure as the previous two paragraphs, or you could introduce a **counter-argument**. For example, if you have previously discussed ways in which the set episode *supports* Neale's theory, you could briefly explore how a certain aspect of the episode might *challenge* the claim that genres change over time.
Concluding paragraph	Summarise your argument and explain your overall conclusion, ensuring that you have answered the question. Your conclusion may be clear-cut (e.g., overall, the set episode either *does* or *does not* support Neale's suggestion) or it may be more nuanced (e.g., the set episode supports Neale's suggestion *to a certain extent*).

Section B: Magazines

The following questions are taken from Section B of the Summer 2018 Component 2 exam.

Option 1: *Woman*

| 0 | 4 | To what extent does the set edition of *Woman* magazine target a particular audience? Explore specific aspects of the set product in your response. [20]

Or,

Option 2: *Woman's Realm*

| 0 | 5 | To what extent does the set edition of *Woman's Realm* magazine target a particular audience? Explore specific aspects of the set product in your response. [20]

Or,

Option 3: *Vogue*

| 0 | 6 | To what extent does the set edition of *Vogue* magazine target a particular audience? Explore specific aspects of the set product in your response. [20]

Section B: Deconstructing the Question

Again, breaking the question down into its component parts can help to clarify the requirements of the assessment task. The key elements of the question have been highlighted and annotated to give you a clearer understanding of the requirements of the task.

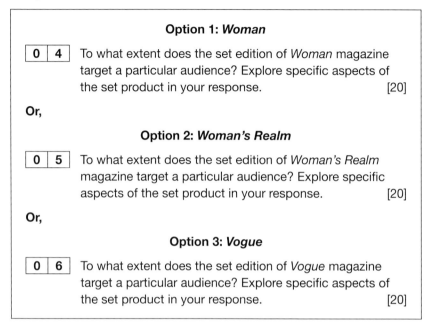

This is another example of a '**To what extent** …?' type question. Again, the question stem tells you that you will be required to make judgements and draw conclusions (**AO2 2**) in your response.

The specific aspect of the theoretical framework that this question is focusing on is **audience targeting**.

To what extent does the set edition of *Woman/Woman's Realm/ Vogue* magazine target a particular audience? **Explore** specific aspects of the set product in your response. [20]

The command word '**Explore**' is often used in questions that assess **analytical skills** and the ability to *apply* (**AO2**) rather than simply *demonstrate* (AO1) knowledge and understanding.

The number of marks available tells you that this is an **extended response question**.

According to the marking scheme, this means that: 'In order to achieve the highest marks, a response needs to construct and develop a sustained line of reasoning that is coherent, relevant, substantiated and logically structured.'

Section B (2018): Planning a Response

Here are the key steps you will need to take when planning a response to this question:

Step 1: Decide on the angle of your argument. Consider which of the following statements most accurately reflects the case you want to argue:

- The set edition of the magazine *does* target a particular audience.
- The set edition of the magazine *does not* target a particular audience.
- The set edition of the magazine targets a particular audience *to a certain extent*.

Step 2: Decide on the evidence that you are going to use to support your argument. Which particular aspects of the set edition of your magazine will you discuss?

Use the following table to identify aspects of the set magazine (e.g., particular images, features, articles or coverlines) that you could explore in your response.

Aspect of the magazine	Extent to which it targets a particular audience

The front cover is one aspect of the magazine that you may find useful to explore.

Step 3: Decide on your conclusion. Think about how you can bring the separate strands of your argument together.

Rather than simply repeating the points you have already made, consider whether you can situate those points within a broader context or put them in a different perspective.

Discussing the wider significance of your findings is often an effective way of concluding an essay.

- What do your findings tell us about the magazine industry, for example?

- Has there been any discernible change in approaches to audience targeting since the set edition of your magazine was published?

Section C: Online Media

Shown below are the Section C questions on online media from the Summer 2018 Component 2 paper.

Option 1: *PointlessBlog*

| 0 | 7 | Explain how representations of identity are constructed in blogs and vlogs. Refer to relevant theories and *PointlessBlog* in your response.   [20] |

Or,

Option 2: *Zoella*

| 0 | 8 | Explain how representations of identity are constructed in blogs and vlogs. Refer to relevant theories and *Zoella* in your response.   [20] |

Section C: Deconstructing the Question

Look again at the way in which we have annotated previous exam questions from the Summer 2018 Component 2 paper and try to do the same with this question:

> **Explain how representations of identity are constructed in blogs and vlogs. Refer to relevant theories and *PointlessBlog/Zoella* in your response.**   **[20]**

Use the following questions as a guide:

- What is the key command word in this question and which particular Assessment Objective do you think the question is targeting?

- What is the conceptual focus of the question? Which particular area of the theoretical framework does it address?

- Is this an extended response question or a shorter answer question? How can you tell?

Take it Further

9.2 Try writing your own response to this question. Think about particular videos or blog entries that you could refer to in order to demonstrate your knowledge and understanding of the ways in which representations of identity are constructed in blogs and vlogs.

As well as considering self-representation, you may also find it useful to discuss the way in which representations of gender are constructed in your set online product. Stuart Hall's theory of representation and his points about stereotyping could be applied here.

- What does the question tell you that you need to include in your answer?

Section C: Annotating a Sample Response

Shown below is a short extract from a sample response to the question on the previous page. Annotate the response, highlighting any examples you can find where the candidate has done the following:

- Referred to relevant theories.
- Used subject-specific terminology.
- Demonstrated knowledge and understanding of the theoretical framework.
- Used key terms from the question.
- Referred to relevant supporting examples from the set product.

Blogs and vlogs provide content creators such as Zoella with a space in which they can construct their own representations. While part of the appeal of these 'new' media forms is the way in which they appear to offer unmediated access to those who feature in them, it is important to remember that the representations we see are always constructed in some way.

As Stuart Hall points out, representation is 'the production of meaning through language'. Therefore, when analysing the representation of identity in blogs and vlogs, it is important to think about how those representations have been constructed through particular aspects of media language such as visual and technical codes. Iconography and mise-en-scène have a significant role to play in this regard. For example, it is noticeable that many of Zoella's beauty vlogs such as 'My Everyday Makeup Routine' are filmed in ordinary, everyday spaces such as her bedroom. This helps to construct a representation of her as the ordinary 'girl-next-door' – a figure that the target audience can easily identify with and relate to.

To many of her fans and subscribers, Zoella also functions as a role model and an aspirational figure. Gauntlett's suggestion that the media provide us with tools and resources that we use to construct our own identities is particularly relevant here, as the feedback provided in the comments section on blogs such as 'Anxiety – the Update' clearly shows that the representations offered in these online spaces have a significant impact on users' own identities. Importantly, these representations are constructed through processes of selection and combination as Zoella chooses which aspects of her day-to-day life to reveal or disclose, becoming the narrator and gatekeeper of her own online identity.

Designing Your Own Questions

Using what you have learned in this chapter, design a series of exam-style questions for each of the three sections of the Component 2 exam – Section A: Television, Section B: Magazines; and Section C: Online media.

When writing each question, make sure you do the following:

- Identify a particular aspect of the theoretical framework that you want to assess. This could be:
  - one of the points from the revision checklists in Chapter 5 (see pages 169, 176–177, 180, 186, 192, 195–196, 201, 206, 213, 218, 222 and 225)
  - one of the required theories (see the table on page 231 of Chapter 6)
  - a particular context (see the table on page 231 of Chapter 6).

- Think about the skills or AOs you want to assess. In particular, consider whether you want to assess the ability to *demonstrate* knowledge and understanding (**AO1**) or the ability to *apply* knowledge and understanding (**AO2**).

- Include a command word or question stem that is relevant to the AO being assessed (e.g., explain, explore, analyse, to what extent … etc.).

- Indicate the set product that should be discussed or referred to.

- Decide how many marks the question should carry (i.e., should it be worth 5, 15 or 20 marks?).

Take it Further

9.3 Once you have composed your exam-style questions, have a go at writing an essay plan for each of them. Then try writing a full exam response to one or two of the questions under timed conditions.

Top Revision Tip

The marking schemes for past papers, which are available to download from the Eduqas website, include indicative content for each of the questions on the exam paper. Although this indicative content is not prescriptive and should not be regarded as a checklist of material that *must* be included in an answer, it provides a useful insight into the kind of material that *could* be included.

When you are creating your own exam-style questions, you may find it useful to do something similar, giving an indication of the kind of material that you might expect to find in the response.

10 Revising Theoretical Approaches

Top Revision Tip

Remember that you don't have to apply every theory to each media product that you have studied. For example, you only need to consider Todorov's theory of narratology in relation to your set television product. You can check which theories are required for particular media forms and products by looking at the assessment overview in Chapters 4 and 6. However, the more you practise applying the theories to different media products the better your understanding of the theories is likely to be.

Here are the main theoretical approaches and named theorists that you will need to revise.

Media Language Theories

Semiotics: Roland Barthes

Semiotics is the study of signs and meanings. As part of your revision, you should make sure that you are familiar with the following aspects of Barthes' theory of semiotics:

- The idea that texts communicate their meanings through a process of signification.

- The idea that signs can function at the level of denotation, which involves the 'literal' or common-sense meaning of the sign, and at the level of connotation, which involves the meanings associated with or suggested by the sign.

- The idea that constructed meanings can come to seem self-evident, achieving the status of myth through a process of naturalisation.

Narratology: Tzvetan Todorov

Narratology is the study of narrative. As part of your revision, you should make sure that you are familiar with the following aspects of Todorov's theory of narratology:

- The idea that all narratives share a basic structure that involves a movement from one state of equilibrium to another.

- The idea that these two states of equilibrium are separated by a period of imbalance or disequilibrium.

- The idea that the way in which narratives are resolved can have particular ideological significance.

Genre Theory: Steve Neale

Genre theory is concerned with the way in which media products are classified and categorised. As part of your revision, you should make sure that you are familiar with the following aspects of Neale's theory of genre:

- The idea that genres may be dominated by repetition, but they are also marked by difference, variation and change.

- The idea that genres change, develop and vary, as they borrow from and overlap with one another.

- The idea that genres exist within specific economic, institutional and industrial contexts.

Representation Theories

Theory of Representation: Stuart Hall

As part of your revision, you should make sure that you are familiar with the following aspects of Hall's theory of representation:

- The idea that representation is the production of meaning through language, with language defined in its broadest sense as a system of signs.
- The idea that the relationship between concepts and signs is governed by codes.
- The idea that stereotyping, as a form of representation, reduces people to a few simple characteristics or traits.
- The idea that stereotyping tends to occur where there are inequalities of power, as subordinate or excluded groups are constructed as different or 'other' (e.g., through ethnocentrism).

Theory of Identity: David Gauntlett

As part of your revision, you should make sure that you are familiar with the following aspects of Gauntlett's theory of identity:

- The idea that the media provide us with 'tools' or resources that we use to construct our identities.
- The idea that while, in the past, the media tended to convey singular, straightforward messages about ideal types of male and female identities, the media today offer us a more diverse range of stars, icons and characters from whom we may pick and mix different ideas.

Industry Theories

Power and Media Industries Theories: James Curran and Jean Seaton

As part of your revision, you should make sure that you are familiar with the following aspects of Curran and Seaton's theory of power and media industries:

- The idea that the media is controlled by a small number of companies primarily driven by the logic of profit and power.
- The idea that media concentration generally limits or inhibits variety, creativity and quality.
- The idea that more socially diverse patterns of ownership help to create the conditions for more varied and adventurous media productions.

Top Revision Tip

Creating flashcards can be a useful starting point when it comes to revising the required theories. However, it is always important to think about how the theories can be applied to media forms, products and contexts rather than just learning them in isolation. Try to think about the theories as a set of analytical tools that can help you to explore and question rather than just a set of facts to be learnt.

Reminder

Remember that the theories listed here are those that are required for the AS Level Media Studies course.
If you are taking the A Level, there are additional theories that you will need to consider. These additional theories are discussed in the Year 2/A Level student book and the Year 2/A Level revision guide.

Audience Theories

Media Effects: Albert Bandura

Media effects theories are concerned with the effects that the media may have on audiences. As part of your revision, you should make sure that you are familiar with the following aspects of Albert Bandura's social learning theory:

- The idea that the media can implant ideas into the mind of the audience directly.
- The idea that audiences acquire attitudes, emotional responses and new styles of conduct through modelling.
- The idea that media representations of transgressive behaviour, such as violence or physical aggression, can lead audience members to imitate those forms of behaviour.

Cultivation Theory: George Gerbner

As part of your revision, you should make sure that you are familiar with the following aspects of Gerbner's cultivation theory:

- The idea that exposure to repeated patterns of representation over long periods of time can shape and influence the way in which people perceive the world around them (i.e. cultivating particular views and opinions).
- The idea that cultivation reinforces mainstream values (dominant ideologies).

Reception Theory: Stuart Hall

As part of your revision, you should make sure that you are familiar with the following aspects of Hall's reception theory:

- The idea that communication is a process involving encoding by producers and decoding by audiences.
- The idea that there are three hypothetical positions from which messages and meanings may be decoded:
  - the dominant-hegemonic position: the encoder's intended meaning (the preferred reading) is fully understood and accepted
  - the negotiated position: the legitimacy of the encoder's message is acknowledged in general terms, although the message is adapted or negotiated to better fit the decoder's own individual experiences or context
  - the oppositional position: the encoder's message is understood, but the decoder disagrees with it, reading it in a contrary or oppositional way.

Answers to Quickfire Questions

1 The Media Studies Specification

1.1 Exploring products alongside the set products familiarises you with the codes and conventions of the chosen form. Also, for Component 1 Section A, you will be required to analyse two unseen products from the forms studied for this section.

1.2 Social and cultural contexts refers to the values and attitudes related to society at the time in which the product was produced. This will have an impact on the representations, themes, as well as cultural influences such as genres.

1.3 In relation to Media Industries you will have covered ownership and funding, including economic factors, regulation, the impact of technology and global production and distribution.

1.4 An extended response question requires learners to construct and develop a sustained line of reasoning which is coherent, relevant, substantiated and logically structured.

1.5 A stepped question is one that is split up into different stages or 'steps'. The marks for each step gradually increase along with the mark tariff.

1.6 In Component 2 you are required to study the set forms and products in detail applying all the aspects of the theoretical framework to the products studied.

1.7 One specification requirement covered is to study products from different historical periods. In Component 2 this is addressed through the study of a magazine produced before 1970. Another requirement is the effect of social, cultural and historical contexts on the representations constructed by the magazines. A further example is how media language and representations convey values, attitudes and beliefs.

2 Revising the Media Studies Theoretical Framework

2.1 Age, gender, ethnicity, culture and the context in which the sign or code appears can affect the audience response.

2.2 The code of technique is the way in which the product is constructed to convey a particular meaning. For example, the use of soft focus and muted colours in a fragrance advertisement suggests the smell of the perfume and constructs a romantic atmosphere.

2.3 For example, a technical code could be the use of close-up shots as a convention of charity advertising campaigns. It forces the audience to engage with the subject however uncomfortable this might be.

2.4 Editing is a process of selection and combination; what is included and what is left out contributes to the construction of meanings. The way in which different shots are edited together creates a narrative and communicates messages to an audience. Other aspects of editing, for example adding sound to create atmosphere, will also construct meanings.

2.5 Audiences may become familiar with the terminology used in particular media products and will feel superior if they understand this vocabulary. For example, regular viewers of crime dramas become familiar with the lexis and may even predict the dialogue at a particular point in the narrative. The lexis used in a niche magazine involves a specific audience in the magazine's community.

2.6 A hybrid genre refers to a product that incorporates the conventions of more than one genre in order to maintain the interest of the audience. For example, some crime dramas also incorporate elements of the horror or science fiction genre.

2.7 The repertoire of elements includes: narrative, characters, iconography and setting, technical codes and audio codes.

2.8 Hall put forward the idea that stereotyping tends to occur where there are inequalities of power, as subordinate or excluded groups are constructed as different or 'other'.

2.9 Gauntlett suggested that while in the past the media tended to convey singular, straightforward messages about ideal types of male and female identities, the media today offers a more diverse range from which we can pick and mix different ideas.

2.10 The images, headlines and copy will have been carefully constructed and manipulated in order to convey a particular point of view with the purpose of persuading an audience.

2.11 In the blogs that are the set products for the Online Media section of Component 2.

2.12 Masculinity is the state of 'being a man', which changes as society changes. It is essentially what being a man means to a particular generation. This is then reflected in the media.

2.13 Newspapers, documentaries, music videos and radio podcasts are more likely to offer representations of issues and events.

2.14 A media product may encourage an audience through a headline or strapline in a newspaper or the introductory voiceover in a television documentary.

2.15 Opinion leaders refers to those in positions of power who aim to persuade an audience of their point of view. For example, newspaper editors and bloggers.

2.16 Curran and Seaton said that more socially diverse patterns of ownership help to create the conditions for more varied and adventurous media productions.

2.17 Demographic profiling is a simple way of categorising audiences, which does not explore the more complex reasons for consumer behaviour.

2.18 Demographic profiling is still used by the print and advertising industries. Advertisers use the information to determine where their products should be placed and it is a useful way for products, for example magazines, to inform potential advertisers of the target audience for their product.

2.19 The New York advertising agency Young and Rubicam first used psychographic profiling to categorise audiences.

2.20 The groups were based on motivational needs and included: Mainstreamers, Aspirers, Explorers, Succeeders and Reformers.

2.21 A newspaper will include content that reflects the opinions of its readers, for example through political bias or mode of address, in this way constructing a particular audience for the publication.

2.22 Hall suggested preferred, negotiated and oppositional readings.

2.23 Contexts are the aspects of the environment that impact upon the product at the time of its production, distribution and circulation, and as a result may affect the meaning.

2.24 The producer of a low-budget film made by an independent film company is under much greater constraints than that of a film made by a mainstream production company.

3 Component 1: Investigating the Media

3.1 *WaterAid* and the *Daily Mirror* have been studied in Section A in relation to political contexts.

3.2 Subject-specific terminology is the specific vocabulary that you must be able to employ when you are analysing media products. It is terminology related to the specific form you are studying, for example when studying your film product you will have used terms that are particular to film and will be different from terms used when discussing other media forms and products.

3.3 Media language refers to the elements used to communicate meaning to an audience, for example the codes and conventions of a particular genre.

3.4 Media processes are the ways in which media products are produced, and the decisions made by producers at each stage (planning, production, editing, etc.) that affect the finished product, as well as distribution, marketing, regulation, circulation and audience consumption.

3.5 Gender, age and ethnicity are all examples of social groups.

3.6 Audience responses to representations may be affected by factors such as: age, gender, ethnicity, socio-economic group, occupation, situated culture, regional/national identity, political beliefs, religious beliefs, etc.

3.7 A repertoire of elements is the key features that distinguish products from one genre or sub-genre.

3.8 An active audience is an audience who actively engages with the messages encoded in media products through the way in which they interpret and respond to those products.

3.9 A paradigm is a set of related signs the encoder can choose from in constructing a product, for example the set of colours or font styles the designer of an advert or film poster may choose from. In choosing one sign which encodes messages rather than another, a paradigmatic choice is made that will influence meaning.

3.10 A syntagm is a combination of signs that are linked together in order to convey meaning. For example, the elements of a film poster including images, fonts styles, language, etc. create a syntagm.

3.11 Intertextuality is when one text is used or referenced in another. In media products an example would be the use of memorable film scenes in an advertisement. The text used will resonate with the target audience.

3.12 The Representation question is a higher tariff question as it is an extended response question. It requires you to develop a sustained line of reasoning which is coherent, relevant, substantiated and logically structured.

3.13 The typical codes and conventions of charity campaigns include: shocking and emotive images, information about the issue presented in a dramatic way with possible use of hyperbole, celebrities directly addressing the audience and appealing for help (white saviour complex), statistics and vulnerable victims directly addressing the audience.

3.14 The use of technical effects, for example CGI, has made music videos more sophisticated. Technical codes and editing, including the use of graphics and animation, have made some examples of music videos highly cinematic in their production.

3.15 Star persona refers to those stars who establish an identity that develops beyond their ability to make music. This may be demonstrated through their personality and be evident across other media platforms, for example magazine interviews. Some stars are adept at changing their image and star persona as part of a marketing strategy and to keep audiences engaged.

3.16 If a band or artist plays an instrument then this establishes them as a serious musician. The inclusion of a performance element reinforces the musical skill of the band/artist. Their style of performance helps to establish their star persona, as well as helping to market them to a target audience.

3.17 Right wing refers to those with a more conservative, ethnocentric viewpoint. They believe in the free market and oppose socialism. They tend to support political parties such as the Conservative party and UKIP.
Left wing refers to people whose view is left of the centre in politics. They broadly believe that existing social inequalities must be addressed, have more liberal political views and tend to support the Labour party.

3.18 The *Daily Mirror* is a left-wing newspaper and explicitly supports the Labour party, and is critical of the Conservative party.

3.19 Newspapers mediate the news for their readers, which constructs a version of the truth but is not the same as real life. This may mean that they re-present the news story in a way that reflects the attitudes and beliefs of the paper and what they believe is the viewpoint of their readers. Consequently, newspapers will present issues and events in different ways.

3.20 The representation of issues and events in newspapers will be affected by the owner of the newspaper, the political leanings of the paper, the readers, and the attitudes and beliefs of the publication.

3.21 Dominant ideology refers to a set of values and beliefs that have broader social or cultural currency. This may be implicit, or, in the case of some tabloid-style newspapers, explicit.

3.22 For some newspapers, for example the *Daily Mirror*, the readership was made up of those who voted for and against Brexit. In order to avoid alienating this readership by explicitly giving a specific

viewpoint, the newspapers had to more careful about how they represented this ongoing event.

3.23 The editorial, the letters pages, political cartoons and any articles covering social or political issues may allow readers to explore the political orientation of the newspaper in closer detail.

3.24 A conglomerate is a large organisation that has interests spanning a number of different businesses or industries. For example, some film companies also have business interests in television, music and radio.

3.25 Vertical integration is a process whereby one company acquires another involved at a different level of the industry. For example, a production company that owns a distributor or retailer. This gives the company greater control over distribution and circulation.

3.26 Diversification is the expansion of a company's operations into new or different areas. For example, newspapers now have websites and apps as well as the traditional print product.

3.27 Emerging media refers to communication through digital technology and on new platforms with interactive elements, for example websites, social media sites, podcasts and apps.

3.28 The BBC is funded by the annual licence fee. At the time of writing, in November 2019, the cost of a TV licence is £154.50.

3.29 A newspaper may use the headline, central image and the way in which it re-presents the story giving a particular viewpoint, to construct an idea of the reader. The aim of the newspaper is to include content that will appeal to the target reader and reinforce pre-conceived ideas.

3.30 Commercial radio stations are owned by private, corporate media industries. They are funded by the sale of advertising and are focused on making a profit. This means that they tend to cater for a broad audience and are ratings driven.

3.31 Radio stations have websites and catch-up facilities (iPlayer/BBC Sounds) to give flexibility to audiences. They also have apps and make their content available as podcasts.

3.32 Interacting with a radio programme may involve texting or emailing the programme and having this read out on air, getting a 'shout out' or a request played on music-led programmes, or taking part in a phone-in where their views can be aired.

3.33 Audio streaming means that a global audience can access radio content wherever they are and whenever is convenient for them. This has widened the BBC Radio audience.

3.34 The choice of topics and the guests on *LNWH* illustrate that the target audience are educated, relatively highbrow and interested in more challenging social topics.

3.35 Useful extracts from the film to help to explore industry issues may include: the opening credits, the end credits, extracts that suggest marketing opportunities (use of stars) and extracts that suggest the production values of the film.

3.36 Synergy is the combination of organisations to create a more powerful body with greater impact than could be achieved by one company alone. For example, Time Warner is a powerful media organisation made up of a combination of smaller companies, with the aim of producing more revenue.

3.37 Technical convergence is the merger of previously distinct media technologies and platforms due to digital advances. For example, being able to watch a Netflix or Amazon film on a smartphone. It also means the combining of different media forms, for example the film industry and the music or video games industry.

3.38 Vertical integration in the film industry is where a film company owns the means to produce, distribute and exhibit the film. For example, where a film company owns a distributor and cinemas/a television channel.

3.39 An example of horizontal integration is Warner Bros, which owns film studios, Rock Steady Games, DC Comics and other related companies.

3.40 A tabloid newspaper would be the *Sun* or the *Daily Mirror*. A mid-market may be the *Daily Mail* or the *Express*. Broadsheets would include *The Times*, the *Telegraph* and the *Guardian*.

3.41 Newspaper websites are immediate and up to date. They offer interactive opportunities. Apps for some newspapers are available for mobile phones and tablets. It is easy to access archived stories and articles. It makes selecting the news and features that appeal to the individual much easier.

3.42 News vales are the criteria that influence decisions made by those in control of the newspaper industry, for example the owners, editors and journalists who select and construct the news.

3.43 The news agenda is the list of stories that may appear in a particular newspaper. The items on the news agenda will reflect the style, ethos and political stance of the publication.

3.44 Citizen journalism is when news is gathered by the general public who are there when the story unfolds. Advances in technology means that they can record and send information quickly.

3.45 Citizen journalism allows the newspaper immediate access to a news story as it happens, through images and interviews. It is cheaper than sending their own journalist to cover the story and having the member of public there means the story can be easily updated.

3.46 The Leveson Report was a public enquiry into the culture, practice and ethics of the British press. It was prompted by the *News of the World* phone-hacking scandal, which brought about the closure of the paper. It had a massive impact on the way in which the public viewed some newspapers and the future regulation of the industry.

3.47 A question on the newspaper industry may appear in Section B Question 3.

3.48 A unique viewer is a someone who returns to a website more than once over a period of time. They can be identified by tracking traffic to the website.

3.49 Three hypothetical positions from which messages and meanings may be decoded refers to Stuart Hall's reception theory.

3.50 An example of a traditional advertising platform would be a newspaper or the television. A digital platform would be a website or mobile phone.

3.51 On the whole, with some exceptions, representations of women are more positive and they are less sexually objectified than in the past. This is to reflect the changing role of women in society.

3.52 The click-through rate refers to the proportion of users of a website who click on a specific link to, for example an advertisement. It is used by advertisers to measure the success of an online campaign.

3.53 This technique was common, particularly in adverts for domestic cleaning products. Two women, who were relatable to the target audience, would discuss a domestic issue, for example how to get a whiter wash. This was usually resolved by one woman recommending the product being advertised. Advertisers thought women would be more likely to buy the product if they could see women like them using it.

3.54 These ideas include: Tide as the brand leader, as nothing else washes as well, the unique selling point of the 'miracle' suds will revolutionise washday, that purchasing Tide will make you happy, that all women should want their wash to be the 'Cleanest', 'Whitest' and 'Brightest'.

3.55 Young and Rubicam advocated psychographic profiling – categorising people according to their values, attitude and lifestyles.

3.56 The current regulation is only applicable to the hard copy of the games. The opportunities available for young people below the age of the PEGI rating to stream or purchase the game online means that they will be exposed to content unsuitable for their age.

3.57 A casual gamer is one who plays more spontaneously and less regularly. They tend to choose games that are less complex and challenging and are harder to target through marketing.

3.58 A core gamer refers to a player with a wide range of gaming interests who regularly actively engages with different types of games.

3.59 Fan communities allow audiences to share ideas about the game and interact with other fans. Some gamers also produce their own walk-through videos to introduce new players to aspects of the game.

3.60 Transgressive behaviour refers to behaviour that goes beyond the norms of social acceptability.

5 Component 2: Investigating Media Forms and Products

5.1 The term polysemic means having more than one meaning.

5.2 Iconography and mise-en-scène are both terms that are commonly used to describe the visual elements within media products such as television programmes or films.

5.3 Diegetic sound appears to come from within the text and is therefore audible to the people or characters we see on screen as well as the audience, whereas non-diegetic sound is only audible to the audience; it cannot be heard by people or characters within the text.

5.4 Genre hybridity occurs when the conventions of different genres are mixed or combined.

5.5 Equilibrium means balance, order or stability. The opposite of this is disequilibrium, which means imbalance, disorder or instability.

5.6 Verisimilitude means having the appearance of truth. It is commonly used to describe the realism of a product (the higher the level of verisimilitude the more realistic the product is).

5.7 Ethnocentrism is defined by Roger Brown as 'the application of the norms of one's own culture to that of others' (*Social Psychology*, 1965, page 183). In other words, the norms and values of one group are treated as if they are universally valid, which means that anyone or anything that does not conform to those norms and values is regarded as suspect, deviant or 'other'.

5.8 Patriarchy is a system of male dominance.

5.9 Misrepresentation means portraying or representing something in an inaccurate, misleading or limited way. Stereotyping is a particularly common form of misrepresentation.

5.10 Tokenism means providing a cursory or superficial representation of those who are under-represented in order to convey the impression of inclusivity, thereby avoiding accusations of inequality and exclusion.

5.11 Publicly owned television companies are designed to serve the interests of the general public and are not-for-profit, whereas privately owned television companies are designed to make a profit for their shareholders.

5.12 A public service broadcaster is one that is required to fulfil certain public purposes, such as satisfying the needs and interests of a wide range of audiences, in order to comply with its public service remit and its licence to broadcast.

5.13 Media plurality is concerned with ensuring that there is a wide range of viewpoints available to audiences.

5.14 The watershed is the time when it becomes permissible to show programmes that are unsuitable for younger audiences.

5.15 In semiotic theory, myth refers to socially or culturally constructed meanings that come to be regarded as if they are not socially or culturally constructed at all but just common-sense or a representation of the way things really are. The process through which constructed meanings come to be seen as self-evident, achieving the status of myth, is referred to as naturalisation.

5.16 The happy housewife stereotype that featured prominently in women's magazines in the 1950s and 1960s is ideologically significant as it could be seen to convey the message that women's place is within the home and that this form of domestic containment should be a source of female contentment, happiness and fulfilment.

5.17 Advertising copy is the written text that appears in an advertisement.

5.18 The white beauty myth is a form of ethnocentrism in which female beauty is defined in terms of white standards and ideals.

5.19 The exotic other is a term used to describe someone or something that is perceived to be different, where that difference or 'otherness' becomes a source of fascination, attraction or pleasure.

5.20 Media concentration refers to a situation in which power comes to be held in the hands of fewer companies.

5.21 Horizontal integration occurs when one company acquires or merges with another that is involved in the same area of business. One magazine publisher buying a rival magazine publisher would be an example of horizontal integration.

5.22 Para-social interaction is the term used to describe the way in which mass media products create the illusion of face-to-face conversation.

5.23 A walk-through video is a video in which a vlogger demonstrates how to play a video game by walking the viewer through the necessary stages or levels. A let's play video is a recording of someone playing a video game, usually accompanied by some form of commentary.

5.24 A haul video is a video in which the vlogger displays and discusses the shopping purchases they have made.

5.25 Gatekeeping refers to a process of filtering and selection. For example, in the newspaper industry, editors perform a gatekeeping function as they decide which stories will make it into the paper and which will not. Vloggers also function as gatekeepers as they choose what to disclose or share with their viewers and what to withhold.

5.26 An advertorial is a specific type of advertisement. The main difference between an advertisement and an advertorial is that the advertorial is presented in the style of the media product in which it appears. An advertorial vlog, for instance, is an advertisement that is presented by the vlogger in their usual editorial style.

5.27 Display ads or banners are advertisements that appear beside or below an online video.

5.28 A pre-roll ad is a video advertisement that appears before the content that the viewer has chosen to watch (e.g., an advertisement that appears before a YouTube video).

5.29 A prosumer is a consumer who is actively involved in the production or circulation of content. For example, many users of online media create, comment on or adapt media content before distributing it online through the Internet or social media.

7 Component 3: Media Production

7.1 In your production you will be required to demonstrate your understanding of media language, representation, media industries and audiences.

7.2 Industry context refers to aspects of production, including the media organisation, production processes, distribution and marketing, and regulatory issues.

7.3 You are required to submit: a production, a Statement of Aims and Intentions and a cover sheet.

7.4 It is advised that learners spend up to eight weeks developing and creating their production.

7.5 The requirements of the brief are there to ensure parity between different briefs, so adhering to them is essential. The completion of them is also closely related to the assessment criteria and your final production mark.

7.6 Primary research is information you gain first-hand from looking at actual examples of existing media products, for example television drama opening sequences. Primary research allows you to formulate your own opinions. Secondary research is found in books and websites, for example, and is written by someone else about the media product you may want to create. It will contain the ideas and opinions of the writer.

7.7 Yes, you can use existing music for a soundtrack but it must be copyright free.

7.8 Yes, the images must be original and taken for the purpose of the production. However, you are allowed to use found images of industry logos and bar codes for magazines.

7.9 In the print and online magazine photographs, consideration of clothing, expression and gesture can help to construct appropriate representations.

7.10 Yes, you can use an existing song for your music video but the track must not have an existing video.

9 Examination Preparation

9.1 These questions carry a low mark tariff, for example 1 or 2 marks.

9.2 It is 3(d), as it refers to industry generally, newspapers which is the in depth study form, and contexts.

9.3 Question 3(d) has two parts. The first part is a broader industry and context focus. The product is referred to in the second part, suggesting that this is not a textual analysis question. The product must be used to highlight the industry issues raised in the first part.

9.4 The first of the two magazine questions is the lower tariff one; this is worth 5 marks. The focus of the question, which requires an explanation of the difference between two semiotic terms, is much narrower than the second magazine question, which is worth 15 marks.

9.5 The extract from the assessment grid suggests that you will need to demonstrate your ability to apply knowledge and understanding of the theoretical framework to analyse your set television product and to make judgements and draw conclusions.

Index

Acknowledgements

p1 iStock/dem10; p5 Rawpixel.com; p7 fizkes; p8 Amir Ridhwan; p9 Ksenia She; p10 Motortion Films; p11 Jacob Lund; p12 (left) Monkey Business Images; p12 (right) panitanphoto; p14 (left) Courtesy of The Advertising Archives; p14 (right) Kiss of the Vampire; p15 (top) Jacob Lund; p15 Courtesy of The Advertising Archives; p16 zhu difeng; p18 ESB Professional; p19 ClassicStock/Alamy Stock Photo; p20 Kiwis; p21 Motortion Films; p22 Dean Drobot; p23 ra2studio; p24 kb-photodesign; p25 (top) marino Bocelli; p25 (middle) Humans Episode 1; p25 (bottom) Beyonce – Formation/YouTube; p26 (top left) Mark Bourdillon/Alamy Stock Images; p26 (top middle) Barnardo's/Believe in Me/TV advert/YouTube; p26 (top right) BFA/Alamy Stock Photo; p26 (bottom left) The Jinx: The Life and Deaths of Robert Durst – Trailer – Official HBO UK/YouTube; p26 (bottom right) Matt Gibson; p28 (top) Claudia Sings Sunshine on a Rainy Day (Full Version)/WaterAid/YouTube; p28 (bottom) Killing Eve/BBC Three Trailer/YouTube; p30 Lenscap Photography/Shutterstock.com; p31 Warm Bodies; p32 Julian Nieman/Alamy Stock Photo; p34 Lenscap Photography/Shutterstock.com; p35 (left) Charity Campaign Video/Not This Girl/ActionAid UK/YouTube; p35 (right) Monkey Business Images; p36 (left) Jeff Morgan 13/Alamy Stock Photo; p36 (right) L'Oreal; p37 (left) Monkey Business Images; p37 (middle) Roman Samborskyi; p37 (right) InesBazdar; p38 (all) We Believe: The Best Men Can Be/Gillette (Short Film)/YouTube; p39 (right) MichaelJayBerlin/Shutterstock.com; p39 (left) Copyright Guardian News & Media Ltd 2020; p40 GaudiLab; p42 Motortion Films; p43 G-Stock Studio; p44 Andrey Burmakin; p46 (top) Jacob Lund; p46 (bottom) nito; p48 (top) The Stable; p48 (bottom) Kevin Wheal/Alamy Stock Photo; p49 (top) Antonio Guilliem; p49 (bottom) Rawpixel.com; p50 1000 Words/Shutterstock.com; p53 TungCheung; p57 Beyoncé – Formation; p59 Lenscap Photography/Shutterstock.com; p60 Claudia Sings Sunshine on a Rainy Day (Full Version)/WaterAid/YouTube; p61 A Nightmare on Elm Street; p62 (top to bottom) Not this Girl/ActionAid UK/YouTube, Pantene Pro-V/Ellie Goulding Superfood Commercial/Pantene UK/YouTube, SCS Furniture Adverts – Grimme 5/Darren Altman/YouTube, COCO MADEMOISELLE Eau de Parfum Intense – Chanel/Chanel/YouTube, Sauvage; p64 (all) Censored/Save the Children/YouTube; p65 (top) Alien; p65 (bottom) Willy Barton/Shutterstock.com; p66 Neil Baylis/Alamy Stock Photo; p67 (all) Crucible of the Vampire; p68 Walkers Crisps; p69 Burying the Ex; p70 Aqua de Gio/Georgio Armani; p71 Courtesy The Advertising Archives; p73 (left) Nike; p73 (right) Dior J'adore; p73 (bottom) The Kiss of the Vampire; p74 (all) Claudia Sings Sunshine on a Rainy Day (Full Version)/WaterAid/YouTube; p74 (bottom) Twocoms/Shutterstock.com; p75 Everett Collection Inc/Alamy Stock Photo; p76 RetroClipArt; p78 (top) Ant Gore; p78 (bottom) Roman Voloshyn; p79 zieusin; p80 (both) George Ezra – Shotgun (Official Music Video)/YouTube; p81 (both) Avicii- Wake Me Up (Official Video)/YouTube; p82 (all) Zedd, Katy Perry – 365 (Official)/Katy Perry/YouTube; p83 (both left) Dizzee Rascal Dream/YouTube; p83 (both right) Beyonce – Formation/YouTube; p84 (both) Taylor Swift – Delicate – Taylor Swift – YouTube; p87 (both) Zedd, Katy Perry – 365 (Official)/Katy Perry/YouTube; p88 Courtesy The Advertising Archives; p90 Marcel Poncu; p91 Lenscap Photography/Shutterstock.com; p92 (both) Lenscap Photography/Shutterstock.com; p94 Mirrorpix; p95 pxl.store; p96 Lenscap Photography/Shutterstock.com; p97 Daily Mail; p98 Mirrorpix; p99 (top) The Sun News Licensing; p99 (bottom) Mirrorpix; p100 (top) romov; p100 (bottom) Shutterstock.com; p101 Angela Ostafichuk/Shutterstock.com; p103 Stocklite; p105

Metamorworks; p107 (top) Assasin's Creed Liberation HD Trailer (2014), GamnewsOfficial, YouTube; p107 (bottom) Twinsterphoto; p108 David MG; p110 (all) Get the BBC Sounds App for Personalised Music, Radio and Podcasts – BBC Sounds Trailer/BBC/YouTube; p111 Late Night Woman's Hour; p112 (top) jax 10289/Shutterstock.com; p112 (bottom) Dmitri Ma; p113 sutadimage; p114 (top) fizkes; p114 (middle) Iakov Filimonov; p114 (bottom) G-Stock Studio; p115 Cheese Scientist/Alamy Stock Photo; p119 rigsbyphoto/Shutterstock.com; p120 AlexLMX; p121 (bottom) Alamy; p121 (top) chrisdorney/shutterstock.com; p122 Willy Barton/Shutterstock.com; p123 (all) Straight Outta Compton – Offical Global Trailer (Universal Pictures) HD/Universal Pictures UK/YouTube; p127 (left) dennizn; p127 (right) Marcel Poncu; p128 (top) Nongnuch_L; p128 (bottom) Bojan Milinkov; p129 waveprintmedia; p130 Tero Vesalainen; p131 chrisdorney; p132 Roasli Othman/Shutterstock.com; p133 Mirror Online; p134 Denys Prykhodov; p135 Mirrorpix; p136 Mirror Online; p137 (all) Mirrorpix; p138 A. Aleksandravicius; p139 Mirrorpix; p141 Lebrecht Music & Arts/Alamy Stock Photo; p144 (all) Claudia Sings Sunshine on a Rainy Day (Full Version)/WaterAid/YouTube; p145 Courtesy of The Advertising Archives; p147 (top) Claudia Sings Sunshine on a Rainy Day (Full Version)/WaterAid/YouTube; p147 (bottom) Doris Rich; p148 (top) Stuart Hall – Some Views on Cultural Themes and Multiculturalism; p148 (middle) The Mean World Syndrome – Media as Storytellers (Extra Feature)/ChallengingMedia; p148 (bottom) Inside the Psychologist's Studio with Albert Bandura/PsychologicalScience; p149 (all) Claudia Sings Sunshine on a Rainy Day (Full Version)/WaterAid/YouTube; p151 (top) Adam Filipowicz; p151 (bottom) PHOTOCREO Michal Bednarek; p153 VSC; p154 Dean Drobot; p155 Gorodenkoff; p156 (both) Assasin's Creed Liberation HD Trailer (2014), GameewsOfficial, YouTube; p157 (top) Pe3K; p157 (bottom) Denys Prykhodov/Shutterstock.com; p158 Courtesy of Newzoo; p159 (top) Natsia27/Shutterstock.com; p159 (bottom) Gorodenkoff/Shutterstock.com; p160 (left) Lets Play Assassin's Creed 3 Liberation Part 1 Louisiana; p160 (right) Gorodenkoff; p161 (all) Assassin's Creed 3 Liberation – Reveal Trailer [UK], Ubisoft/YouTube; p162 Dean Drobot; p163 Assassin›s creed liberation HD Trailer (2014), GameNewsOfficial/YouTube; p165 panitanphoto; p166 Lipik Stock Media; p167 fizkes; p168 (left to right) BBC – Life On Mars – Trailer/YouTube, Humans/AMC Networks, The Jinx: The Life and Deaths of Robert Durst – Andrew Jarecki Interview (HBO)/HBO/YouTube; p169 Monkey Business Images; p170 (both) Life On Mars/dailymotion; p171 (left) Life On Mars/dailymotion; p171 (middle) Humans Titles/MOMOCO Film Titles/YouTube; p171 (right) The Jinx: The Life and Deaths of Robert Durst – Andrew Jarecki Interview (HBO)/HBO/YouTube; p174 (top) The Jinx (2015) HQ – EO1: A Body in the Bay/dailymotion; p174 (bottom left) Life On Mars/dailymotion; p174 (bottom right) Humans Series 1 & 2 Recap/The Story So Far/Channel 4/YouTube; p175 (both) Life On Mars – S1EO1/dailymotion; p176 (both top) Humans Titles/MOMOCO Film Titles/YouTube; p176 (both bottom) Humans Series 1 Episode 1/Channel 4; p177 Rawpixel.com; p178 (both) The Jinx: The Life and Deaths of Robert Durst – Trailer – Official HBO UK/HBO UK/YouTube; p179 (top) Life On Mars – S1EO1/dailymotion; p179 (middle right) Humans Trailer/Roadshow Entertainment/YouTube; p179 (middle left) Life On Mars – S1EO1/dailymotion; p179 (bottom left) Humans Trailer/Roadshow Entertainment/YouTube; p179 (bottom right) The Jinx: The Life and Deaths of Robert Durst – Trailer – Official HBO UK/HBO UK/YouTube; p180 Stuart Miles; p183 (top two right) Life on Mars An

integrated campaign for a drama set in 1973/vimeo; p183 (centre) Life on Mars/Amanda Paul; p183 (bottom two) Persona Synthetics: behind Channel 4's 'Humans' campaign/Campaign/YouTube; p184 (top) Humans/AMC Networks; p184 (bottom three) The Jinx: The Life and Deaths of Robert Durst – Trailer – Official HBO UK/HBO UK/YouTube; p185 Ofcom; p186 (top) Andrii Yalanskyi; p186 (bottom) Rehan Qureshi; p187 iQoncept; p188 (top) Diego Cervo; p188 (bottom) Andrey_Popov; p191 (left) Woman; p191 (middle) Woman's Realm; p191 (right) Vogue; p194 (top) Max Factor Crème Puff; p194 (bottom) Australian Sultanas; p195 Imperial Leather; p196 (left) Breeze; p196 (right) Cutex; p197 (both) Woman; p198 (top) Woman's' Realm; p198 (middle) Australian Sultanas; p198 (two up) Imperial Leather; p198 (bottom) Vogue; p199 Gor-Ray; p200 (top both) Woman; p200 (bottom) Vogue; p201 (top to bottom) Woman, Woman's Realm, Vogue; p201 Bohboh; p205 David Burton/Alamy Stock Photo; p208 (top to bottom) Imperial Leather; Woman, Woman, Vogue; p209 Woman's Realm; p211 zefart; p212 (left) Alfie Deyes Vlogs; p212 (right) Zoella; p212 (bottom) Rawpixel.com; p213 BUNDITINAY; p214 (top) rvlsoft; p214 (bottom) Alfie Deyes; p216 (top left to right) Alfie Deyes, Alfie Deyes Vlogs, PointlessBlogGames; p216 (bottom both) Zoella; p217 (top) Alfie Deyes Exploring the Most Haunted Prisons Part Three; p217 (bottom) Zoella; p218 Rawpixel.com; p219 Alfie Deyes; p220 (top left) My Everyday Makeup Routine/Zoella/YouTube; p220 (top right) Alfie & Joe Gym Workout!/Jalfie Deyes Vlogs/YouTube; Seeing A Therapist/Alfie Deyes Vlogs/YouTube; p220 (bottom left) Girls Night in with Tanya Burr/Zoella/YouTube; p220 (bottom right) The Manly Challenge/PewDiePie/YouTube; p222 (top) Sutipond Somnam; p222 (bottom) TierneyMJ; p223 Zoella; p224 (top) GRWM: Everyday Festive Glam Look/Zoella/YouTube; p224 (bottom) Big Nutella Celebrations in the Office/Alfie Deyes Vlogs/YouTube; p225 quinky; p226 (left) The Mad Lib Story Challenge/Alfie Deyes/YouTube; p226 (right) Tanya Burr and Zoella 5 Minute Makeup Challenge/Zoella/YouTube; p227 (top) Ricky Of The World/Shutterstock.com; p227 (middle) The END Of PointlessBlog/Alfie Deyes/YouTube; p227 (bottom) Zoella; p229 Zoella.com; p230 wavebreakmedia; p231 Flamingo Images; p232 Janelle Lugge; p234 everything possible; p235 Humans Trailer/YouTube; p236 (left) Javi Az; p236 (right) LADO; p237 (left) Osadchaya Olga; p237 (right) smolaw; p238 Andrey_Popov; p239 (left) GuruXOX; p239 (right) Giovanni G; p240 (top) bodiaphvideo/Shutterstock.com; p240 (bottom) MaxFrost; p241 (top) World History Archive/Alamy Stock Photo; p241 (bottom) charnsitr/Shutterstock.com; p242 (left) Pink – Walk Me Home (Official Video)/Pink/YouTube; p242 (right) Gorodenkoff; p243 (bottom left) oliveromg; p243 (top) Nikkolia; p243 (bottom right) Marwood jenkins/Alamy Stock Photo; p245 (top) mimagephotography; p245 (bottom left) Chaosamran_Studio; p245 (middle) Elnur; p245 (bottom right) Rawpixel.com; p247 (top) stockfour; p247 (bottom) sutadimage; p248 Mr. Thanachat Ousagui; p249 Tatiana Popova; pp251–2 Ed Sheeran – Shape of You [Official Video]/Ed Sheeran/YouTube; p253 (top) Everett Collection Inc/Alamy Stock Photo; p253 (bottom) Courtesy The Advertising Archives; p255 Calvin Henderson; p256 (left) Jag_cz; p256 (right) andrewvect; p257 chainarong06; p258 Mirrorpix; p259 Daily Mirror; p260 Assassin's Creed; p261 Rawpixel.com; p262 picoStudio; p265 A.J. Pictures; p266 Iqoncept; p268 Life on Mars; p272 (left) Woman; p272 (middle) Woman's Realm; p272 (right) Vogue; p273 Artur Szczbylo; p274 Casimiro PT; p275 Jacob Lund; p276 (top) Zuraihan Md Zain; p276 (bottom) sodafish